A BRANDED WORLD

Adventures in Public Relations and the Creation of Superbrands

Michael Levine

WILEY

JOHN WILEY & SONS, INC.

Published by John Wiley & Sons, Inc., Hoboken, New Jersey.
Published simultaneously in Canada.

For general information on our other products and services please contact our Customer Care Department within the U.S. at (800) 762-2974, outside the United States
at (317) 572-3993 or fax (317) 572-4002.

Wiley also publishes its books in a variety of electronic formats. Some content that
appears in print may not be available in electronic books. For more information about
Wiley products, visit our Web site at www.Wiley.com.

ISBN 0-471-26366-4

Printed in the United States of America

10 9 8 7 6 5 4 3 2 1

To the victims of the September 11 tragedy

CONTENTS

ACKNOWLEDGMENTS

A book is many things but certainly not a solo effort.

Expessing my endless gratitude to the following extraordinary people who generously supported me before, during, and after the writing of this book is a privilege that I take seriously. To each, my love and deep appreciation:

To Jeff Cohen for his tremendous support in creating this work. Jeff helped immeasurably and assists me in continuing to create the concepts that you are reading.

To Alyse Reynolds—A woman whom I affectionately refer to as "the Fixer." She is an invaluable, loyal friend and associate.

Blessed associates and friends, who assist, support, and encourage me when it is not always easy to do so: Peter Bart, Marilyn Beck, Craig Black, Adam Christing, Paul Coughlin, Tara Griggs, Bill and Ann Hartley, Richard Imprescia, Karen Karsian, Arthur Levine, Patty Levine, John McKillop, Nancy Mager, Cable Neuhaus, Steve Shapiro, Michael Viner, and David Weiss.

My brilliantly talented literary agent and friend, Craig Nelson. My extremely smart, gifted and strong editor, Airié Stuart.

Note: Interns interested in working in Mr. Levine's Los Angeles office can contact him at levinepr2@earthlink.net.

INTRODUCTION

If you're in business and you're not branding, you're already three steps behind everyone else. If you're talking about Branding or embarking on Branding efforts, but you're not really clear on what it means, you are part of an uninformed majority that is doing itself more harm than good. If you think Branding is something done to cattle with a hot iron, you have purchased the wrong book.

You'd have to labor to shield yourself from the power of Branding; it's hard to avoid it in today's business and social climate. Even in the backwoods of very, very small-town America, you couldn't emancipate yourself from the in-your-face concepts of Branding messages from all over the world. Even in conversations that don't discuss it (and those are becoming few and far between), Branding is present. On television, in the supermarket, at the movie theatre, in your car, Branding is constantly with you. If you're in business—*any* business—you are involved in Branding in some way. If you are a sole proprietor, you may, yourself, be a brand.

It is no longer enough to simply be the best—or even the best-selling—product on the market. It has become necessary to establish a brand identity, which can lead to additional products, deeper market share, and expanded consumer loyalty.

As Cable Neuhaus, editor in chief of *Folio* magazine, says: "Branding is so paramount. A car to many, many people is an extension of themselves. It's an extension of the way they see themselves. Relatively few people go down to the dealership that's closest to their home and say, 'What can I get for $22,500?' That's not the way people buy cars for the most part, and that's the reason the car companies spend billions of dollars worldwide, in all likelihood, on the Branding enterprise. GM just fired the guy who's in charge of Branding because they feel he wasn't very successful there. They have a succession of car lines and you can move up the lines: Chevy, Pontiac, Buick, Cadillac. There isn't all that much difference between a Buick and a Pontiac; they're usually built on the same frame. The difference is how they market themselves to the audience. Pontiac is 'We build excitement.' Buick is 'American luxury.' "

Introduction

In the world of public relations, where I work to brand some of today's hottest stars, it's virtually impossible to avoid talking about Branding. Working in Hollywood for 20 years, I've never heard the kind of buzz around a concept that I've experienced with Branding. Everyone is looking for the key to the concept; everyone is saying the word, although most have misconceptions about its meaning.

The problem is, only the select few people know what Branding really is. And even fewer understand the essential role public relations plays in the Branding process. As Duane E. Knapp, president of BrandStrategy, Inc. and author of *The Branding Mindset,* says: "Most people do not have a clue what *brand* means. The common misconception is that brand is hype. They have this concept that one of the ways to be a successful brand is that you've got to hype the brand, you've got to have a lot of activity, a lot of communications, a lot of advertising, which is the antithesis of the true concept of brand. I think [PR] is the most important role. The company should decide what their promise is. If you don't have a brand promise, you have nothing, and it's not the advertising tagline. It's what the employees and the company promise to consumers. It's not a promise unless it's written, unless every single employee in the company can tell you what they have to do to deliver that promise. They might not be able to recite the exact two or three sentences, but for example, at L.L. Bean, they know that there is no such thing as an unhappy customer."

> "I think (public relations) is a massively important, and even more massively underleveraged, role in the Branding process. I don't think people fully understand the value of setting up an interview with a major magazine or somebody else endorsing your brand. 3M talks about how you perceive your brand in three different ways: one, 'customer satisfaction,' two, 'would you buy the brand again,' and three, 'would you recommend it to a friend.' I look at PR as an analog to 'would you recommend it as a friend.' "
> —Scott M. Davis, managing partner of PROPHET's Chicago office and co-author of *Brand Asset Management*

It's impossible to look at Branding without the public relations perspective, and my business happens to be public relations. In doing business

Introduction

with high-profile celebrities from Barbra Streisand to Fleetwood Mac, Demi Moore to Kareem Abdul-Jabbar, Charlton Heston to Michael J. Fox, and corporate clients like Pizza Hut, I deal with concepts like advertising, marketing, market research, and sponsorship. Public relations is part of all those disciplines. And since public relations is, we'll discover, an integral part of the Branding process, I have a unique perspective on the business of Branding. I work with people who create and perpetuate some of the most successful brand names and brand identities. I've worked with the highest-level actors, actresses, entertainers, directors, and Hollywood insiders, all of whom strive to become brands and some of whom have done exactly that with unparalleled success.

I know the advertising executives and marketing professionals who create brands, and I know the editors, producers, studio executives, and television moguls who present them to the public. In fact, you'll read about their experiences and hear their opinions throughout this book. They'll help me to explain why some things work and others don't. It's not alchemy; it's not voodoo. There may be magic involved, but magic is usually the product of intense drudgery, endless practice sessions, and just a touch of inspiration. Branding isn't the wave of a magic wand; it is a discipline that can be taught and learned. It can be practiced and examined, discussed and analyzed. The better it is understood, the more successfully it will be utilized.

There will also be a total Branding experience: the creation of a fictional brand of ice cream that we'll see grow from an idea into a full, mature brand through the best use of public relations practices. The concept of the product, the name, the presentation, and the advertising and marketing will all be influenced and shaped by the uses of public relations. The brand will emerge through its promise to the public, and through the way that promise is communicated and reinforced. That is pure public relations.

The journey we're about to take will be a fascinating one. We'll examine brands that are practically sacred in many households, and discover how they got that way. We'll look at the most inspired choices and biggest Branding mistakes ever made. And through it all, we'll keep an eye on what you can do to use public relations techniques to help create that once-in-a-lifetime brand.

CHAPTER ONE

WHAT *IS* BRANDING, ANYWAY?

"[Branding is] a 15-second elevator pitch that every employee in the organization can not only get and articulate, but can talk about their role in bringing that to life."

—SCOTT M. DAVIS, MANAGING PARTNER, PROPHET CHICAGO

There is no concept as vital, as discussed, as mentioned, as of the moment in the world of marketing and advertising today as *Branding*. Everyone uses the word in every conversation, there are countless self-proclaimed experts on the subject, executives want it, account managers plan it, strategies are formulated, money is spent, advertising is done. But the fact is, very few people actually know what the word *Branding* really means in this context.

Is it really important to put the concept into words? Everyone seems to understand Branding, even if they're not always able to communicate their understanding in eloquent terms. They "get" Branding, even if they can't define it as accurately as Webster's dictionary. So, why bother to codify something that seems so pervasive?

First of all, most people who "get" Branding as a concept don't really understand what it means to create a brand and build it into a dominant market position. The majority of businesspeople do not have a strong working definition of Branding, and therefore can't determine what is and is not a successful brand. Some confuse a brand with a product, which can be a devastating mistake with terrible consequences.

Before defining *Branding,* it's important to define what it is *not*. Branding is not simply a matter of creating the name for a company or a product

1

and repeating it ad nauseam to the public until it becomes a household word. There have been plenty of brand names that have come and gone in what amounts to the blink of an eye—and advertising and marketing executives who have come and gone just as quickly, who can attest to that truth.

Branding is not just taking the name of a successful product and slapping it on the box of a new product to "expand the brand." Diversification is only possible when so much goodwill and trust have been established with the consuming public that the name will be followed wherever it goes. And even then, the product must deliver what it promises, or the brand name itself will be diminished, not enhanced. That is the polar opposite of what a Branding campaign sets out to do, yet it happens on an alarmingly regular basis.

Branding is not an advertising campaign, a marketing slogan, or a logo. It doesn't have to apply to a product, a company, or a title. Michael Jordan is a brand. Coca-Cola is a brand. Bill Clinton is a brand, and so are George W. Bush, Martha Stewart, and Julia Roberts. But this book is not a brand, because it doesn't meet the necessary criteria. And that's not simply because the title is too long; it's because one product doesn't equal a brand. An author can be a brand, but a title can't, because it is only one product being sold. An author creates many products, while the title of one book is just that: the title of *one book*.

Some legitimate questions can be raised about whether or not Branding is a fad. Until now, it has seemed that Branding is something that can only be done by huge corporations with budgets at the very least in the millions of dollars. But that's not true. Given the proper information, anyone trying to make an impression on consumers can create—or *become*—a brand. It's not impossibly complicated, it's not something only a select few people "in the know" can do, and it doesn't have to be prohibitively expensive. That means smaller companies will be competing on the Branding level, but it also means that even larger companies are going to have to do more work to maintain their existing brands and especially to launch new ones.

There are many techniques and concepts that go into every Branding campaign that can be used by anyone at all. It's important, for example, for a brand to be consistent, and that is true of the Walt Disney Company and the drugstore down the street. It's important to tell the truth, and that is as much the case for Microsoft as it is for a local supplier of jams and preserves.

> "There are so many parity products out there that the only way to differentiate yourself from the others is to create an aura, an image, around your brand. Consumers need a road map; they need to find a way to get from their need to a product purchase that's simple, easy, not full of a lot of noise, and most brands get lost somewhere between the shelf and the consumer mindset."
> —Karen Benezra, editor of *Brandweek*

In 1998, Jennifer Lopez was an actress. By 2000, "J. Lo" had become a brand. The difference came with brilliant handling, good career choices, and a very revealing dress, as part of a calculated and well-planned campaign that was designed to accomplish exactly the result it produced. Through careful use of public relations in a Branding campaign, Lopez managed to make the leap from interesting personality to brand in a remarkably short period of time. And it was by no means either an accident or a phenomenon. It was the result of a very well-calculated series of events.

Because Lopez was aiming at a multifaceted career—acting and music, as well as any pursuits she might still have up her sleeve—the campaign was intended to brand her personality with the public, rather than simply her range of performance. A brand promise—that this would be an exciting, unpredictable personality—was made. So the timing of a strong album at the same time Lopez had a movie debuting, and especially the appearance in the astonishing dress at the Grammy awards, was aimed at conveying a daring, sexy personality not unlike Madonna's, and doing it in a rush of publicity, all at once.

It worked brilliantly.

A TRUE WORKING DEFINITION OF BRANDING

Branding is a complex process, but its goal is simple: It is the creation and development of a specific identity for a company, product, commodity, group, or person. It is carefully designed to present qualities that its creators believe will be attractive to the public, and it is meant to be developed and perpetuated for the long haul. An ad campaign launches a product. Branding, when it's done right, creates an institution. Branding brings about so many benefits it reminds me of the saying, "You can count the number of seeds in an apple, but you can't count the number of apples in a seed."

> "[Branding has] always been a critical subject, and has everything to do with instant recognition in a very instantaneous society. The ability to establish your name quickly and have your customer respond to that quickly is the name of the game."
> —Mark Lacter, editor of *LA Business Journal*

Perhaps the best way to illustrate the concept of Branding is to explore the new car market. Everyone knows instinctively the difference between a Chevrolet and a BMW. And it's not just a matter of price: Consumers who are asked about cars will describe a Chevy as reliable and comfortable, while a BMW will be described as exciting, luxurious, and brilliantly engineered. We know the personality of a BMW or a Chevy (or for that matter, a Volkswagen, Ford, Kia, or Hyundai) without necessarily being able to articulate it. We make presumptions about a person who gets out of a car in the parking lot based on what kind of car it may be. And even though some of these identities may have gotten a little diluted over the years (Is there much of a difference between a Chevy person and a Pontiac person?), they are awfully hard to shake. We know what the nameplate on the back of the car means.

There's a difference between Coca-Cola and Pepsi. There's a difference between CBS and Fox. There's a difference between *Star Trek* and *Star Wars*. All of these are successful brand names, and they each have a distinctive personality, which may defy definition, but is easily understood by the public at large.

Examine the decades-long competition between Coca-Cola and Pepsi: On the surface, these two companies' products seem interchangeable. But more effort and money have gone into creating differences between the personalities of the brands than into differences in the products themselves.

What *Is* Branding, Anyway?

In the seventies, when the word *generation* was being used in any number of contexts, Pepsi commandeered the young adult segment of the population and dubbed them "the Pepsi Generation," in an attempt to make Coca-Cola seem old and staid. In the 1980s, Coca-Cola executed what was perhaps the most celebrated marketing mistake in history, discontinuing production on its core product, the most recognizable brand name in the world, in favor of a more Pepsi-like formula it dubbed New Coke. This Grand Canyon–size blunder eventually worked in the company's favor when consumers revolted with startling vehemence and Coca-Cola quickly announced it would bring back its revered product, now under the name Coca-Cola Classic. Sales rebounded, and more media attention was lavished on the Cola Wars. The campaign also managed to underline the loyalty and affection so many consumers had for original Coca-Cola—which might very well have been the goal of the company to begin with. Coca-Cola eventually dropped the word *Classic* from its name, and remains the most widely recognized brand in the world to the present. Try finding a can of New Coke today.

> You can change your product, but if you tamper with a beloved brand, the public will kill you. A successful brand, however, is a joy to behold. It conveys its strong personality proudly. It is consistent. It is confident without being cocky. It is friendly without fawning. It never wavers, doesn't put a foot in the wrong place, and assumes the public will accept it but never takes its place for granted. A successful brand seems to chug along effortlessly, when in fact it is the product of exhaustive research, dedication, backbreaking work, and inexplicable inspiration. It is, to paraphrase Thomas Edison, "10 percent inspiration and 90 percent perspiration." What is remarkable is the way the exhausting work is hidden, with all the gears and wheels behind the curtain, so that the brand seems to emerge on its own with no telltale signs that this isn't the brand's personality but actually the product of endless market research projects. In Branding, as in magic, the effect is lost if the effort is visible.

A *brand* is an end result. *Branding* is the process by which a brand comes to be. A brand is many, many things, but it is never an accident.

THE THREE COMPONENTS OF BRANDING

If Branding is the creation and development of a personality—an iden-tity—for a product or company, it is the result of work by a number of dif-ferent professionals, all aiming at the same goal. While the roles of advertising and marketing have been well documented, the third prong within the Branding process, public relations, has largely been overlooked. For the most part, Branding professionals fall into three categories:

1. *Advertising*. It's a wonderful thing to create a unique, user-friendly brand that the public is sure to embrace. However, if the public doesn't find out about the brand—and much of the public will find out through advertising—all that effort, time, and money will go to waste. The look and attitude of the advertising also help define the brand in the public's mind.

2. *Marketing*. In devising the personality of the brand and determining how it will be presented to the public, marketing, which is usually done in-house and through consultants, helps to create the entity that the brand will become. It's a fine thing to own the recipe for Oreo cookies, but if you decided to sell the recipe and not the cookies, you would be making a very large marketing mistake. Marketing is not just selling; it is knowing what to sell and how to sell it as part of a larger plan.

3. *Public relations*. If advertising is the juggernaut of public attention, pub-lic relations is the stealth bomber. PR generates publicity for the brand, helps solidify the public's opinion of the brand, and defines the brand—all without being perceived by the public.

Advertising is obvious, marketing is invisible, but public relations is the most difficult of all things to be: subtle. It is also arguably the most valuable, indispensable part of the Branding process. Without public rela-tions, it would be impossible to create a truly world-class brand, no matter what the budget or how exciting the product. Public relations is absolutely essential to Branding.

What *Is* Branding, Anyway?

For a new brand to be successful, all three of the Branding components must be firing on all cylinders. They must be working in tandem, but they also have to succeed individually.

Advertising

In today's business climate, even the most secure brands need to advertise. As it sells its billions and billions of hamburgers, McDonald's doesn't cut back on its ads; it increases them. Nike is well known for spending millions on celebrity endorsements for advertising. Its ads are legendary, and its "swoosh" logo is known the world over without a word being said.

A good advertising account executive will be involved in the birth of a brand, even if others have already decided on a good portion of the brand identity. How to present that identity—to introduce the public to the personality of the product—is advertising's job, in conjunction with public relations.

The look of a television or print ad is as important as the message being delivered in print or dialogue. Quick edits, bright colors, extreme close-ups, and changing landscapes may appeal more to younger viewers, and will convey a different personality than golden sunsets, slow camera pans, and traditional storytelling.

Sound, too, will change with the kind of brand being developed. Loud music might be fine for a soft drink ad, but won't work for a feminine hygiene product. If the product is meant to appeal to young, urban-based men, it's probably a bad idea to use music from *Swan Lake* to make your point. If the product is intended to have a sassy, feminine attitude, Sheryl Crow will more likely achieve the goal than Barry Manilow.

But advertising isn't just about creating TV commercials. As Marshall McLuhan noted decades ago, "The medium is the message." The programs during which the ad can be seen will make a statement about the personality of the product, as will the choice of publications in which print ads will run. If your product is supposed to be irreverent, young, up-to-date, and unconventional, ad buyers will probably be more successful in *Rolling Stone* than in *U.S. News and World Report*. Remember, each media outlet has as clearly defined a personality as its advertisers. In fact, the advertising often helps define the media outlet's personality, and vice versa. CBS has, whether correctly or not, been identified as the "older network" for a number of years, and savvy advertisers will probably be very careful about aiming youth-oriented ads at viewers of that network. More specifically, the ads will be purchased with a very careful eye on which programs appeal to the target audience.

Account executives get involved earlier on with the concept of the ad campaign itself. When a brand is new, it's important the target audience be able to identify the brand, and identify *with* the brand, very quickly. So after it's decided what kind of brand identity is being introduced, and the target audience to which the brand is being marketed, advertising creative executives begin deciding what message to convey and how to convey it. As Grace Ascolese of Ascolese Associates says, if you were advertising a new soft drink, "You can argue about taste, but in order to get tried, you have to come up with a personality" for your product.

Consider the TV ads for Mentos, the breath mints aimed at teenagers and young adults. While viewers over 30 might consider the ads annoying and obnoxious, the commercials identify the product's identity well, and they are perfectly aimed at the target audience. In each of these ads, which are filmed without dialogue, a young person is presented with some obstacle (a traffic jam, parents returning home too early), and, popping a Mento, concocts a cheeky solution to the problem while a bouncy jingle informs us a few times over that Mentos are "fresh and full of life."

Now, from a storytelling standpoint, that doesn't make a great deal of sense. Mints don't actually help you solve your problems, unless your problem is a mouth that reeks of garlic. In fact, even in the commercial, the mint doesn't solve the problem. But in presenting the kind of person the ad celebrates, having the target audience identify with that person (through the rudimentary story being told), and then having the character enjoy the product, a number of messages are being conveyed. First, if you want to be like this person, you should try these mints. Second, this is a cool kind of person to be. Third, isn't it fun to be young and irreverent? These mints are young and irreverent. If you want to be seen this way, you'd better have the mints with you at all times. All this, and not a line of dialogue has been spoken.

What *Is* Branding, Anyway?

Advertising doesn't create the identity, but it does choose how to present the identity, and it certainly helps define the identity of the product, and, by extension, its users. With a clever choice like that made for the Mentos ads, it expresses the advertiser's message very well. But ads can't do the job alone. And they can't determine what the image should be. That part of the process is accomplished through marketing.

Marketing

Before there can be a brand, there has to be a product. The bridge between product and recognizable brand is marketing.

It is sometimes difficult for people outside the business to understand marketing, because they confuse it with advertising. The two are totally different processes. Their goals are not the same, and their methods are not in the least similar. They are performed by separate groups of specialists, and can often be at odds with one another until a compromise or alternative solution can be reached that satisfies both disciplines.

If advertising is the way the public usually discovers a product, marketing determines what it will discover. If the look and sound of advertising are important, the decisions made by marketing executives will determine the tone of the ads. In other words, marketing takes a product and assigns it a personality. Based on the target audience for the product, marketing will determine which traits that segment of the population is likely to find appealing, and will do its best to ascribe them to the product being marketed.

For example, when Apple Computer was experiencing some sales difficulties a number of years ago, and cofounder Steve Jobs returned to guide the company, the iMac computer was the first product to be released by the "new" company. The personality of the product was going to be very important: It had to remind loyal Apple users why they liked the computer to begin with, and to convince new users to try something that required a large outlay of money and was going to look different from anything they'd seen before. In fact, the future of the entire company was going to hinge on acceptance of iMac, and if it was seen as too much like IBM-based PCs, it would be rejected by the loyal Apple following. If it came

9

across as too different or too strange, the product would fail to expand Apple's market share—which was dwindling at the time—and the company would be in very dire straits indeed.

What the company did was to analyze the strong points of Apple and the iMac. It marketed the iMac as something new, something fun, and something that younger users who were just beginning on the Internet could appreciate.

Marketing executives made sure the iMac was presented as a young, innovative, smart, and easy way to enter the online world, something that American consumers were just beginning to do in large numbers at the time. TV ads emphasized the look of the computer and the ease with which it could be installed and connected to the Internet.

So, before the product came out, there was already great anticipation. But once the iMac—which was considered a wildly revolutionary design at its inception—was unveiled, the focus was all on the product. It helped that the iMac *looked* different: Its colorful, all-in-one bulbous design was certainly a change from the beige boxes that had dominated the computer industry for years.

Certainly, the iMac turned the fortunes of Apple Computer around. Apple increased its market share and sold millions of iMacs, and a company that appeared to be on the brink of extinction not long before was assured a solid foothold, if not a dominant position, in the home computer market.

The iMac campaign worked because the personality assigned to the product was appealing to enough consumers who could afford to buy it. It worked because the advertising choices were made correctly. It worked because the product could actually deliver the innovation and ease it promised. But mostly, the iMac campaign was successful with consumers because the marketing executives involved had correctly defined its target demographic, had been careful to identify the characteristics that market would find attractive, and had successfully conveyed that personality through the product to the public. People believed that the iMac was innovative and exciting because the marketing choices made were the correct ones.

What *Is* Branding, Anyway?

If the computer hadn't worked well, if it hadn't delivered on its promises, no marketing campaign would have been able to achieve the success of the iMac. But by the same token, if the marketing campaign hadn't been thoughtfully worked out and executed, the product could have been superior to all others on the market and it still would have been swallowed up by the competition. Remember Betamax? Sony's original video recording system was considered by most experts and many consumers to be the superior format in terms of performance, but it was quickly eliminated from the market because Panasonic and other companies managed to position VHS as a more user-friendly, longer-lasting (the cassettes were bigger, and held more tape) product. Quality was no longer the issue, and Betamax is now a half-forgotten curiosity.

> Marketing doesn't determine what a product will be or how high its quality will be. It does determine how the product is perceived by the public, and it is best done when working from strength—in other words, a strong product can be more easily marketed—but that doesn't mean every great product will market itself. Nor does it mean that every successfully marketed product is the best in the field.

What marketing does is to determine the proper audience for a product, and then deliver to that audience what it wants. The target demographic can be as narrow as 15-year-old boys living in the suburbs, or it can be literally anybody. That will depend on the product. But once the demographic is identified, marketing professionals analyze it, make sure the characteristics of that demographic are compatible with the product, and then emphasize the strengths of the product. The strengths of the product here are very specific: They are the strengths that will best convey the personality the demographic wants to see in itself.

For example, if Philips had tried to market its flat-screen TV to an audience over 65, which traditionally is not warm to change, it might not have been successful, no matter how innovative the product may have been. Instead, the company aimed its ads at people in their twenties and thirties, emphasized the newness and difference of the product, and had a great success.

Some of this type of success is due to market research, which is a branch of marketing. Through focus groups, surveys, and other tools, market research helps determine what people want. Marketing is more the art of taking what already exists and making it more attractive to the public through positioning and Branding techniques.

It is a natural and easy mistake to confuse marketing with advertising. (Advertising is what happens when marketing has already been done.) And marketing is not public relations, the discipline we are about to examine. Public relations also works with what marketing professionals have already done, but does different, less obvious things with it.

Public Relations

"A lot of clients don't understand the difference between Branding, PR, advertising and marketing," says Rob Frankel, author of *Revenge of Brand X.* "Personally, I prefer PR to advertising. I like PR because a lot of my Branding program is based on third-party endorsement. It's way more credible and fast-acting than when you pay for ads."

People often confuse public relations with publicity, and it's easy to see why. Public relations is actually the craft of attracting publicity, and not publicity itself. That statement is not simply a trick of semantics; it makes an important distinction that will determine pivotal, essential components of a Branding campaign.

> Public relations is not advertising; advertising is what you pay for, public relations is what you pray for. It does not consist of devising or purchasing ads that you see on television, hear on radio, or read in newspapers and magazines. What is said about you is more valuable than what you say about yourself. PR is not marketing, since public relations does not decide on the message to be conveyed or the personality of the product being marketed. Public relations does not create the product or its identity. Its role in Branding is considerably more subtle.

What public relations does is to attract attention, preferably from news media, since the media will eventually tell many more people than the PR person could reach individually. PR people are adept at finding the news in a story and making sure it is packaged properly and aimed at the correct media to best exploit the information and generate the most publicity.

> Public relations is possibly the most organic, central part of Branding, one that will help make the campaign successful or doom it to failure. Once marketing executives decide on a perfect identity for the product, and once the advertising executives have packaged a message to deliver directly to the public, public relations professionals are responsible for the messages the public gets through indirect channels—that is, through the news media they consider more credible than anything they see between acts of a television show.

One problem, however, is that some businesses are leery of the press overall, and don't realize the boost that PR can provide. "Most companies have a fear, not just of the *Wall Street Journal,* but of all major publications. I aim to get my clients to realize that when I can get other people writing about them (hopefully in a favorable light), thinking about them, talking about them, and using them as an example in a conference or speech, that is called free publicity, and that is brand building," says Scott M. Davis, author of *Brand Asset Management.*

The job of public relations is to combine what marketing and advertising do, and then use the information in different ways. Marketing determines the personality, or *brand identity,* being publicized. Public relations professionals are given that information and are asked to find the proper news media to carry the message. For example, in the case of the iMac, Apple made sure (quite often by donation) that school systems around the country had iMac computers as soon as they were available. This helped familiarize very young computer users—possibly those who had never used a computer before—with Apple's product first. This brilliant public relations move demonstrated that Apple had strong interests in education and a history of helping children. These are not bad messages to give a consumer.

The move into schools also made sure that iMacs were perceived as unusual and innovative. This reinforced the famous print ad campaigns that showed no computer, but rather photographs of innovative thinkers (Albert

Einstein, Martin Luther King, John Lennon) with the slogan "Think Different" and the Apple logo. The ads were meant to precede the iMac to the market with the message that Apple was the "different" computer company. But it managed to be different while identifying itself with comfortable, interesting personalities, and therefore did not come across as threatening or strange. This brand identity appealed to traditional Apple customers by identifying them with forward-thinking geniuses, and also tweaked the interest of new users, who wanted to see themselves in that light.

Brand identity is the most vital part of the Branding concept. With the wrong identity, even a perfect product can fail to become a brand. With the proper identity, one that has been crafted carefully and thoughtfully, a product can launch a brand and eventually become what every Branding practitioner hopes for—a household word.

> Public relations doesn't create the brand identity, but it helps to present and define the identity in ways that are not so blatant that the consumer is on the defensive before the message is communicated.

Local newspapers, radio programs, and television news programs are the beginning of the PR person's quest, which will eventually lead to national TV shows like *Dateline* and *60 Minutes*, as well as more chatty, but perhaps more user-friendly, outlets like *Oprah* and *Today*. The most widely read publications in the country and the world, such as the *New York Times*, the *Washington Post, USA Today,* and *Parade* are all targets on the public relations dartboard.

But before news of the new product, service, or personality can reach the media, the public relations professional has to analyze the brand identity. The characteristics built in by marketing executives will help guide the message. Sassy younger women read different magazines than successful middle-aged men. The audience for Conan O'Brien is not the same as that for Regis Philbin.

And at the core of the public relations activity comes the question of news. Public relations professionals don't create news stories; they find the newsworthy aspect or unique selling proposition of a company's story and try to attract attention to that. In other words, PR is the art of telling the truth in the most positive light possible, like wearing your best suit for a job interview.

In order to understand the role of public relations in Branding, first we have to understand how public relations works. It's a business unlike any other, and its rules are very specific. Public relations can help create a brand, establish it, promote it, develop it, and keep it healthy, all without being detected by the general public. It is as central a component of Branding as any other, and its importance is immeasurable.

CHAPTER TWO

THE ROLE OF PUBLIC RELATIONS IN BRANDING

As I explained in the previous chapter, public relations is a seriously misunderstood discipline. Even people in business tend to confuse it with publicity, which is a completely separate concern. In actuality, public relations is much more than the art of attracting publicity.

Because PR can be difficult to control, it is often discredited. According to Dick Lyles, president and chief operating officer of The Ken Blanchard Companies, a full-service consulting and performance improvement company, "People tend to migrate to things they can control. Even now, when an executive looks at an advertising message that's exactly what they want to create, with exactly the right positioning and so forth, they say, 'That's the message I want to send.' That's great, even though people may not read it, or people may give it less value and discount it, because it's advertising. . . . [On the other hand], if you get a well-placed article in a trade journal or you get some ink, people give it more credibility. The impact is greater, but because it may not come out exactly the way it was intended to come out, [businesspeople frequently] discount it."

The concepts of Branding and public relations are closely intertwined. The job of public relations is to encourage the public to have positive thoughts about a particular company, product, service, or individual. Branding is the idea that a particular set of attributes will encourage the public to have positive thoughts about a particular company, product, service, or individual. It's a subtle distinction, but an essential one.

The Role of Public Relations in Branding

In order to best understand Branding and how it is done, it is necessary to examine and explain public relations. Many experts on Branding espouse the opinion that public relations is a vital part—if not the most vital part—of the Branding process. Public relations practitioners are particularly well suited to the Branding concept, since they are well versed in the techniques and practices that create a public identity very close to the central idea of a brand.

Unlike marketing or advertising, which are essential activities and indispensable to the creation of a brand, public relations is not devoted to a tangible object. Advertising executives create television, print, and radio ads; these are concrete, identifiable things. Marketing creates a product—be it a physical product or a service—and presents it to the public. That is an obvious, noticeable thing; it is not hard to understand.

Public relations does not do either of those things. When properly conceived and executed, a public relations campaign is next to invisible; the public does not know it's there. More to the point, public relations does not create a physical manifestation of its effort: When PR is done right, it doesn't leave the trace of a newspaper or magazine ad, a videotape, or an audiocassette that will win awards—and that can sometimes overwhelm the message being delivered.

What public relations does is to encourage third parties to deliver the message. Why? Because the third parties are news organizations, print journalists, and television and radio news programs and talk shows, which by definition have more credibility for the general public than an advertisement or the word of a company spokesperson.

In other words, public relations is meant to generate news coverage. It does so through planned events and through news stories (*true* news stories, it should be emphasized) suggested to reporters and their editors. When a newspaper runs an article about the unusual new promotion being done by a local business, that's public relations. But to the reader of that newspaper, it appears to be an article generated by the editorial staff of the publication itself: There is no advertisement disclaimer that runs over a PR-suggested news article. That makes sense, because the news editor always has the option of ignoring the suggestions made by public relations people. Editors and producers will rely on public relations for news leads, but will not simply act as a conduit, presenting the message from the public relations company's client unedited and unconfirmed. Public relations can suggest, but not control, the message being sent. It is a very difficult tightrope to walk.

For example, in 2000, when the Beatles song compilation *1* was being released by Capitol Records, it presented (believe it or not) a public relations dilemma: how to promote an album full of songs that the entire target audience almost certainly owned in another form already.

The problem was solved in a number of ways. First of all, it was emphasized that these were the 27 number one songs the band had produced during its legendary career. Press releases noted over and over again that these songs had never been compiled on one album before. It was intimated that many in the group's core audience might not have heard these songs on CD before, having bought them on vinyl records when they were originally released.

But more than anything, the public relations executives managed to generate publicity for the album with something that no other project could possible offer: access to the (at the time) three surviving Beatles for interview. News programs, interview shows, publications, and talk programs were all given opportunities (albeit brief ones) to interview at least one Beatle, and therefore the album was mentioned on countless airwaves and in publications for weeks before its release, and given very prominent placement.

The album went on to become a smash hit, reaching number one almost 40 years after the initial release of some of the recordings. It was yet another triumph for a legendary recording group, but it was also something of a coup for the public relations personnel involved. Yes, they had the luxury of three of the most famous faces on the planet, and the ability to use them. But the PR people who worked on that project also knew that they had to make something that wasn't necessarily new seem vital and important, and they knew where the news story in the project was kept. Making sure the news got out was their job, and they did it admirably.

The best part: The public was never aware there were PR people involved at all. What average fans saw on TV was Paul McCartney, George Harrison, and/or Ringo Starr. They heard snippets of the songs they had loved for decades. And they were told that this was different; it was new; it was unique. That's all the public needed to know. The fact that this message had been carefully constructed and the interviews painstakingly arranged was irrelevant to consumers; all they needed to know was that the Beatles were, more or less, back.

Public relations works behind the scenes, but its impact on Branding is enormous. Because PR generates interest, and precisely because it is working offstage, it is as valuable a part of the Branding process as can be imagined. And best of all, it's often the least expensive component in a sophisticated Branding machine.

As Adam Christing, president and founder of Clean Comedians, a company that provides meeting planners with G-rated comedians, says, "Public relations takes the brand and makes it mobile, makes it more visible. It's like taking a band that's been successful in a local neighborhood and taking it out on the road so more people can experience it."

Of course, when the message is not delivered in the form that was initially intended, that means the public relations professional has not done the job properly. The mistake can be in the design of the message itself—in particular, if the message that has been designed is a false or misleading one—or in the method of its delivery. It's a fine thing to have a vital, exciting news story to tell, but if the presentation is ineffective, that story will not be told, or will be told in such a way that its original intention is lost.

Public relations is about messages and their delivery, but that isn't all PR is. In correlation with Branding, the goal of public relations must always be to create a feeling in the mind of the target audience for which the message is being tailored. If Branding is about creating an identity for a product, service, or entity (company or individual), public relations' contribution to Branding is about making that identity friendly and likable for the public—specifically, the public for which the message is intended.

Obviously, the feeling most PR aspires to create is a positive one. But the intention is vastly more complex than that: In truth, public relations seeks to create and maintain a consistent feeling of familiarity, trust, reliability, and confidence with the targeted public. If advertising is about getting the public's attention, public relations is about delivering the message once the attention has been commanded.

When people express an opinion about a product or a company, initially they'll say they like or don't like it, without offering further explanation. But when they're given specific questions about their opinions, the effects of public relations become clear. When products are assigned personality traits or attributes by the public—"friendly," "environmentally aware," "concerned with quality," "accessible"—it means that public relations, in conjunction with advertising and marketing, has done its job. But because the public is naturally wary of advertising and marketing, and because those disciplines are considerably more visible than public relations, it is possible that PR makes the most honest, and deepest, impact on the public's psyche.

How is the feeling created? Unlike advertising or marketing, public relations aims to influence public opinion without being noticed. So efforts made by companies to create goodwill through advertising and marketing are effective, but will be met with a higher amount of resistance from the public than a public relations campaign.

ANATOMY OF A PR CAMPAIGN

An effective public relations campaign must begin with a clear message. In other words, the point being made to the public must be focused, well conceived, and uncluttered; there is no point in trying to deliver two messages at once, since both will inevitably be diluted upon delivery, and therefore less effective. Simply expressing the company's chosen identity in easily identifiable terms is enough for an initial campaign, and if that message is delivered successfully, the campaign is a success.

The message is determined by analyzing the brand being marketed, and doing so with clear vision and self-knowledge. Too many marketing executives rely on their own concept of the brand's identity, and never bother to discover what attributes the public has assigned to a product. Just because you've decided that you want to project a certain image doesn't mean that's the image you're projecting. Extremely high-profile marketing campaigns have failed because not enough market research and communication with the consuming public were done.

The Role of Public Relations in Branding

For example:

- When AT&T Wireless decided to consolidate its wireless phone, pager, and Internet technology into something called mLife, it gave the public examples of what the company meant. Unfortunately, the public still doesn't understand, and has no idea what the *m* stands for (it is *messaging*).
- United Airlines has long invited the public to "fly the friendly skies of United." The public has noticed that the experience on the plane is not terribly friendly, and is now distrustful of all airlines' claims.

The criteria for effective public relations messages should be: (1) Is it true? (2) Is it unusual? (3) Is it interesting?

On the other hand, if a company already exists in the marketplace, a new message will have to be identified. For retail companies, the addition of a new product category or a price reduction are always effective messages. Sales promotions, particularly very public or extremely unusual ones, make good messages. Anything out of the ordinary being done by the company in the name of public service or community aid is a legitimate message.

In order for the message to be even rudimentarily effective, it absolutely must be true. Remember, the message is being disseminated by the legitimate news media; a false message will be discovered and exposed, and will immediately brand the company negatively. It will do more damage than having no message at all, and such situations must be avoided at all costs.

Unique messages are going to be more noticeable and more attractive to the gatekeepers who determine which stories are told and which are not. So an unusual message—something a company is doing that no one else has considered or been creative enough to conceive—will be considerably more successful than one that seems tired or old simply because it has been seen before.

It goes without saying that the message must be interesting. If it is unique, unusual, and true, but without any interest to the general public, the message being delivered will most likely never find the light of day. If it does, it will undoubtedly be ignored, or worse, ridiculed.

A BRANDED WORLD

Many companies make the mistake of assuming that if a message seems unusual and interesting to them, it will be those things for the general consuming public. People in business tend to find their business fascinating; it is the thing they spend most of their time thinking about, so they are more knowledgeable about and concerned with their business than any casual observer or consumer would be. That is only natural and proper. But it is far too easy to make the miscalculation that a message that might be fascinating to an industry insider—for example, "Ours is the only paper bag made with 100 percent maple fibers"—will also be of interest to a casual user of the product. In almost every case, that assumption will be proven untrue.

So, communication with the consuming public is an essential component to any successful Branding venture. Discovering from the public what its true feelings are about the brand identity being contemplated, as well as any changes being discussed concerning an existing brand identity, can help a wise marketer avoid miscalculations that can prove disastrously costly and possibly fatal to the brand, the product, or the company.

This is not to imply that the public must be allowed to dictate all Branding decisions, however. What's more important is for anyone involved in Branding to have a clear-eyed view of their brand identity. Wal-Mart remains a wildly successful brand by not trying to be Tiffany's. McDonald's, although it has slipped precipitously as a trusted brand in recent years, still has the good sense not to hire Wolfgang Puck to rethink its hamburger recipe.

When a Branding professional loses sight of the original mission—that is, the brand identity—and tries to be all things to all people, the results are almost always calamitous. The archetypal example of New Coke works as a warning about so many different Branding errors that it seems clichéd to mention it, but consider: The fundamental miscalculation being made was the level of loyalty the average Coca-Cola drinker had for what was, and remains, unquestionably the most well-known, best-loved brand identity on this planet. To think it was a good idea to remove this beloved product—in favor of a formula that emulated the competition and was bound to alienate Coca-Cola loyalists who had stuck with the brand, in some cases, for decades—is astonishing.

A FEW BASIC PROMISES

Public relations can operate effectively only when a clear, realistic brand identity has been conceived. Certainly, PR professionals can be part of the team that establishes that identity, but it must be, above all else, a true identity. That means it must have specific attributes, specific philosophical tenets, and, most important, a few basic promises made to the consumer that will never, ever be broken.

These promises, which should be written down in the simplest language possible and distributed on a regular basis to every employee of the company, are a covenant made with the public. They define the brand identity; they provide reasons to patronize the brand; and they offer, at the most basic level, differentiation from all competing brands. They are never to be taken lightly by any employee, and under no circumstances are they ever to be broken for any reason.

If your business is a store that sells items that cost $1 apiece, you must never charge $1.05 for anything. If your restaurant prides itself on cleanliness, the rest rooms have to be absolutely spotless anytime anyone walks in. If your promise is that every customer will be served within 30 seconds of entering, you'd better have a stopwatch on every employee's wrist and be sure it's operating accurately.

The promises your business makes are the central core of that business. If you've promised to provide the longest hot dogs in town, and you provide them, no reasonable person is going to complain that you don't have the best crêpes suzettes as well—unless you've promised that too.

It's extremely important that the promises you make flow from your brand identity. Understand what you are to the public and what is expected of you, and you can make bold but realistic promises. Try to provide every solution to every problem, and you will end up providing nothing that is the least bit effective.

Consider, for example, the Disney brand. Here is a company whose name and logo are recognized in every country on the planet, whose message is received and understood everywhere from Beverly Hills to Beirut. It was once estimated that Mickey Mouse was the most recognized figure anywhere on Earth, more than the president of the United States, more than Tom Cruise, actually more than Santa Claus (who is famous in only about one-third of the world's countries).

On the surface, Disney might appear to offer all things to all people. Besides its movies and television programs under the Walt Disney name, it also produces entertainment under the Touchstone and Hollywood Pictures banners. Disney has a network television show on a network it owns (ABC), and also provides programming on cable TV via the Disney Channel and ABC Family. The company owns theme parks in California, Florida, Japan, and France. It also owns ESPN, publishing companies, video distribution companies, real estate, and retail stores. Disney logos appear on merchandise ranging from souvenir Mickey Mouse ears to fashions created by respected designers, electronics, calendars, furniture, musical instruments, sound recordings, and timepieces. Disney produces Broadway shows. It even owns a town in Florida.

But no matter how widely it casts its net, Disney always promises its customers the same things: high quality, fanatical customer service, and a dedication to the family. It might produce some R-rated movies under its Touchstone, Miramax, or Hollywood Pictures umbrella, but never with the Disney name. It will provide scary thrill rides in its theme parks, but you'd better believe the streets in that park will be clean and the "cast members" who work there will find a way to solve virtually any problem a guest might have during the stay. Guests at Walt Disney World are never told, "We can't do that"; they are always given at least an alternative solution. Maybe the ABC network will broadcast *NYPD Blue,* which offers controversial language and partial nudity, but the Disney Channel won't ever consider such a thing. If Disney produces a show on Broadway, you can rest assured that children will be admitted and the content will not offend their parents.

Disney has become the tremendous conglomerate it is today by making promises to its consumers and keeping them consistently since the company's inception. Anything that bears the Disney name has a special trust, a covenant with the consumer, and Disney lives up to that covenant every single time.

It's easy to ridicule the seemingly fanatical insistence Disney has on referring to its employees as cast members, in considering the consequences of every word spoken on every program its networks air, in not allowing its male employees to grow beards, or in its sanitized image that seems unrealistic in modern society. But it would be foolish to attack the surface of the Disney brand and overlook the unprecedented success it has enjoyed for a number of decades. The company continues to grow, but never for a moment does it take its covenant—the promises it makes to its audience—for granted.

Go to the Disney Web site at www.disney.com and you'll see the company's dedication to its core philosophy at work with every click. Want to discuss a vacation at Walt Disney World in Florida? You can book your vacation, including airfare, car rental, hotel, and theme park tickets, through Disney online. If you need personal assistance, phone numbers are always available. News about upcoming movies from the Disney studios can be found, including coming attractions trailers. Games are available for children and adults. Want to buy some Disney merchandise? The Disney Store has an online catalog. There is always the option of speaking to a Disney representative with any question or concern you might have. And the Disney Web site is careful not to provide links to ABC, Touchstone, or Miramax, because those companies deal in material that, although affiliated with the parent company, does not conform to the Disney brand. They are separate brands and are treated separately. They have their own Web sites.

While the philosophy is not directly presented to the consumer in words, it is not in the least difficult to discern or understand. Disney will provide you with high-quality, attentive customer service and a dedication to family. It's there on the Web site, in the theme parks, and in the entertainment provided by the company under its own name. Under no circumstances does the Disney Company ever renege on those promises, and it holds firm to them in every aspect of its branded business.

On those occasions when there is even the suggestion of a break with the covenant, Disney works swiftly to correct the situation. When some video copies of its animated film *The Little Mermaid* were rumored to have an off-color visual joke in three frames (⅛ of a second), the company made sure the rumors were dispelled, and the offending three frames, although they really didn't contain what the rumors said they did, were cut from subsequent copies. Disney takes its covenant very seriously.

BRANDING IS ESSENTIAL

Everything impacts on Branding—the smell of the bathroom, the signs in the window, the product being sold in the store, the things people say. One of the most powerful things that impacts all people's perceptions is what they read, see, or hear about in the media, because it carries with it the imprimatur of the media outlet.

To illustrate: If a garage band pays to produce its own CD and sends out fliers to every record store in the country saying the album is a breakthrough collection, it won't carry a fraction of the impact that same CD will have if someone on MTV uses the exact same words, because now the brand of the garage band has been enhanced with the brand MTV.

The old saying, "There is no such thing as bad publicity" is absolutely incorrect, however. Having a brand's name mentioned in the media is a very strong influencer, and it can cut both ways. Should a media outlet say something negative about a brand—even if the information is proven to be totally inaccurate—the negative repercussions on the brand identity can be devastating. It can take a lot of damage control, in the form of advertisement, retractions from media outlets, and strong statements from the brand itself, to undo one misplaced comment from a credible media outlet. Sometimes the damage can't be controlled or undone.

When public relations is done properly, an item of information is disseminated to media gatekeepers, who then decide to report the information either directly or indirectly. Reportage is done, research is accumulated, interviews are performed. Eventually the information item becomes a media report, and it is at that moment that the public relations professional can no longer control it entirely. Media outlets—particularly the most desirable, most credible ones—operate autonomously, reporting the information they deem necessary or interesting and excluding all else. Time constraints, space limitations, and the realities of economics play as prominent a role in the decision-making process as the newsworthiness of the information being considered.

If a company is launching a new brand, the temptation will exist to try to saturate the market with information on that brand. Often, when my company is contacted about the creation of a new brand or a new product, the request will be, "Get us as much exposure as you can." That is absolutely the wrong thing to request at that time, because it is not a strategic position.

Such a company should be requesting a strategic plan that is consistent with their short-, middle-, and long-term goals. (Short-term is defined as 6 months, mid-term as 18 months, and long-term as 36 months.) It's very important to define those goals before seeking media exposure, because the lack of a goal is the lack of a plan, and that will obliterate any hope of Branding before it ever has the opportunity to begin.

In Lewis Carroll's *Alice's Adventures in Wonderland,* there is a marvelous moment in which Alice, trying to find her way through the maze that is Wonderland, asks the Cheshire Cat for direction. The cat asks, quite logically, where Alice's destination might be, and she replies that she doesn't care where she ends up, but needs to know which road to take. Told that Alice doesn't care where she's going, the Cat replies, "Then it doesn't matter which way you go."

Companies that want to create brands but don't know what their specific goals are for the next 6, 18, or 36 months can't possibly be expected to define their brand identity or the proper kind of media coverage they need to best exploit their brand's possibilities.

A good percentage of Americans believe that Elvis is still alive; there's no accounting for what people might think. But the reality is that a Branding campaign, fueled by public relations efforts, will fail miserably if it doesn't have specific, well-defined goals in place for various points in the future before it begins.

How do the elite Branding experts determine their goals ahead of time and pass that information on to public relations professionals? It helps to be first in your field. Those companies that came to the marketplace before anyone else—Wal-Mart, Johnson & Johnson, Kleenex, Coca-Cola, Disney, McDonald's—had an advantage before they generated their first media placement. Nobody was ahead of them, and they knew precisely what they intended to do.

Keep in mind that most of those brands established themselves very early with very little (in many cases, close to no) advertising budget to work with. They managed to create an impression in the minds of consumers without spending millions in magazines and newspapers or on radio or television (in those cases when radio and television existed at the brand's inception).

They did it almost exclusively with public relations. These companies had a plan, a course of action, long before they had a brand name or a brand identity. They projected the possible sales for their products and services and had realistic goals for the coming six months, the coming year, the coming three years. In many cases, those goals were far exceeded, due in large part to the brilliant public relations campaigns that had been launched and executed to establish and support the brand. Without those plans, goals, and projections, there would have been no road map—and, as the Cheshire Cat would say, there would be no point in choosing one road over another, since it wouldn't matter where you ended up anyway.

It is extremely important, then, to set realistic goals. In order to do that, the smart Branding practitioner needs to have a clear-eyed view of his or her own product and company. Only with that can a true brand identity be created, one that will capture the imagination of the targeted consumer and differentiate the new brand from whatever competition currently exists or will exist in the future. Keep in mind that even those who were first ended up dealing with competition. Kleenex may be the most famous brand of tissue available today, but it is far from the only one on the market.

THE POWER OF PR

It is impossible to isolate one individual aspect of the Branding process and examine its effect on the psyche of the consuming public, since an effective Branding campaign is more than the sum of its parts. Would a campaign be as effective without advertising as it would be with advertising? Certainly not. Without a strong brand identity designed by marketing professionals, would a brand still be able to establish itself as more than simply a product? I think not.

But by that same token, removing public relations from the Branding overview would be an extremely serious mistake. Because the public finds information it receives from the news media to be the most credible of all the messages it receives publicly (as opposed to messages from friends or loved ones, which are received privately), public relations serves an absolutely indispensable purpose in Branding. It provides information about the brand to the public, without the stigma of being from the source itself. Messages received from the source—such as advertising messages—are perceived by the public to be less credible, since self-interest will invariably cloud the information being provided.

Public relations provides perhaps the clearest access to the public, but not the most direct by any standard. By definition, information that is disseminated through the media will be filtered by the media as well. In some cases that filtering takes the form of self-censorship; in other words, the media choose not to disseminate the information at all. This can happen because of the space, time, and financial limitations mentioned before, or because the media outlet has deemed the information unnecessary, not newsworthy, or just plain uninteresting.

But even when a media outlet chooses to use information it has been given through public relations, the message is not guaranteed to be delivered in its original form. In fact, most of the information delivered by news media and provided initially by public relations professionals is altered in some way by the time it reaches the public. This is simply part of the news gathering and reporting process. Often, the original data provided by the public relations professional will be expanded into a wider-ranging news story, which will sometimes include not only the company that generated the original information, but other news sources as well. These can include competing brands, since there is no control over a news item once it has been presented to the news media.

Even if the originating company is the only source of information, almost always the reporter and gatekeeper who decide to report the story will gather their own data, conduct their own interviews, and write their own copy without consulting the public relations professional. The company creating or promoting the brand in question will not be consulted before the news item is published or broadcast, so even if there are inaccuracies in the reporting, they will be dealt with after the initial report, and will not be prevented so much as repaired.

Press coverage does not guarantee success. When the New Coke campaign was beginning, for example, and the date for the old Coke to leave store shelves approached, an entire half-hour of network television on ABC's *Nightline* was devoted to the topic. It was the kind of coverage a public relations professional dreams about, and still the product was one of the most notable failures in recent business history.

Public relations can't disguise a bad brand, and it can't create a brand where one doesn't exist. What PR exists to do is to tell the story as truthfully as possible, but in the interest of the client. Sometimes that will be part of a much larger overall campaign designed to help create or establish a brand in the mind of the public or to keep that brand fresh and positive in the public's collective sensibility.

When PR meets Branding, the result is a stronger, healthier brand in many cases. That happens when the criteria for public relations success mesh with those for Branding success; and those conditions come together more often than not if the proper planning has been done.

It would be a very serious miscalculation to assume that public relations alone can create a brand. But the corollary assumption—that public relations is a frill and not an integral component in the Branding process—would be potentially more devastating. Public relations exists to create in the general public's mind a positive image of a particular product, company, individual, or entity. That is about as close to a working definition of Branding as you are likely to find.

Public relations must be utilized alongside other business disciplines to make a Branding campaign work. There must be strong marketing plans, there have to be business models, there should be market research to determine the public's true opinions, and in almost every case there should definitely be advertising. However, the role of public relations within the Branding process has traditionally been deemphasized. Overlooking public relations—which provides the truest, most credible sources of information to the public—has proven to be a very shortsighted decision indeed.

CHAPTER THREE

BIRTH OF A BRAND

In this chapter, in order to illustrate the steps included in creating a brand, we will create a fictitious brand and develop it for the optimum Branding plan. We will create, refine, and develop our brand to illustrate how marketing, advertising, and especially public relations play into brand creation.

For our purposes, the brand we devise should have a few prerequisites:

1. It should be situated in a market that has no overall dominant brand.
2. It should make very specific promises and state them clearly.
3. It should have a well-developed brand identity that encompasses these promises.
4. It should have a specific target audience whose identification is enhanced by market research.
5. It should develop its identity based on achievable goals.
6. It should remain absolutely dedicated to the promises, to the point of obsession.
7. It should distinguish itself through its identity, which must be clear and easy for the public to understand.
8. It should police itself—in other words, there should be safeguards to ensure that the promises are constantly being kept, and if possible, exceeded.
9. It should create, besides a brand identity, a marketing identity, which will be the symbol the public will first recognize in conjunction with the brand.
10. It should never confuse or combine its identity in order to expand, but it must be expandable.

A BRANDED WORLD

First, let us identify a market into which our fictitious brand can be introduced. In accordance with the prerequisites we just listed, this must be a market that has no single dominant brand, such as Coca-Cola, Nike, Disney, or McDonald's. Our brand can certainly have competition, but we don't want to compete with a giant on the same day we introduce our first product. In Branding, it is always best to be first.

For the purposes of our exercise, we'll choose the ice cream market. While there are a number of formidable brands, such as Häagen-Dazs, Ben & Jerry's, Breyer's, and Edy's, all competing in that market, there is not yet one brand so dominant that attempting to sell a competing product in its marketplace seems pointless. Also, the ice cream market has enough separate niches to conquer that a well-conceived, well-developed brand could certainly make a very big impact on the current marketplace.

For example, it is possible to dominate the supermarket ice cream market, the premium ice cream market, the ice cream novelty market (cones, pops, etc.), or the ice cream storefront market (cones and cups sold for immediate consumption). We will have to choose the market for our brand carefully; carve out a niche by crafting a very specific, very attractive brand identity; and then make the right marketing and advertising moves, in conjunction with public relations campaigns, to convey the idea of the brand and its promises to the public.

Our first step should be a thorough examination of the ice cream market to determine the appropriate niche for our brand to dominate. Given the costs of setting up individual stores and establishing a retail take-out ice cream brand, we should immediately eliminate the storefront business from our plans. That's the kind of thing that can be an ancillary business after our brand has become a household name.

The novelty market, which consists of supermarket cartons with individual items inside (Dove Bars, Good Humor, etc.) or separate items sold at stands or from ice cream trucks, is also probably not the best market to target. Research indicates that, by a very wide margin, the bulk of ice cream is sold in supermarkets. So supermarket sales are the most obvious niche to attack.

Within that supermarket niche, the super-premium market, in which such brands as Häagen-Dazs, Ben & Jerry's, and others have done well, has shown strength. These brands, which generally have a higher percentage of milkfat and a more upscale profile and market identity, are considered the crown jewels of the ice cream business and are correspondingly more expensive than other supermarket brands.

What most of the super-premium brands have done so far is to concentrate on exciting flavors that are not traditional. Ben & Jerry's has cultivated a fun, sixties-type persona, aligning its flavors with such cultural icons as Jerry Garcia. The flavors are often new, complex variations on old themes, including elements that have not traditionally been used in supermarket ice creams.

Cable Neuhaus, editor of *Folio* magazine, is a brilliant observer of brands and Branding. He has watched Ben & Jerry's, and he is impressed with the company's ability to create a brand. As he says, "I think most people buy Ben & Jerry's for two reasons: They really like the product, and it is a premium product, and Ben & Jerry's is very good at marketing the fun. The names of the ice cream are fun, and that's brilliant marketing."

Häagen-Dazs has been more traditional, emphasizing high quality and an upscale image to attract higher prices. Its flavors are less unconventional than Ben & Jerry's, but go beyond the traditional smooth, plain flavors that were considered supermarket fare before the super-premium brands began selling their ice cream in local markets.

In order to find an area that does not compete directly with the larger brands, and to distinguish our brand from all the rest, it will be necessary to find a niche that has not yet been explored. Sometimes, entering a market between two established niches is the best way to carve out a portion of the market for a new brand. As Al Ries says, "The way you build a brand is by creating a new category you can be first in."

Therefore, one way to enter the ice cream market and establish a brand unlike anything else already in that area would be to start with a very specific product line, one that seems narrow but can be expanded easily once the brand has been established successfully.

To establish a unique brand identity that we ourselves clearly understand, we need to analyze the identities of our most successful competitors.

A BRANDED WORLD

In supermarkets, Häagen-Dazs and Ben & Jerry's are the most recognizable, most successful super-premium brands, so they will be the personalities we'll observe. Keep in mind that our goal here is not to emulate our competitors and do what they do, or we'll be doomed before we start. Our aim should be to analyze what the competition is doing, and then do something that will fill a niche they have not yet considered. If we maneuver successfully, we can establish a brand that doesn't copy the competition, but steals some of its market share by appealing to a larger segment of the population in a way the competitors haven't considered.

Right now, basic flavors like chocolate and vanilla are dominated by less expensive bargain brands, such as "house" brands with the name of the supermarket on the carton, or by national brands like Breyer's and Edy's, which offer higher-quality, but not super-premium, products. Yes, Häagen-Dazs and Ben & Jerry's make chocolate and vanilla (Ben & Jerry's, in fact, has a flavor called "The World's Best Vanilla"), but they do not emphasize those flavors, and offer them more out of a sense of not ignoring the old standards than one of reinvigorating old favorites or finding something new about them.

Our brand, then, will be a super-premium ice cream sold through supermarkets that will feature only three flavors—chocolate, vanilla, and strawberry. These are the three basic flavors, which were sold in supermarkets for decades before super-premium ice cream was established, so the consuming public is used to them in that venue. But these flavors have never been emphasized in high-quality, super-premium form, so our brand will be unique to the market. In other words, we will be first—an absolute necessity for a recognizable, successful brand. Our niche becomes clearer with analysis. Right now, our core product—super-premium chocolate, vanilla, and strawberry ice cream sold in supermarkets—is not being duplicated by any of the competition. When it is offered by recognizable brands, it is either sold in half-gallons and not of the high quality we're going to offer, or deemphasized, sold only in pints, and given less shelf space than flashier names like Chunky Monkey and Dulce de Leche.

In order to stand out, we will have to emphasize our high quality and offer value. We can do this by packaging our ice cream not in pints or half-gallons, but in quarts. Since we will be offering only three flavors, we will not be losing shelf space if we make our packages larger, but we can avoid the "bargain/low-quality" stigma that half-gallon containers might evoke. Our ice cream will be of the highest quality, but since we are selling more of it at a time, we can offer it at a lower per-ounce price than any super-premium pint.

We do want to emphasize quality, but we don't want to jettison the image of fun and excitement that has made Ben & Jerry's so successful. So we should emphasize the experience of ice cream we all remember from childhood, when ice cream was the ultimate treat and we would behave ourselves all day for the promise of a cone at night.

So let's call our product Ultimate Treat. This name—which could have been Just the Best, Just Rewards, More Better, Evening Cone, or Best Basics—conveys the idea we're trying to express to the public. The word *ultimate* is a superlative; you can't do any better than this, and that is the message we are conveying. *Treat,* however, is more playful, and will evoke the childhood sense memory we are hoping for with this product.

Ultimate Treat's brand identity will be that of a friendly, easy-to-know product, one that combines the wistful nostalgia for a simpler childhood time with the desire for something that's better because it is made to be better—not pretentious, but basic and confident. It will have some of Häagen-Dazs' attention to ingredients and quality, coupled with a touch of Ben & Jerry's fun, but a gentler, more innocent type of fun than can be associated with Cherry Garcia.

Our aim will be to conjure up images of summer days with an ice cream cone in one hand and a parent's or grandparent's hand in the other. It will be the research and development department's responsibility to make sure the product lives up to the reputation we will create for it, and already marketing experts have been involved in the positioning of the product in supermarkets and the brand identity we have developed. Later, public relations (in concert with advertising and marketing) will introduce the identity, define it to the intended audience, and reinforce it through the introduction of the product itself and beyond.

REFINING THE BRAND'S PERSONALITY

Creating the brand, as discussed earlier, is more than simply creating a product and an advertising campaign. The brand will be defined by its identity—its personality—and everything that happens from that moment on will be based on that concept. The success or failure of the brand will very clearly be based on the identity and how well it is presented and maintained. "People don't understand that first you have to create the brand before you can raise awareness of that brand," says Rob Frankel, a world-renowned Branding expert and author of the book *The Revenge of Brand X.*

Our brand, Ultimate Treat, is already a very well-made product. And we have identified the niche of the market we're going to target. Now we need to determine what that niche finds attractive and how to best sculpt a brand identity.

Remember, that doesn't mean we're going to ask people what they want us to be. We're going to find out what people want and then emphasize those aspects of our brand's personality. In order to appeal to the target audience, we will find it necessary to specify the target audience's expectations so that we can then exceed them. This process will entail market research.

Focus groups, surveys, questionnaires, and polls have taken on something of a negative quality among the public, but they are still very useful tools in determining the mood of a targeted population. They are also very helpful in identifying that population.

For Ultimate Treat, our goal is to enter the supermarket ice cream market and eventually to dominate that market's super-premium subsection. Our efforts will be centered around the three basic flavors—chocolate, vanilla, and strawberry—that are the most popular, and the simplest, available on the market. And in order to avoid being a me-too product in an area already dominated by another brand, we will not try to emulate the high-end elegant appeal of Häagen-Dazs or the retro-hippie fun approach of Ben & Jerry's. Our aim is to carve out a new niche, perhaps drawing a bit on each of those market areas, but targeted at a broader range of consumers who might have some nostalgia for bygone days of ice cream cones and want to reexperience that feeling or pass it on to their children.

But our assumption that such an audience segment exists is, at this moment, strictly a gut feeling. If we find that people really *don't* long for a high-quality chocolate cone at the end of a hot summer day, we will have wasted millions of dollars on a premise that could have been revised with a comparatively small outlay of funds, effort, and time.

Therefore, market research personnel should be involved as early in the process as possible, according to Grace Ascolese, president of the Arlington, Virginia-based market research firm Ascolese Associates. "I would argue as a researcher that [research should be involved] at the very beginning so you don't develop something and then have to retrofit it," she says. "You get to the point where you have a car, and all you do is throw in twentysomethings drinking latte inside, and that's your Branding. Branding should be organic to the product so you can build it in and develop a sense of 'This is who I am,' if you keep it broad enough."

Having worked with brands ranging from Nickelodeon to AOL/Time Warner, Ascolese understands the power of Branding, but she also knows that research can make Branding more powerful if it's done properly. She does not advocate creating a product based simply on the test scores from research documents, but she does say paying close attention to what the public wants can help make any brand a household name.

According to Duane E. Knapp, author of *The Brand Mindset,* "most companies don't know what they are in the consumer's mind. Very few brands get to be genuine because very few companies know that's what they want to be. You have to understand, and you have to have a promise, and that promise has to be unique. Webster's definition of *brand* says it has to be distinctive, it can't be like anybody else's. The only attribute of *brand name* in the dictionary is 'well-known.' It has to be a promise that the customer cares about. It can't be a promise that a bunch of people made up over a good glass of Chardonnay like a lot of the tech companies did. 'We're going to have the biggest, most powerful network in the world.' Who cares about that? What I care about is that I want to pick up my phone and hear the other person without static."

In the case of Ultimate Treat, if we hire a market research firm like

Ascolese Associates, we'll need to ask a number of questions. In order to determine if our product has been designed properly, we'll need to find out if people want a super-premium ice cream in the three basic flavors. If they do, we'll have to begin our work on the brand's identity: In other words, Will consumers respond to the nostalgic but playful image we've determined the product should have? If that, too, turns out to be the case, we'll test the name *Ultimate Treat* versus some others to see which one the public responds to most positively and why.

The *why* becomes important when we consider the many reasons people might have for answering affirmatively on a form. In some cases, people respond to the first suggestion they're given more strongly than they will to subsequent suggestions. Others will have a negative reaction to either of the words in our brand name, or might have a particular image that resonates for them in one of the other choices. Names can be difficult, and sometimes they are decided less on research data and more on a gut feeling, if the data are not overwhelming.

A *focus group,* then, will be the place for us to start exposing our brand and its identity to the public. This is a small cross section of the public at large: Focus groups include about 8 to 10 people. They are either recruited in a common place, like a shopping mall, or through premailed questionnaires. Participants are paid a fee (usually $50 to $75 for consumers). Some professional focus groups are held within industries, and professionals are usually paid as much as $175 to participate, depending on their seniority and position within the company. Research firms keep lists of those who have participated before, and can sometimes put together a group based on income, gender, or other considerations, depending on the product and the type of audience the brand is trying to attract.

Sometimes the focus group is presented with the product itself. Other times, the idea, the name, or the concept of the product can be suggested. The questions are designed so that they are rarely answered with "yes" or "no." The group leader (the moderator who represents the product involved) makes sure to ask questions that begin with *how* or *why,* to get the group members to talk, expand on their opinions, and start discussions.

Market research done for a consumer product is not all that different than the same research done to gather data about an entertainment personality, a political candidate, or a television program. The questions are often about likes and dislikes; the choices are often between titles or names of products, advertising copy, images, and logos. And every scrap of information collected in the process can easily be ignored by marketing executives if they feel strongly enough about something else. It's not an exact science.

For example, "A friend of mine used to do movie positioning and was testing these titles," Grace Ascolese says. "There were two titles—*Flashdance,* and *Pittsburgh Ballerina*—and *Pittsburgh Ballerina* won. But whoever was in charge said, 'I'm not going to call this movie *Pittsburgh Ballerina,*' and so it was *Flashdance.*"

When I was helping to establish the Michael J. Fox brand at the time of *Family Ties,* the network had done testing, and one of the things that had been suggested was to recast the role of Alex P. Keaton. But Gary David Goldberg, who created the program, refused to do so, and a major television and (eventually) movie star was born. Sometimes, the right thing to do is to go with your gut.

A good deal of excellent, helpful information can be gained from market research, and quite often it can help conceive, establish, and maintain a very successful brand. While marketers have to be wary of the obvious trap—the urge to become whatever the public wants, merely to be accepted—market research information can warn them of possible missteps before they are taken, and can save huge sums of money spent on misguided campaigns.

However, one focus group or even one market research study will not be enough to launch a successful brand. In many cases, entrepreneurs trying to establish their product and brand identity will find market research too expensive and will have to bypass such activities for the alternative, which is merely to trust their initial instincts and hope they are right. Later, when brand extension or maintenance is the goal, market research might be a very useful tool.

In the case of Ultimate Treat, some basic assumptions will have to be made. First, our imaginary market researchers will have the task of determining if there is a market for the product as it has been envisioned. Our funding should be substantial, but not unlimited. We'll have to make sure the research that is done is done efficiently and is to the point. So, with these criteria in mind, how would a researcher answer the first question: Is there a market for Ultimate Treat?

The members of the first focus group, recruited from previous groups dealing with supermarket-based grocery products, would be asked to describe their most indulgent dessert treat. After a round of conversation that might include such candidates as crème brûlée or crepes suzette, the field can be narrowed. With Americans leading the world in ice cream consumption, it's a pretty sure wager that once the topic is brought up, a relatively quick consensus on ice cream can open the discussion to more specific concerns.

When the focus group has concluded that ice cream is a fine dessert, it will be possible to narrow the focus to what the group considers a good ice cream, and what it desires from an ice cream dessert.

Our research should have begun long before the focus group convenes, however. In order to know which questions to ask, it is essential to have the facts on the current state of the ice cream market. For that, we can find much of what we need on the Internet.

For example, the data on annual ice cream consumption in the United States as opposed to other countries comes from the URL www.tigerx .com/trivia/icecream.htm. (Second in ice cream consumption is New Zealand, by the way, and the results are not statistically guaranteed.) More brand-specific (and more reliable) information can be found at a Web site for the University of Guelph in Canada (www.foodsci.uoguelph.ca/ dairyedu). That site, with far more academic and scientific data, reveals that the United States is (or, at least, was in the year 2000) far and away the leading producer of ice cream, but only the second leading consumer of the product per capita. (That fact will be significant.) New Zealanders eat 26.3 liters of ice cream each per year, according to the data, but the United States, with a much larger population, comes in second at 22.5 liters. China is the second-largest producer, followed by Canada, Italy, Australia, France, and Germany. After New Zealand and the United States, residents of Canada, Australia, Switzerland, and Sweden eat the most ice cream per person. When we expand our business globally, these numbers will factor into our expansion plans.

Birth of a Brand

From other data available on the Guelph University site, we can determine that in 1999, vanilla was easily the most popular ice cream flavor, accounting for 29.3 percent of all ice cream sold by volume. Chocolate was second at 12.2 percent, but strawberry, at 3.4 percent, came in only eighth. Does this indicate a flaw in our thinking? Should we reconsider our inclusion of strawberry in the three basic flavors that will form Ultimate Treat's product line?

Not necessarily. First, the university's research is a few years old, but we can assume that consumption patterns have not shifted drastically since 1999. In addition, upon closer examination, the third-place flavor listed in the research is not one flavor but many. "Nut flavors" came in third, accounting for 11.1 percent of ice cream sold. That umbrella can include such wildly varied flavors as butter pecan, almond, and pistachio. Fourth was Neapolitan, a specialty flavor, and fifth was a category called "cookies and bakery," which doesn't apply to our product. After that come two other "combination" categories: fruit flavors except strawberry, and candy flavors. So strawberry really does come in third when dealing with single-flavor categories.

Still, does the large drop, from 12.2 percent to 3.4 percent of all ice cream sold, mean we should reconsider strawberry's inclusion in the line? Perhaps that's something our focus group can help to clarify.

Other questions we will broach include public acceptance of the brand name Ultimate Treat and a clear direction in terms of the brand identity. If we discover that the public is repulsed by the idea of a nostalgic, playful childhood treat, that consumers prefer ice cream to be either goofy (Ben & Jerry's), stately (Häagen-Dazs), or generic (Breyer's, Edy's), we might have to rethink our entire brand identity or make a much tougher decision—one that would mean ignoring the research and going with our initial impulse. That is a much riskier response, and one that can cause tumultuous reaction through company ranks, even if it ultimately proves to be the right choice.

The *U.S. Business Reporter* (www.activemedia-guide.com/icecream .htm) offers startling insight into the ice cream market we are about to invade. While Ben & Jerry's or Häagen-Dazs may have the most visible names (and, the uninitiated would say, the most famous brands) on the market, they are by far not the leaders in market share. Breyer's sells the most ice cream in the United States. In 2000, the company's market share stood at 12.0 percent, followed by Dreyer's (Edy's on the East Coast) at 10.0 percent, Blue Bell at 5.6 percent, and then Häagen-Dazs at 4.5 percent and Ben & Jerry's at 3.7 percent. Brands like Well's Blue, Turkey Hill, Dreyer's/Edy's Light, and Healthy Choice round out the top brands.

This throws some of our assumptions about the market into turmoil, but reinforces others. Notice, for example, that the biggest brand in the ice cream market holds only a 12 percent share of the marketplace. There is no one huge, dominant brand here, no Coca-Cola or Disney to dethrone—even Ben & Jerry's with its brilliant Branding does not dominate the field. This is largely because, until recently, it has been very difficult to establish a national brand of ice cream. Transportation of the product was slow and expensive, and this was a product that required very specific conditions to be transported properly.

In the past decade or so, that has changed. With manufacturing plants set up nationwide (and even worldwide), it has become possible to create and maintain a truly universal brand of ice cream, which is how Häagen-Dazs and Ben & Jerry's managed to grow from regional businesses into larger, more global corporations. Internet sales have made it possible for a small company like Lappert's to sell ice cream from its home in Hawaii (the idea is that local, fresh ingredients like pineapple and coconut are used in the product) to points anywhere on the globe for a relatively hefty shipping fee. The market is primed for a dominant brand, but none has emerged. It might very well be time for Ultimate Treat.

Our initial focus group, which is now discussing the merits of ice cream and the types of feelings and memories it evokes, can help us determine a direction for our brand identity. While we have hired a market research firm to conduct the focus group, the data it reports following the group session will definitely address our initial assumptions, as well as concerns we might have taken for granted.

Grace Ascolese explains the focus group process further: "The moderator guides the conversation from a very loose guide. Questions are open-ended; not too many yesses and nos. Usually clients are in a back room behind a two-way mirror. Groups are taped (audio and usually video).

Birth of a Brand

Follow-ups depend on the research objectives. If testing creative work (advertising copy, footage of TV personalities, posters, etc.), sometimes qualitative research is all that's needed. Often it's used as a preliminary step to a quantitative project. In these cases, groups are used to explore the range of responses and questions as well as to refine the questionnaire that will be used to measure consumer reaction."

That questionnaire is a next step. Consumers are called on the phone either at random or from a list purchased by the research firm, based on specific demographics or previous willingness to participate in a survey. Once the consumer agrees to participate, very specific questions—in our case, about ice cream, nostalgia, flavors, and brand names, among many other topics—are asked in a multiple choice format, in order to best qualify the answers when assessing the data.

Questions on our form could include: "Ice cream reminds me of: (a) summer evenings; (b) carnivals; (c) salespeople in trucks; (d) childhood treats." Answers of (a) or (d) might support our proposed brand identity, whereas (b) could mean something other than supermarket-style ice cream and (c) definitely refers more to ice cream novelties rather than scoops, something we are not marketing at the moment.

In other words, if our final report from our market research firm indicates a 30 percent response to answers (a) or (d), we might have to seriously consider reinventing our brand identity, or at the very least revising it. If we get 60 percent or better from those two responses, we can safely assume we are on the right track.

Another question might be: "I consider ice cream: (a) a rich reward; (b) the ultimate treat; (c) just the best or (d) sweet revenge." While this question does not directly address the name of an ice cream product, it is exactly that issue we are trying to gauge here. Because it deals with the consumer's feelings about ice cream, the question can help tap into emotions that will strike a chord with consumers in the name of a product. Should we find that answers to (b) are disappointing, or that one of the other choices is especially strong, our name might have to change.

Various questions on the form will address the issues of nostalgia, what associations the consumer might make between ice cream and fun, whether children or young adults would respond to the playful nostalgia we intend to convey, and whether the absence of wild, unconventional flavors would help or hurt a new brand trying to enter the supermarket ice cream marketplace.

"Groups are great for questions like: How? Why?" Ascolese says. "The preferences should be on creative, in-depth responses. You don't quantify the number of consumers who will choose a product. That's in a follow-up phase." In other words, it's the consumer's impressions, the feelings and emotions associated with the product, that are examined in a focus group, while more quantitative work, with real percentages and hard numbers attached, will be found in the follow-up telephone questionnaires and responses.

Group polls are one indicator of how a brand is being accepted (or rejected) by the general public. Public relations is more a science and an art of influencing the public to accept a brand, and uses polls as a guideline but never a law. My work in public relations has led me to create a concept I explained in *Guerrilla P.R.,* called the Tiffany Theory, which has been taught in the 25 top business schools. The Tiffany Theory states that a gift delivered in a box from Tiffany's will have a higher perceived value than one in no box or a plain box. That's not because the recipient is a fool; it's because in our society we gift-wrap everything: our politicians, our corporate heads, our movie and TV stars, and even our toilet paper.

How does that relate to Ultimate Treat? Because the perceived value of a product will be increased with its association to other products, names, or concepts that already have value in people's lives, the idea of a warm summer night with a pure, smooth ice cream treat is essential to our success. In other words, ice cream alone won't make the difference in the market, or someone would have dominated by simply putting out the best product. We need to make a great product and have the public associate it—wrap it in Tiffany paper—with a pleasant memory of a seemingly lost experience that our product will recreate.

Dick Morris took a trait of President Clinton—his propensity for making people feel like he would give everyone whatever it was they wanted—and turned it into a positive attribute. Clinton wasn't a manipulator; he was a statesman who could broker peace agreements with some of the least probable parties on the planet. The reality was there; if Clinton hadn't walked away with the agreement he did, Dick couldn't have manufactured one to make the president look good. But once the work was done, Dick could take it and wrap it in his best Tiffany paper, to make what had been perceived as a negative Clinton trait and turn it into an asset.

We can take what could be seen as a questionable move (associating our ice cream with an earlier, simpler time) and transmogrify it into something much more positive, something marketing textbooks years from now could hail as a bold move that helped establish a dynamic brand identity. But we have to look first at our market research data to see how much room we have to maneuver.

For the sake of our fictional product, let's examine a fictional market research report compiled after a nonexistent focus group and telephone survey. The focus group indicated that consumers are very attached to the idea of ice cream, that they are emotionally pleased with the idea of a rich ice cream treat after a hot day, and that the two most popular flavors by a wide margin are vanilla and chocolate. But beyond that, what can the data tell us?

First of all, we must resolve the question of our flavors. Will we stick with the two most popular, vanilla and chocolate? Should we add strawberry? Or will the consumers tell us that more exotic flavors are exactly what they've been craving, and that our loyalty to the simplest flavors is misguided?

Our research, taken primarily from the telephone survey, indicates that while vanilla (35 percent) and chocolate (22 percent, strongest on the East Coast) are the favorite flavors chosen by consumers, our audience does not want to stop there. Other flavors were widely split in terms of preference: Among single flavors, strawberry (the only kind we surveyed) was third, but far behind chocolate, at only 7 percent in a survey of 1,422 consumers across the country. Not far behind it was butter pecan at 6.4 percent and chocolate chip at 6.1 percent. No other flavor managed a number above 3.2 percent.

However, consumers were overwhelming in their desire for a third flavor. Asked if they would prefer an ice cream brand that sold only vanilla and chocolate or one that offered vanilla, chocolate, and one other flavor, an impressive 71 percent of consumers responded that three flavors are better than two. The question now is which flavor to add.

Because strawberry came in third, it would seem the logical choice. However, it was not an overwhelming favorite by anyone's standards, and it has another difficulty attached to it. If we are to adhere to our philosophy of high quality and the best ingredients, we would want to add fresh strawberries to our ice cream. This would add prohibitively to our manufacturing costs, and might even compromise the quality of the product, since fresh fruit tends to freeze in ice cream and sometimes includes pits or debris. By the same token, nuts (such as in butter pecan) add many steps to manufacturing, including processing the nuts to maintain sanitary standards and avoid bacteria, and storage at a specific temperature to reduce rancidity.

On the other hand, chocolate chip, which was not far behind butter pecan, is easier to produce, particularly since we are already manufacturing vanilla. The addition of chocolate chips adds a step to manufacturing, but does not seriously complicate the process. So chocolate chip will be our third initial flavor for Ultimate Treat.

Asked about a brand name, consumers in our market survey were not terribly enthusiastic about the name Ultimate Treat. In our multiple-choice question, our chosen name actually came in third, behind Just the Best and Rich Reward, although it did beat Sweet Revenge (which might be a better name for a low-fat ice cream, anyway). In fact, Just the Best was far and away the most popular choice, with 33 percent of the respondents choosing it. Ultimate Treat was favored by only 17 percent of the consumers surveyed.

Clearly, our product name was not well chosen. It's better to know that now rather than after the brand identity is cemented and the product is in stores, but it is a warning sign that not everything we've assumed can be trusted to resonate with the public. After much debate among the members of our marketing team, it is decided that Just the Best is a better fit for our brand identity, and it is adopted as the new product name.

Luckily, our chosen brand identity has scored much more favorably among the target demographic audience. In the question regarding the consumer's feelings about ice cream ("Ice cream reminds me of:"), our choices—(a) summer evenings and (d) childhood treats—were much more enthusiastically received than (b) carnivals and (c) salespeople in trucks. This, along with responses to six other questions in the telephone survey, indicates that our brand identity of a playful nostalgia will be warmly received by the public.

Market research has reinforced some of our original perceptions, it has deflated some assumptions we made, and it has given us a clear direction in which we should be moving. Public relations can take this research and interpret it, as we just did, to better determine our future moves. When we use the research data as an indicator, rather than a bible, for future choices, it is a useful tool. If we become slaves to the research, we may not make any huge mistakes, but we are almost as certain to create something that will never have a chance to dominate its market.

Remember what Dick Lyles said in Chapter 2: The message may not come out in exactly the wording you intended, and it might be distorted in one way or another or grouped with the message from other corporate entities, even competitors. But while control of the message is important, it is the fact of the message itself—the placement, in public relations terms, in a media outlet that tells even part of your story through a third party that is seen as credible—that is the ultimate goal here.

The Tiffany Theory once again is at work. If you wrap your message in the imprint of the *Wall Street Journal,* some of the cachet of that brand will rub off on yours. It's impossible to overestimate the impact that a message delivered by a third party—not by you through advertising—can have on a consumer. And now that Just the Best has an identity to launch, we can do so confidently, knowing that the power of public relations can help consumers understand what we are and why they're going to love us.

CHAPTER FOUR

MAKING THE BEST FIRST IMPRESSION

Have you ever wondered why movie producers pay all that money for a big, splashy premiere when their film is being advertised via television, radio, magazines, and newspapers? Why bother to get a star to appear on a red carpet for an event that might predate the opening of the film by a week or less? Will the public really care what stars think about the film before they've seen it?

There's an extremely good reason the tradition of Hollywood premieres has continued since the days of the silent film. If anything, such events are more beneficial now than they were before the days of television. They can perform the very definition of public relations service: coverage in credible news media for a product, service, event, or personality that will be seen as more trustworthy and serious coming from a third party (the media outlet).

How valuable is a minute of time on *Entertainment Tonight?* Have you tried to buy a minute of advertising on *Entertainment Tonight?* It can be prohibitively expensive to all but the largest companies, very few of which are launching new brands. And, as I've stated before, advertising is a potent outlet for your message, but it does not encapsulate the same kind of credibility you can get from a third-party source like *Entertainment Tonight.* If your film's premiere is covered on a syndicated entertainment news show, or if a picture appears in *People* magazine, you have paid less for the premiere than you might have for analogous advertising placements, and you have gained a very strong measure of credibility. That is why movie premieres are still an important, meticulously planned and executed ritual of the film business.

It is a cliché that you only get one chance to make a first impression. However, clichés get to be clichés because, for the most part, they are true. The first impression a brand makes, particularly when it is the first in its category, is more than critical; it is an essential of the Branding process. And public relations, which thrives on creating impressions, is the most integral, vital part of the first impression a new brand will make.

As Adam Christing, founder of Clean Comedians, says: "One of my favorites is Federal Express. The word *express* denotes speed; that's the coat of arms right there. There's a bond there—when I think that I've got to get a package to Chicago by tomorrow morning, I don't think of anyone else. Of course, the advantage is very clear. Often a brand makes the impossible possible. [In the beginning] no one believed that FedEx could do what they said. But when Fred Smith found a way to do it, and they did it, suddenly there was a brand that was created from nothing."

Brand inception is perhaps the most crucial, jugular moment in the Branding process. Everything that is to come will flow from the decisions made at the onset; it is very difficult to undo a first impression, and reweaving a tattered brand identity may be the most daunting task for a marketing professional. It is infinitely preferable to avoid miscalculations at the beginning, rather than to have to correct them later. After all, the legendary producer Robert Evans always says, "once branded, always branded."

When a brand campaign begins from scratch, every decision made will certainly have an impact on the reception the final brand will have when it is introduced—not to mention consumer confidence and acceptance of the brand for years, and hopefully decades, to come. From the concept of the first product to the names and logos associated with the brand, each aspect of the campaign will require careful thought, deep knowledge of the market, and a golden gut.

PR plays a critical role in the birth of a brand. As Al Ries, a marketing strategist and coauthor of *The 22 Immutable Laws of Branding,* says, "The only way to launch a new brand is with PR."

BRAND BEGINNINGS

When the Walt Disney Company began, its product was short animated cartoons in black and white. Things have changed.

The intelligent marketer does not expect his or her brand to remain the same from the moment of conception to the time when the name is known in virtually every household. But there are certain constants that will indeed be present throughout: The promises made when the brand is conceived can and must be fulfilled every minute of every hour of every day that brand is on the market, and the public must be certain that will be the case. Disney made its promises at the onset, and no company has been as consistent and as successful in communicating those promises to the public in the past seven decades.

I have had considerable experience in developing new brands and using public relations to introduce them, particularly in the case of young actors and actresses who were eager to become household names. When I met and started working with Vanna White, she had not yet become the letter-turner on *Wheel of Fortune*. Kirstie Alley was a former interior decorator and a young actress when I met her. I have also helped to establish a number of other performers whose names you know quite well.

In the early 1980s, I was asked to help a young actor who was beginning his first major role in a TV series to create his public identity. When I first met Michael J. Fox, he had performed in some Canadian television programs and had small parts in a few low-budget movies. Now, he was starting a role as Alex P. Keaton, the conservative son of liberal parents, on a new sitcom called *Family Ties*.

Because the public at large had never heard of Michael J. Fox, we decided to present him as the character Alex P. Keaton. In interviews, Michael wore a tie, and while he didn't espouse a political point of view, his presentation was that of a conservative young man with a sly sense of humor, much like the character he was about to play.

What I was doing was helping Michael to create an image, which would become the identity the public would first see of him. While it wasn't the image that Michael would keep through the years, it was the first one to make an impression. And if that impression was favorable, it would allow Michael the opportunity to expand his identity later—as he has done so successfully.

Public relations is so important in brand creation not because it determines the direction the brand will take, but because it makes the first impression and reinforces this impression over time. In Michael J. Fox's case, we were lucky to have what became a hit series, and a very talented actor in a role that would define him for the early part of his career. But PR played its part, establishing the Michael J. Fox brand in the public's attention, and making it a brand people wanted to experience again and again.

PR AND BRAND INTRODUCTION

When you're creating a brand, you have to establish an identity. People don't know what a brand is the first time they hear its name, and the public won't necessarily get the message you are trying to communicate simply through the brand name.

The first thing to do is to establish the name. Many teaser advertising campaigns will deliberately obscure the brand's function in favor of its identity, and capture the public's attention using only the name before the product is introduced to the marketplace. Products such as Red Bull energy drink and the iMac were introduced in just such a way, whetting the public's appetite for information about the product before the product itself was available. Sometimes that works like a charm; other times the public doesn't care about the product and won't seek the information.

When I was involved in promoting Michael J. Fox in his *Family Ties* role of Alex P. Keaton, some of the work had been done before I began. Obviously, the role had already been written by Gary David Goldberg, the show's creator, and Michael had been cast before I began. Michael's talent and that of Gary Goldberg helped to make an impression on the public's mind no matter how well I did my job. Michael J. Fox became a TV star with a role that was perfectly conceived and that he performed brilliantly. Public relations didn't do that.

However, we did manage to attract a good deal of attention for the actor and the role before the public discovered them. We made sure

Michael was interviewed about the role and the way he was cast in it at every opportunity. We cultivated the image he would put forth at each interview, including the clothes he wore and the attitude he projected. When someone interviewed Michael J. Fox in those days, they were really interviewing Alex P. Keaton.

By the same token, when I began working with Mary Hart, *Entertainment Tonight* was not a 20-year-old broadcasting institution. It was a new and unfamiliar program, a gamble being taken by some syndication executives and local stations, and Mary Hart was simply the woman who sat behind the desk and read the TelePrompTer. But she was ambitious, and wanted to become the human equivalent of a brand. She wanted the public to know who she was and what she did.

We set to work at establishing a brand reputation, an easily recognizable identity, for Mary Hart, whom the public had no opportunity to know at that point. And in evaluating the many wonderful points we could have emphasized, we couldn't help but notice that Mary did, in fact, have extremely lovely legs, and they were visible quite often during *Entertainment Tonight* broadcasts. If people hadn't already noticed Mary's legs, they certainly should have their attention drawn to them. Mary's legs would help to make her more recognizable and more unique—after all, if you can't stand out on your own two legs, how will you ever make an impression on a fickle public?

It was especially important to establish the Mary Hart brand without appearing too eager or lascivious. *Entertainment Tonight* was always conceived as a family show, and Mary's image was meant to be wholesome and friendly, nonthreatening to women or men. We needed a way to emphasize how lovely Mary's legs were without seeming to be sexist or demeaning about it.

The solution that I helped implement was having her legs insured for $1 million by Lloyd's of London. This move, which was well covered in newspapers and broadcast media, made the public take notice of one (actually, two) of the assets we wanted to emphasize, and made a point of communicating how special and interesting a talent Mary was. It got people to tune into the show to see Mary Hart as well as to hear her read entertainment news reports. At the same time, we also made sure Mary was included on a list of the 10 best hairstyles on television at around the same time, to attract more attention and plant the suggestion that she wasn't just a pair of legs.

How do Mary Hart's legs relate to super-premium ice cream? The fact is, the image being communicated isn't all that different, although the two examples couldn't be less similar. We have decided to give our new ice cream brand, Just the Best, the same wholesome, non-threatening image that Mary Hart projects. While we can't insure an ice cream for $1 million, we can discuss the assets of our product, which in this case is chiefly the pure, wholesome, top-of-the-line ingredients being used to make the super-premium ice cream in such familiar flavors. We want the public to know that they may have had vanilla, chocolate, and chocolate chip before, but they've never had those flavors like *this*.

First, we can send people into the streets of some major cities around the country, clearly identifying themselves as market researchers, asking passersby one question: "Are you a chocolate person, a vanilla person or a chocolate chip person?" Depending on the answer, the consumer will be given a button to wear that reads, "I'm a chocolate person" (or "a vanilla person" or "a chocolate chip person"). The consumer will be instructed at the time to wear the button on a certain day in the coming week and be eligible for a prize. No mention of the product name will be made.

However, public relations will be at work. Newspapers and local TV and radio stations will be alerted that a certain day of the coming week will be "Just the Best Day," and that everyone who wears a button and is spotted by a Just the Best representative will be eligible for a grand prize (a year's supply of ice cream, a chocolate, vanilla, or chocolate chip colored car, a sum of money, etc.) given to one special winner whose button has the words *Just the Best* hidden on it, visible only to a special scanner.

On Just the Best Day, representatives will be back on the city streets, stopping people who wear the buttons, scanning the buttons, and giving out coupons. Those whose buttons don't have the special message will immediately be given a one-scoop sample of the flavor they have chosen via the button. The one lucky person with the prizewinning button will be given the prize identified in the promotion.

Again, all local media outlets will have been notified ahead of time, to let the public know why someone is stopping people in the streets and scanning their flavor buttons with a machine. The brand name will be emphasized in all promotion, and everyone will be looking for the words *Just the Best* on the buttons, again making the name memorable.

By the time the prize is awarded, the name of our brand will be well known in each city we visit, and hundreds if not thousands of people will have been given a free sample and a coupon for more. If our product is as good as we think it is, we will have a very strong customer base to begin with when we introduce the product to stores, which should be very soon after the promotion is held, in order to retain the public's memory of the promotion and its attention to the product.

Thus, when our advertising campaigns begin, the product will already have a foothold and a head start in the marketplace. Hopefully, the flavor question (and the coverage it will have gotten in local media) will help consumers understand the concept of a basic-flavor, high-quality ice cream. The flavor buttons will reinforce that information, and if the person really is an aficionado of one of our flavors, our sample should convince him or her that this is a new, exciting version of something that seemed familiar, but is now being done much better.

A public relations campaign designed to introduce a brand identity shouldn't try to do too much. Name recognition is first, which is why the promotion (and the grand prize) should be geared to the repetition of the name Just the Best. But the public also has to understand the concept of the brand, the identity being created. So the explanation of the three-flavor, high-quality concept should be emphasized in all press releases, with the hope that local media will mention these features in whatever coverage they give the event itself.

With the establishment of the brand identity and the beginnings of name recognition for the brand, public relations professionals have a groundwork on which to build. And just as the Michael J. Fox brand was built on talent and quality, matched with public relations expertise, so the Just the Best brand can succeed based on a high-quality product being promoted properly.

Keep in mind the power of the promise. Charlie Koones, publisher of

Making the Best First Impression

Daily Variety, the most recognizable and respected brand in business-to-business media, says that all of Branding is based on a promise: "Branding is about the establishment of a promise with customers. What that product is going to do for [them], what it will deliver for [them]. The brand is a communication of a benefit. Ninety percent of a brand is the experience you get once you get where you're going."

There is nothing public relations can do if you promise the best chocolate, vanilla, and chocolate chip ice cream in the world and then deliver something that isn't immediately distinguishable from every other brand. It's important to make a promise you can keep, and to keep that promise every day. As we continue, we'll assume that Just the Best delivers what we have promised. We'll leverage public relations in order to communicate that promise.

The most important thing, which should never leave any employee's radar screen, is that the agreed-upon identity is what reaches consumers' eyes first, and that consumers recognize and understand the message of that identity immediately. A good example of the perfect first impression is the case of Amazon.com. When this service was launched on the World Wide Web in 1994, there were 3 million new users who were potential customers for Amazon.com. Most people had never purchased anything online, and a very substantial percentage of the population was not connected to the Internet at all.

The first time most people experienced Amazon.com, then, they were unfamiliar with the procedures and practices for online buying that we take for granted today. Now, with over 125 million potential Amazon.com customers, the concept of buying books, music, and electronics (among many other items) via computer is not at all daunting. But in 1994, the very idea of committing a credit card number to a computer purchase was intimidating, and the question most often asked about Amazon.com was, "Why?"

It made no sense to those who were used to buying books in a store that they should pay for delivery to their homes. The population in general did not consider going to Barnes & Noble an inconvenience. The same books available on Amazon.com were available at Borders, at the local bookstore, and at the public library. Why bother with the computer?

Why pay for shipping? Why take a chance that your credit card number would be broadcast to anyone using the Internet at the time you transmitted your order?

Amazon.com answered the question with two words that continue to dominate the company's mission statement and overall philosophy to this day: customer service. Yes, the Web site's slogan was "Earth's Largest Selection," but that was merely the lure. Once on the site for the first time, a consumer would be dazzled with the availability of products and the impeccable customer service offered to everyone, every time.

Never underestimate the value of customer service to Branding, and never think for a moment that customer service is not a form of public relations. In fact, because it requires, by definition, contact with the public (often initiated by consumers themselves), customer service might be the purest form of public relations. Make a friend here, and you have a customer for life. Make an enemy, and that person will tell everyone he or she knows how unreasonable you are.

It was in that area that Amazon.com excelled immediately. Customers who have questions are dealt with quickly and efficiently. Shipping is completed as close to the time of order as possible. Product availability is always a priority. In short, everyone does everything to make sure that the first time you use Amazon.com, you are impressed enough to become a habitual customer. And that strategy has worked enormously well, defying all business predictions at the time of the company's inception.

The Amazon.com strategy is consistent with the parameters set up for a successful brand: It determines a brand identity, it makes specific promises, and it keeps or exceeds those promises. Making promises and fulfilling them is absolutely the best way to make a first impression. There is no substitute.

When customers first encountered Amazon.com, the promises were clear: We will have the largest selection possible, we will deliver it to you promptly, and we will discount much of our merchandise. In the beginning, Amazon.com dealt strictly in books, and the company was always sure to have access to as much product as it needed through warehousing space and agreements with distributors. If a book was unavailable, Amazon.com would try to find a used copy. If the wrong product was shipped, the company made sure it accepted returns and provided the correct item as quickly as possible. Customer service, when necessary on the phone, was polite, accommodating, and positive. There were no disgruntled customers, and word began to circulate.

Today, Amazon.com is perhaps the best-known bookseller in the world. Its customer base is truly international, its product lines have multiplied, and it even began turning a profit recently, defying predictions once again. Because it was the most visible, most trusted e-commerce site anywhere, Amazon.com more than survived the dot-com disaster and is thriving to this day.

Jim Robinson, chairman of Partners In Charge, says, "Good service doesn't have to be expensive. Some of the new suites hotels provide good, clean suites but they don't have a restaurant. They don't have a gift shop. Poor service, in the long run, is more costly."

The value of public relations in a first impression is enormous. Consider that Amazon.com's Jeff Bezos has appeared on the cover of *Time* magazine as the 1999 Person of the Year. That didn't occur by accident; there was public relations work done behind the scenes that allowed the story to happen. Without stunts, events, or celebrities, Amazon.com managed to develop a reputation by doing what it could do better than anyone else. Word of mouth did have an enormous impact, but public relations work at the grass roots level managed to get news items about Amazon .com, all tied to the company's reliability and enormous selection, placed in publications and on the airwaves. Amazon.com was truly first to the marketplace in a number of different ways, and it managed to deliver on every promise the company made to its consumers. It is a model of Branding. Today, when you say the word *Amazon* to a friend, the river is not the first thing the other person will think about; Amazon.com has truly become a household word.

Never underestimate that first impression. Marketing guru Al Ries says, "The biggest mistake that big companies make is not seeing the enormous opportunity of being first. Take, for example, Coca-Cola. Here's a company that owns the world's most valuable brand—$72 billion. Interbrand .com lists the value of the world's most valuable brands. You ask Coca-Cola how Coca-Cola became such a valuable brand, and I'm sure they'll say it's the marketing, it's the distribution, it's the filing system, it's the mission statement of the founders—and it's all baloney. I look at Coca-Cola and I say, 'That's the first cola brand, the first brand in the category.' "

How does a first impression take hold? Dick Morris, a brilliant political consultant, says it's a question that can fundamentally define the Branding process itself: "*Reputation* is a calcified or fossilized encoded word for *characteristic*. You start with behavior, then you go to characteristic, then you go to reputation, then you go to brand. The first thing I do is crack a joke and you laugh; that's behavior. Then I crack a lot of jokes and you laugh a lot, that's a characteristic: Dick's funny. Then, I keep cracking jokes, and you really like it, and you start to tell your friends: Dick is funny. At that point it becomes a reputation. Then the reputation becomes known by a great many people, who are willing to pay for it—and I think Branding always involves paying for it with money or votes or something—at that point it becomes a brand."

To utilize Morris's model for branding for Just the Best, first we should define the behavior that we intend to make the defining characteristic of our brand. Does ice cream have a behavior? Certainly: It has a taste, which is ultimately the most distinctive difference between one brand and another. So the taste of Just the Best will be its behavior, and, hopefully, the people designing and producing our ice cream have crafted the most distinct and appealing taste possible for our three initial flavors.

Now, we need to define the characteristic that we want to emphasize to the consuming public. That is, what will the first, clearest, and most central promise for our brand be? The name *Just the Best* should give us a direction. Not only do we want people to remember our name, we want them to believe it. So the characteristic we want to emphasize most strongly is our quality: Our ice cream will be just the best.

The first thing we as public relations representatives want to do, then, is to introduce our characteristic to a select group of people. That will be done through our on-the-street events, asking passersby whether they are chocolate, vanilla, or chocolate chip people and handing out the analogous buttons. The characteristic being demonstrated here is our dedication to quality, which we show by limiting our product line to the three flavors that we believe we can make best. The public will be given the message that Just the Best delivers the highest quality by focusing obsessively on a limited number of flavors.

Keep in mind that, at the beginning, the product will not be the center of the promotion. The people given buttons in the street will not hear the name Just the Best at the time of the initial meeting, but will hear it repeatedly over the next few days as the promotion reaches its second stage—the awarding of coupons and prizes. Media outlets will be given the name of the product in press releases and promotional materials throughout the period of the promotion, and will be free to use it in print or on the air.

Keeping the name of the product off one of the first and most visible promotional events the brand will have may seem counterproductive. But because the name will be used in the media (again, providing Tiffany wrapping and extra third-party credibility), and because everyone with a button will be encouraged to make a return trip to the same spot in order to determine eligibility for a prize, the public will certainly discover the name of the product (and the brand) through means that will seem more trustworthy to consumers.

By establishing alliances with local radio stations, we can increase our promotional budget and the visibility of the promotion, but we will be limiting our exposure to the audiences of the stations with which we have agreements. It might be better to stay within our own budget, present all media outlets in the market with the promotional materials, and take the coverage we can get from each individual station, since ice cream is not a product that appeals only to one demographic or age group.

Once the behavior has been refined into a characteristic, the next step in Dick Morris's model is to develop a reputation. This is done through a natural process, as the people who have been given flavor badges on the street will tell their friends, relatives, and coworkers about the experience. They'll also talk about the sample of ice cream they've been promised and the chance to win a very attractive prize in a few days.

Duane E. Knapp, author of *The Brand Mindset,* says: "The dot-com implosion was caused by all these people thinking they wanted to be a brand name. So they spent a huge amount on advertising. They have no clue how to make the customer happy. They spend a ton on advertising, yet their customer service is terrible. You buy one of these pieces of gear, you send it in, and you go through a nightmare to get it back. I have never heard of a company that went out of business because they had a 100 percent guarantee of satisfaction and delivered on it."

Our customer service reputation will be especially well cemented on Just the Best Day. When the time of the promotional climax comes in each test city, consumers will be given samples of Just the Best in large numbers, and one will win the prize that has been designated. Assuming that the product is everything we have said it is, conversations about the experience will ensue. We will have recruited an army of civilian ambassadors who will have coupons for our product in their hands and will want to share the experience they've had with others. Everyone gets a chance to taste the product, we assume most of them will find it enjoyable, and a reputation has been born.

Finally, the reputation must be turned into a brand. While this process is different for a consumer product than for the political candidate Dick Morris might have been advising, the fundamental points are roughly the same: Instead of votes, we want people to take some money and pay for a quantity of Just the Best. The coupons encourage larger numbers to sample the ice cream, and by the time the Just the Best promotion has reached the end of its multi-city tour, there should be a very substantial number of converts to the product. If sales begin to take off the way we project they should, a brand will have been born.

While all this is going on, however, the full identity of the brand, meaning more than just the one characteristic we have chosen to emphasize, will be exposed to the public. It's one thing to be a high-quality ice cream; it's another to be Just the Best. Häagen-Dazs is seen as a high-quality ice cream; so is Ben & Jerry's. Their brand identities, however, are very different, and are also quite different from the one Just the Best hopes to cultivate.

In order to convey the kind of warm, playful, nostalgic feeling we want for Just the Best, public relations will have to play a large role, but no one element can carry the entire workload. Advertising and marketing will be major factors, graphics will be important, and the message we present will have to be unified and focused to project the information we want the public to remember.

Making the Best First Impression

How does a company project image without seeming heavy-handed and obvious? Clearly, a good deal of the responsibility will lie in the work of public relations, where the Tiffany Theory dictates that well-wrapped information, preferably delivered from an outside source, adds credibility and import. But every aspect of a brand is open to scrutiny, and every decision made about the brand will contribute either positively or negatively to the overall brand identity.

The image conveyed in all publicity, advertising, and any other public statements will have to be consistent as well as being consistent with the agreed-upon identity. That is an important distinction: If two messages are being sent by two different departments of the company, the brand will be seen as confusing, or worse, dishonest. If the information being disseminated is not consistent with the brand identity, the company—and its brand—will be considered by the public to be false, and any trust established with the consumer will be lost.

"Message alignment is the name of the game today in effective communications, and ultimately gets you, in our view, to Branding," says Merrie Spaeth, founder and president of Dallas-based Spaeth Communications, a worldwide leader in business communications. "It is the snapshot which over time will create brand integrity. Messages out of alignment are what screw things up and the easiest targets today are the banks, because when you look at the advertising, they all promise personal service. When I say to my audience, 'How many of you see these ads?' all the hands go up. 'And how many of you are getting personal service?' All the hands go down."

So, not only does the communication from the company to the consumer have to be consistent, the implicit message—the experience the consumer has with the company through the product or service—has to be consistent, and true as well.

CHOOSING THE RIGHT WORDS

Merrie Spaeth says that the words chosen to convey the message can be as important as the message itself. She contends that even if people aren't paying attention to the specific words, they will file away what they hear, and even on a subconscious level will remember the impression the words delivered.

"Words are how most people pluck things out to remember them. Most of us pick a couple of words, pull up recollections around them, and pass that on," she says. "That's what governs how reporters pick out quotes. The question is which words are memorable. We divide them for strategic business purposes into good words—the words you want people to remember—and bad words—the words you don't want them to remember. Jargon is a subset of bad words, and our definition of jargon is a word or phrase that your listener does not use on a daily basis."

What makes some words good and others bad? Mostly, according to Spaeth, it is the feeling they conjure, rather than the direct meaning of the words in the context of the sentence as spoken. Hearing the word *cancer,* even in a sentence like, "Well, it's not as serious as cancer," is going to have an emotional effect on the listener, one he or she might not even be aware of, but one that will color the memory of hearing that message, and could change the listener's impression of the speaker and the company the speaker represents.

It can be argued that even bad words can be used strategically to positive effect, but that is a very risky and dangerous course of action, and one that should not be entered into casually. A company spokesperson can be conveying a message that can be construed as negative, but using good words can lighten that message and create a more positive emotional memory for the listener to retain.

"If you are Arthur Andersen right now, good words would be *excellent reputation, long tradition, skilled personnel, deep relationship;* those are all truthful, good words," Spaeth says. "Obviously, bad words would be *shredding, scapegoat, renegade, failure, risk.* Generally, in business terms, *layoff* is a very bad word; *opportunity* and *job growth* are very good words. When you ask people which words are more memorable, the bad ones generally drive out the good ones. *Shredding* is crowding out a lot of words [in the case of Arthur Andersen]. You want to have a clear understanding of which words you want pushed ahead and which words you are competing with."

Spaeth suggests starting with two lists—one of good words, and one of bad words—and then crafting any statement, any advertising, any communication with the public at all, by using as many of the words on the first list and as few of the ones on the second as possible. The goal is never to lie; the truth should be able to withstand the use of predominantly good words. Lying to the public is the worst possible public relations move, and must be avoided at all costs. That doesn't mean a company has to commit media suicide by painting itself with the most negative brush possible, but it does mean that at no time—even when the reputation of the brand is on the line—is it acceptable to tell a flat-out untruth. These will always be discovered and publicized, and the lie will end up being far more damaging to the brand's reputation than even a negative truth ever could have been.

For example, in branding a political candidate, if you lie, people will eventually find out. The trick, then, is to take something that might be perceived as negative and make it seem positive. That is public relations at its best.

As Dick Morris says, "When I first began to work with Clinton, when he was president, he had a reputation for wanting to please everybody," Dick recalls. "Everybody walked away saying he was in their corner. And it wasn't malleable; it was manipulative. The more serious accusation was that he was a phony. We changed that from a negative into a positive by creating the idea that he was a peacemaker.

"When he went to Northern Ireland, he met with the Orangemen and the Catholics, British and Irish, and he persuaded them all that he felt their pain, that he knew where they were coming from, that they had empathy with him, that they could trust him, and that in their trust of him, they found a common basis for peace.

"He did it first; he created the reality," Morris says of the former President. "What I did was to take the reality that he had succeeded in the Irish peace negotiations and explain it as being an extension of the characteristic that we all knew he had, but up until now we didn't like. Another example of that was that Clinton used to be seen as a con artist. We changed that into the Great Communicator, someone who could take very complicated concepts that were very important for the American people to understand, like the global economy, and could explain them, FDR-like, in simple enough terms that everybody got them, and as a result was able to mobilize his nation to move forward."

DATA SMOG

It is important to remember that any company trying to create or maintain a brand has exponentially more competition than it would have 20 years ago. The unprecedented proliferation of communications outlets in the past few decades has turned this society into a battered, dazed, overwhelmed race of receptors, fielding information nuggets hurled at us at an unprecedented, seemingly incomprehensible rate of speed, and at a volume the like of which has never been seen before.

Bob Nelson, president of Nelson Motivation, Inc. and author of *1001 Ways to Reward Employees,* says, "If you don't stand out, you don't get noticed. There used to be less noise out there in the marketplace. Today, there's such a din of messages, from our shopping carts to our door fliers to our e-mails and faxes, which of course didn't exist before. We were bombarded 20 years ago as well, but we've gotten better at turning all the messages off. I don't look at a book unless I've heard about it from a few people."

It is estimated that the average teenager today receives more messages—either news reports, advertising, phone calls, e-mails or whatever—in one hour than his or her grandfather did at an analogous age in a week. And that might very well be an underestimate.

Let that statistic sink in for a moment and you can see how utterly different this information age is than any that has ever existed. The vapor of information with which we are constantly barraged adds to a societal condition I call *Data Smog,* which makes it hard to hear or see anything—including the messages that create the condition.

According to Rob Frankel, a world-renowned Branding expert and author of *The Revenge of Brand X,* "There are so many choices in the media; it's not really about the three big networks anymore. It's about people having all these choices about where to go, what to watch, what to see. They're driven by their own problems, their own issues, their own agenda. It's much more important now to make sure that they have a favorite choice, and that's what Branding is all about."

Data Smog has turned us into a race of Mr. Magoos. Quincy Magoo, you'll recall, is the myopic cartoon character who mistakes a traffic sign for a policeman or his neighbor's hat for a nest of eagles. Because of Data Smog, most people walk around in a stupor that allows for no serious penetration of any one message. It's more the cumulative effect of all the messages one remembers, rather than a singular piece of information. It makes us all nearsighted.

This makes the task of establishing or enhancing a brand more daunting than it would have been when Coca-Cola, Disney, or even Nike were beginning their remarkable Branding runs. Data Smog has raised the stakes, but it has also raised the bar: It is as infinitely more profitable to build a successful new brand today as it is more difficult.

"If Branding is more important today, it is because of Data Smog," says *Variety* publisher Charlie Koones. "How do you cut through? How you get a consumer to sit up and take notice? Therein lies the challenge. To me, the Internet is such an interesting arena for analysis of Branding. You go into space, and how do you find something in space? How do you navigate all this, when there are tens of millions of Internet sites out there? How do I find something, and what does that something do for me? What does it mean? Whether it be on the Internet or driving down Sunset Boulevard, I've got more stuff coming at me than ever before. I'm listening to my radio, I've got my cell phone working. I've got the billboards popping at me. I've got e-mail coming at me while I'm driving."

Of course, the best way to cut through Data Smog is to be new, to be first, to be brilliant, and to be well-funded. But, through public relations, it is possible to make an impression the old-fashioned way—by getting someone else to talk about you. It isn't easy, but nothing worth doing is easy. If anybody could do it without training, public relations would immediately become obsolete; everybody would be communicating their message in exactly the right way, and there would be no need for anyone who could present it better.

Data Smog has increased the importance of Branding. Dick Lyles of The Ken Blanchard Companies says he believes Branding has taken on a

more essential role in modern business, in large part, because of the proliferation of media messages and their impact on the average human's psyche.

"[Branding is] only more important today because the marketplace is
more crowded," says Lyles. "Branding was attributed to people's success
20 years ago, and certainly those who had established brands could succeed
and succeeded way better than those that did not. I think today it's essential. It used to be essential for achieving the highest levels of success. Now,
it's essential just to survive.

"I think the pressure is immense. A big part of Data Smog is because
of the crowded marketplace, obviously. I think what's going to happen
in the very near future, within the next couple of years, is that we'll all
be connected even more. This whole technology will mean 24/7 con-
nectivity. Mobilization is just going to enhance that. Data Smog is going
to get thicker. It's going to get more oppressive; it's going to be more
intimidating."

How, then, does the smart brander go about cutting through the
smog, something that will become even more central to survival if Data
Smog thickens? The key will remain in good, solid public relations practice, but with twenty-first-century technology and awareness.

There are role models to help pave the way, of course. The true
household names, the brands that everybody knows in every household in
most countries, have a few common traits, and observing their courses of
action (although it's important not to copycat a specific campaign or
event) and analyzing them will provide a useful road map through the
Data Smog–clogged information highways of the future. Lyles says the
Walt Disney Company is a prime example of a successful brand. "Disney
has one of the strongest brands going from a broad consumer market segment. They've treated every demographic around the world, and they
continue to exploit that," he explains. "They've protected it, and they
maintain the brand integrity. In terms of positioning in a wide-branded
market, in terms of maintaining brand equity, they've been brilliant."

In other words, keeping the essential promises made at the company's
inception, and making sure the consumer knows those promises and
the fact that they're being kept, has been key to Disney's phenomenal

success. These consistent messages have allowed Disney to break though the Data Smog.

With Just the Best, we should never take that lesson lightly. In order to establish our brand with the public, we must make basic, easy-to-understand promises that are important to the consumer, and then make absolutely sure those promises are kept in every circumstance, with no exceptions.

What should be our promises?

1. Our ice cream will deliver the highest quality through the finest ingredients.
2. Just the Best will deliver value through larger containers at lower comparable price.
3. Just the Best will refund the purchase price to any consumer unsatisfied with the product's quality.
4. Just the Best will deliver the best taste to the market through the freshest ice cream.

These are basic, simple promises that we can communicate clearly to consumers. But our employees must first understand the promises and realize that we are absolutely, obsessively dedicated to keeping them. From the delivery personnel who drive the trucks to the plant managers in every production facility, it must be clearly comprehended that high quality, freshness, and customer satisfaction are not variables, they are absolute constants.

If a consumer calls our toll-free line with a problem, that problem must be satisfactorily resolved before the consumer hangs up. If our product has not sold within our self-imposed freshness period, it must be returned or discarded by the retailer. Frequent taste tests must be held with randomly chosen consumers to ensure that the taste of the product remains as highly rated as it was at the brand's inception. Again, none of this has any room for variation; it must be done every day the company is in business.

"You have to be consistent. People have such short attention spans, and you have so little time to grab the consumer and try to invent yourself in their brain, that you have to be effective and you have to be consistent.

If you're not, their attention span is not going to allow for that," says for-mer *Brandweek* bureau chief T. C. Stanley, now a freelance writer.

Our four promises must be printed on every container of Just the Best, but that merely communicates the company's promises, not the brand's identity. In order to build the identity, we will have to invoke advertising and public relations in tandem, beginning with an initial advertising cam-paign that will lead up to the brand's introduction event, otherwise known as a launch party.

As we approach the product launch, it is necessary to develop a visual identity for the brand. Nike's swoosh logo is so powerful an image that the company rarely uses its name in advertising; it merely shows the icon. Coca-Cola's classic bottle, and its nostalgic typeface for its logo, are unmistakable. And the Mickey Mouse ears need only be glimpsed to make sure that the Disney Company is involved in a project, a product, or a theme park.

For Just the Best, the message being delivered is one of playful nostal-gia, a warm remembrance of a simpler time—but not one so drenched in tradition that it becomes stodgy or unapproachable. We want our con-sumers to associate the product with fun, but also with deeper feelings: love, home, warmth (a difficult concept for ice cream), and safe fun.

Our logo image, then, should be something that conjures up such feelings. The old-fashioned ice cream cone is an obvious choice, but is best avoided in this case, since our product will be sold in supermarkets, and not in cones at all. Images of our pure ingredients—a vanilla bean, a piece of chocolate, a chocolate chip—are too esoteric. The cow pattern has been taken by Ben & Jerry's.

Perhaps the best way to convey our core values is to visualize that day long ago when a parent or grandparent bought us an ice cream cone at the end of a hot summer day. That gesture, with implied love and the antici-pation of a fun treat, encapsulates exactly the combination of emotions we're attempting to stir. So our logo might be a larger adult hand offering a luscious-looking ice cream cone (deemphasizing the cone and promi-nently featuring the delicious ice cream) to a smaller, eager-looking hand.

With this image comes a visual brand identity: Our print ads, and all materials from our company, will feature the logo prominently, along with its summer evening color scheme of orange and red broken only by the glistening image of the white or brown ice cream in the cone.

In other words, every image we generate will stem from the design and the intention of the logo, since the logo comes from the brand identity, and that is our most cherished, prominently featured possession. The logo isn't the brand, but it does convey as precisely as possible what the brand's characteristics are intended to be.

Now it is time to share the logo, and its brand, with the rest of the world.

CHAPTER FIVE

PLANNING A POWERFUL LAUNCH

George M. Cohan once offered this piece of advice to a young actor: "Whatever you do, kid, always serve it with a little dressing." The young actor was Spencer Tracy, and he remembered the advice.

Because Data Smog has impaired our vision and hearing, distorted our comprehension, and shortened our attention span, it is more difficult now to attract and hold the public's attention than it has ever been before, as I discussed in the preceding chapter. And since this condition seems to be getting worse rather than better, we can assume that 10 years from now it will be more difficult still. The task of establishing and maintaining a successful brand is much more an uphill climb now than it was when the best-known of today's brands—McDonald's, Coca-Cola, Disney, and so on—were starting their remarkable runs. This begs the question: Is it possible, in today's information-drenched society, to create a true brand?

Certainly it is; ask the people at Home Depot, Nike, Starbucks, Federal Express, and Lexus, or the publicity professionals who diverted your attention to Jennifer Lopez, Julia Roberts, George Clooney, Brad Pitt, and P. Diddy. Talk to the people who created the ultra-successful brands Bill Clinton and George W. Bush.

In each case, the brand managers (the people who created, designed, and established the brand in question) knew enough to serve everything with "a little dressing." Jennifer Lopez's dress at the Grammy Awards, which threatened to give the worldwide television audience a very good look at all that is Jennifer Lopez, created such a stir that the actress/singer became a brand almost literally overnight. There was talk about the dress

70

at water coolers, on telephones, via e-mail, on Web sites, and perhaps best of all, from David Letterman and Jay Leno the next night. Even if you hadn't watched the awards show, you certainly knew about Jennifer Lopez by the end of that week.

Think of the dress as Jennifer Lopez's launch party and you can start to get the idea of the importance a first impression can make on the public. And if you think that it was something Lopez had lying around in the closet and just decided to wear on a whim, you have missed the point of this entire book. Jennifer Lopez knew exactly what she was doing when she put on that garment, and it had been designed to deliver precisely the type of reaction it engendered. The moment at which the public saw her in that dress had been planned for weeks, and the ensuing onslaught of comments and publicity were the exact response that had been nurtured and hoped for. Nothing had been left to chance, and the result was a public relations dream come true.

The concept of a launch party—an event meant to introduce a brand and establish the beginnings of its identity—is hardly new. Each moment of the event is planned to the second, there is no room for surprise (except to the public, which hopefully will be pleasantly surprised), and there is no margin for error. Making a bad first impression is the Branding equivalent of calling Dr. Kevorkian; it is assisting in your own demise.

A launch party does not, technically, have to be a party at all; it can be any kind of event that makes a splash for the brand, draws attention to it—preferably from the media, that third-party group we are always hoping to attract—and explains some part of the company's promise to the public, enough to get consumers interested in sampling the product for themselves. Hopefully, at that point, the product will speak for itself and help to build a brand.

Dr. Robert Epstein, a brilliant observer and analyst of the role psychology plays in business solutions and Branding, notes that psychologists sometimes consult with corporations and advertising agencies to anticipate, and in some cases, dictate, the reaction consumers will have to a product, service, or personality.

In the case of Just the Best, the launch party will include the contest and the street presence outlined in previous chapters. But with a new product, particularly one that is intended to have a major presence in its market, a formal introduction event is probably a good idea as well. Remember, the goal is to attract the maximum amount of attention possible while spending the minimum amount of money on such things as advertising. Public relations is about not paying for placement in print or on the air.

But the proper introduction for a product must mesh with the product's brand identity as well. Just the Best is projecting an image of fun, nostalgia, and quality, and the event planned and executed to launch the brand must exude those qualities in unprecedented amounts.

In some cases, a brand will attempt to interest a celebrity in acting as a spokesperson for a new product. The upside of such an endorsement can be quite formidable: Celebrities tend to attract media attention, the very thing a new brand can use more than anything else. They also project a certain image, and if that image is especially compatible with the brand identity being projected, the association can help define the brand in the public's mind and cause a positive impression at the same time.

Howard J. Rubenstein, president of the legendary PR firm Rubenstein Associates, says a celebrity spokesperson certainly helped reestablish the brand identity of one of his longtime clients: "We've had Weight Watchers for most of 36 years, absent a few years of hiatus. We understood, and they understood and understand, the importance of Branding and the power of giving a face to the brand. I introduced them to the Duchess of York, Sarah Ferguson, who was also a client of ours then, and our effort was to help update the image of Weight Watchers. We thought that by generating enormous publicity and promoting the logo of Weight Watchers, we could maintain their high top-of-the-line brand awareness."

According to Rubenstein, Fergie was precisely the right person at that time to endorse the Weight Watchers program. "She was in the right age category, she lost weight largely with Weight Watchers, and she was and is keeping it off with Weight Watchers," he notes. "We were trying to appeal not to a 60- or 70-year-old person, who might have been the audience we had 35 years ago, but to people maybe in their late twenties through the thirties and forties. Because Sarah was a popular figure internationally, we figured that she was right for that campaign."

The downside of having a celebrity spokesperson, of course, is complicated. For one thing, celebrities expect to be paid handsomely for endorsements, and that can be daunting for a new brand. Particularly with a product that is not a brand extension, a large drain on the budget from a celebrity endorsement may not be cost-effective. In addition, celebrity endorsements can sometimes backfire when the star in question behaves in a way that might not reflect the brand's image (as any company that used O.J. Simpson as a celebrity spokesman might attest).

Another problem can occur if the celebrity really doesn't use the product he or she endorses. All the good work done by the association with that star can be destroyed, and even worse, turned into animosity from the public, if such a thing is uncovered. "I've found that if you found a paid spokesperson who isn't an adherent or user of the product, that has high risk to it. You might surface with disbelief in the media," Rubenstein says.

For Just the Best, a celebrity spokesperson is probably an errant move. Establishing a new brand without an unlimited budget is difficult enough without having to devote a substantial portion of those finite funds to an endorser who will serve primarily as an advertising tool. It will be more judicious for us to concentrate on the establishment of the product's assets and the brand identity rather than tying it to a personality that—although already established—might distract from the message the company is trying to send.

Rob Frankel, author of *The Revenge of Brand X,* understands why one brand succeeds and another might fail. He emphasizes the idea that a brand has to appeal to the consumer, and must not have an identity that people within the company launching it or the industry in which it is launched find exciting, but the general public won't understand. "The term *Branding* before was used to describe a unique selling proposition. I believe that's obsolete at this point. Now, it's a unique buying proposition," he says. "A selling proposition is: 'Here's what we have to sell, and here's why you should buy it.' A unique buying proposition is: 'We know what you need, and here's why you should buy it.' One is from the customer point of view, and the other is from the corporate point of view. One of the problems with traditional Branding is that it really comes down to a lot of corporate chess meetings, and focuses on what you've got to sell, as opposed to what people want to buy."

A BRANDED WORLD

Keeping a clear picture of your value to the consumer is essential to the Branding process. People who believe they can outguess public opinion, anticipate exactly what the general populace will want, and deliver it without actually determining whether the public agrees are fooling themselves and will bring down their brands around their ears.

However, having determined what the public wants through surveys, market research, and market analysis, the intelligent Branding executive will make sure that message is conveyed to the public in the perfect Tiffany-style package. The launch event may be the only chance you have to capture the public's attention, and it will certainly be the best chance you have to present your brand message unadulterated and unfiltered. After all, advertising is very effective, but is seen by the public as a somewhat suspect message, since it is clearly coming from the company whose interests lie in convincing consumers that the product is desirable. With a launch event, coverage will either come through more credible established media outlets, or, better yet, firsthand from the Branding company to the consumer.

The best launch offers direct consumer contact and generates enough publicity to be included in media reports. The first Just the Best gambit partially achieves this goal—giving people buttons, then samples and prizes in the street, combines some direct contact with enough of an unusual event to garner press coverage. But that isn't quite enough. For one thing, it would be tactically impossible to give buttons and samples to a large segment of the population of any major city; the cost would be too high and the probability of running into huge percentages of the population too remote. After the initial exposure, and once some word of mouth has been generated, it will be time to present a larger, more general, and much higher-profile event, one that will formally introduce the brand and the product and convey the brand identity to consumers in the purest, simplest way possible.

THE MAIN EVENT

What makes a consumer choose one brand over another? If two companies are competing in roughly the same marketplace, what are the assets that tip the scales in one direction and not the other? These are the questions that have to be answered before a launch event can be planned, because they will help determine exactly what qualities of Just the Best should be emphasized and how to best communicate them to the ice cream consuming public.

In some cases, the amenities or features one brand offers over another—the most concrete of advantages—make the consumer's choice for him or her. But when products are too similar, when the tangible advantages each one offers become indistinguishable from those of the other, the brand identity must do the persuading. If the product doesn't have demonstrable features that are clearly superior to those of the competition, then the identity of the brand, or the feeling the brand engenders in the consumer, is the most obvious difference, and therefore the aspect that should be most widely exploited.

Grace Ascolese of Ascolese Associates, a market research firm, says: "I went to a convention, and they had this whole presentation about W Hotels, which is Weston. And they have the Heavenly Bed. The person who took my reservation on the phone said, 'Oh, you're going to love our beds.' I went to the convention, and was beat up by the time I got to California. They put such a presentation on the beds that I left thinking, 'I have to stay at a W whenever I can because I love these beds.' They were really comfortable, but W's whole premise, their core value, is that they want to pamper the business traveler."

In this case, the concrete advantage—that of the extremely comfortable bed in the hotel room—melds with the brand identity point, which is that W Hotels will pamper the business traveler and make him/her feel special. It's an example that bears examination, since it combines the two objectives of the product becoming a brand and has the intended effect on the business traveler, who is the target audience for this brand.

For some markets, cost is going to be the driving factor in a brand choice. Generally, consumers tend to buy the lowest-priced gasoline they can find in their area (although location and convenience also play a large role in such choices). They buy books by John Grisham (a brand if ever there was one) based on past experience, having read a Grisham book and expecting to duplicate that experience with a new one.

A BRANDED WORLD

Adam Christing, president of Clean Comedians, says, "There are only three ways to offer an advantage: price, premium quality, or personalization. It's important to focus on which of those three the business offers the customer. It's important not to try to be more than one of those. McDonald's doesn't try to have the best burger, offer the lowest price, and customize every order."

> When dealing with a new brand, consumers are wary, but curious. Given a clear reason to sample something for the first time, they generally will. But if the experience they have on that first occasion isn't a combination of familiar and different—that is, if they are not both rewarded for their curiosity and impressed with the experience they have on the first try—the consumers will usually maintain brand loyalty and not switch to the new brand.

That scenario, of course, assumes that the brand will be in direct, head-to-head competition with at least one other brand. In the case of Just the Best, we are dealing with some competition on more than one front, but nothing that is exactly in a direct position to compete for the exact same consumer. We will expect our brand, if successful, to funnel consumers from both the super-premium brands like Häagen-Dazs and Ben & Jerry's and from the supermarket brands like Breyer's and Edy's. We are not marketing to be a niche brand between the two segments of the market, but to be a broad-based product that will eventually cut across all ice cream consumer segments to be the first true national brand in the ice cream business.

My experience in Branding with Hollywood celebrities has often taken a similar road. After all, there are plenty of actors and actresses, and a fair number of them become famous. But there's only one Michael Jackson, there's only one Barbra Streisand, there's only one Charlton Heston, and there's only one Michael J. Fox.

Granted, in many cases, when I began working with the celebrity, the brand was already in place. Some were in need of a brand makeover (we'll get to that later in the book), while others were trying to go from being a well-known performer to being a star, or from being a star to becoming a superstar.

Planning a Powerful Launch

In Michael J. Fox's case, the brand was an unknown, about to be flung into the ultra-competitive world of network television. So the objective was to make him stand out in the crowd, to communicate the brand identity (in his case, the character Alex P. Keaton), and to make that identity an attractive and likable one for the viewing public, which was our target demographic.

There were various launch events, most of which were aimed at introducing more general themes than "Michael J. Fox, hot new talent." In many cases, the events were aimed at familiarizing the public with the television show *Family Ties,* which at that point was very much focused on the characters of the parents (played by Meredith Baxter and Michael Gross). In fact, the opportunities to make Michael J. Fox stand out were not as plentiful in the beginning.

Before the first episode aired, however, the media covering the television industry did begin to hone in on certain personalities. That was when a series of launch events—in this case, interviews with various members of the general and entertainment press—were held, and that was when we made sure Michael was presented in exactly the way we had planned, to establish his brand.

Luckily, Michael is a gifted performer who has a sly and quick wit, so he was what the press likes to call a "good interview." He answered questions as himself, not as Alex Keaton, but we made sure he was always dressed the way Alex would dress (which was not Michael's own style) and that his attitude was compatible with the show's and the character's, even if Michael and Alex were two very different types—and they were.

Eventually, Michael's natural charm and the brand image developed for Alex Keaton merged in the public's mind. Later, when he began to take on other roles in movies and on television, he had to break free of the original brand identity and prove that he wasn't only Alex P. Keaton, but Michael did that in a number of venues and the result was a very successful brand expansion.

"The people who have been the most successful at Branding are the people who were the most successful in identifying what their product was," says Larry Thompson, a successful producer and manager for high-level Hollywood stars. "You have to know what the product is. Look at the top brands in America. They knew what they were and they marketed themselves based on what they were. The quickest way to brand yourself is to buy an ad in the Super Bowl. Well, I still don't know what mLife is, and I must have seen 27 commercials."

In other words, no matter how widely your message is circulated, it will fail if it is not circulated clearly. Advertising people are generally interested in putting out exciting, attention-grabbing advertising, but often their motivations can be clouded by the possibility of winning advertising awards or moving to other branches of the media. Many commercial directors are now moving to television and feature films based on the striking visual images on display in their work. That is a serious advantage for them, but it does not necessarily serve the brand or the product being advertised to the maximum effect.

If the ad is striking, dramatic, colorful, startling, beautiful, or hilarious, but doesn't communicate the message of the brand, don't be fooled—it is a bad advertisement. Public relations events, like launch events of any kind, can do more in one afternoon than a two-week ad campaign on national TV can do if the public relations event is well conceived and executed and the ad campaign is not.

For Just the Best, the stage must be national. One of the differences between this brand and many of the supermarket ice cream brands already on the market will be that Just the Best is designed to be sold nationwide. Due to the volatile nature of the product (ice cream has a tendency to melt and doesn't transport across long distances well), many brands have opted to serve a particular geographical region rather than attempt to dominate the market across the United States, and, eventually, in other countries. Just the Best will have manufacturing and distribution plants across the country, like many of the smaller, more specialized brands, and thus will be the first true dominant ice cream brand sold in supermarkets.

Therefore, the event calculated to introduce Just the Best to the nation of consumers must be seen as a nationwide happening. But it should also reinforce the brand identity trait of a playful, nostalgic product whose values may owe more to the small town than the countryside. How can these elements be expertly blended to convey the brand identity image and still emphasize the unique nationwide availability of the new brand?

Planning a Powerful Launch

The Just the Best launch event should emphasize the coast-to-coast aspect of the brand introduction, while at the same time organization should be done on a level as local as our budget will allow. You might remember Hands Across America, a nationwide event that was orchestrated in 1986. People from the West Coast to the East Coast formed a human chain across the nation. The event was meticulously organized at the local level, but it garnered national attention as well. This combination is our goal as well—the more local groups are involved, the better our opportunities for local news coverage will be, while the nationwide flavor of the event itself should garner a good deal of attention from the larger media with more wide-ranging reach.

If the brand is being launched during an election year, the event can take the shape of a national election for the favorite Just the Best flavor. This reinforces key elements of the Just the Best brand identity. It introduces the brand as an ice cream company that concentrates on the quality of its flavors, and explains which flavors they are and why there are only three. It also demonstrates the nationwide distribution of the product (since every state will be involved in the election, including Hawaii and Alaska) and celebrates the personality of fun and small-town nostalgia upon which the brand intends to play. And, in naming the mock election, it presents the brand name and logo for the consuming public to discover and learn. In fact, this element of discovery can be quite powerful.

People tend to develop affection for, and remain loyal to, the things they feel they discovered on their own, as legendary film producer Robert Evans notes in his book, *The Kid Stays in the Picture*. Consumers who believe that they found a certain product "first" and then recommended it to their friends and relatives will often be the most loyal proponents of that brand for life.

The idea of the Just the Best flavor election is to provide that "sense of discovery" for consumers who try Just the Best on its introduction. And the idea of having a very large-scale, high-profile event to launch the brand means the maximum number of people will have the opportunity to be "first" with this brand and gain their own sense of discovery. Loyalty is going to be an essential quality for the Just the Best consumer, especially in the brand's first year, so that thrill of being the first on the block must be impactful and impressive.

The election will be organized much like a political one: The candidates will be vanilla, chocolate, and chocolate chip. Volunteers (and Just the Best employees in each state) will organize grass roots supporters for each flavor. Television ads will include debates. And, of course, there will be plenty of coupons and free samples available for consumers to form their own opinions. The fact that the ice cream is packaged in larger quantities than most other premium brands—quarts rather than pints—for a comparable price will demonstrate the high quality and value of the product.

To emphasize the fact that Just the Best is sold not in "scoop shops" but in supermarkets, the election itself will be held on a specific date (preferably not the same date as the governmental elections are held, but close to it) in supermarkets across the country. Representatives of the company will be on hand acting as "election personnel," there will be voting booths in each supermarket, and it will have been made quite clear that the winning flavor will be distributed free on the day of the election (polls close at 3:00 P.M.).

A national winner will be announced after each supermarket calls a central number and adds its tabulations. Television spots will be purchased to announce the winner as close to the end of the election as possible, to give consumers time to get their free quart (or coupon for a free quart) of the winning flavor in their local supermarkets, or to buy another flavor with a value-added coupon.

It would be possible, of course, to perform preelection "polling" and have a winning flavor ready for Election Day, to cut promotional costs and render the actual in-market voting meaningless. But that would be a very bad idea from a public relations standpoint; once consumers found that their participation was not essential, they might feel betrayed and the promotion would end up having an effect diametrically opposed to the one the brand hopes to achieve. It will be worth it to spend the extra money on the promotion and let the election be "legitimate."

Subsequent ads will show "real" consumers in towns across the country talking about the high quality of the ice cream and why they voted for one flavor or another. The winning flavor will issue a statement thanking its competitors and reminding the public of the promotion. After the first day, coupons issued on Election Day will continue to be honored.

The Just the Best Flavor election promotion is a launch event that serves a number of purposes: It raises awareness of the brand, it explains the general promises the brand is making, and it encourages consumers to sample the brand very quickly after introduction. It establishes the venue in which the product is sold and the fact that the product is sold in quarts, as opposed to the pints most super-premium brands typically market, and more than anything else, it introduces and reinforces the brand identity of a fun, down-home product that will meet and exceed the expectations of its target audience.

The campaign can begin as long as a month before the designated Election Day to build anticipation among consumers. It can continue for a week or two after that day to remind the public of the fun the brand provided and continues to provide, and to encourage repeat business, preferably sampling flavors other than the one that won the election.

Once the launch event has been executed and achieves the level of success anticipated for it, the time will come to begin building on the initial rush of attention. Public relations will play a large role, but so will marketing and advertising. In the next flurry of events, it will be necessary for all three disciplines to work in tandem, and for the goal to be the same for each—to dovetail with the introduction and never let the momentum lag.

CHAPTER SIX

MARRYING PUBLIC RELATIONS AND ADVERTISING IN BRANDING

The difficulty with discussing the role of advertising in Branding is that so many people mistake advertising for Branding. The fact that a particular product has an attention-getting ad campaign and a recognizable spokesperson, logo, or slogan does not necessarily make it a brand. As we've established throughout this book, a brand—particularly a successful brand—is a series of promises being not only met but exceeded, and a carefully crafted brand identity being communicated and maintained from the brand to the public.

Advertising, while enormously helpful in accomplishing all that a successful brand does, cannot create a brand all by itself. By definition, a brand is something that combines advertising, public relations, and marketing into a package so seamless it becomes impossible to tell where one discipline leaves off and the next begins.

It would be irresponsible and erroneous to suggest that advertising is not a vital part of the Branding process, however. It is often the most public face a brand displays, and (when public relations isn't doing its job properly) can be the first, most memorable impression a brand makes on a consumer. For example, consider how the Nike swoosh logo would have evolved had it not been for the advertising campaigns the company has unveiled over the past 15 years. Michael Jordan could endorse the athletic shoes all he wanted, but without the "Just Do It" campaigns, the emblem of an extremely successful brand would still be an incomprehensible symbol.

In the Just the Best introduction campaign detailed in the preceding chapter, it would have been patently impossible to conduct a national election campaign without at the very least a limited advertising presence. Public relations could have devised the campaign and implemented the election in local supermarkets, and it might even have been a moderately successful launch, but unless some television, radio, and print advertising were in place to back up the word of mouth and media coverage, most consumers in any given market would have been unaware of the promotion, and in all likelihood confused by the election booths and Just the Best personnel present in their local supermarket on the day of the election.

In most cases, advertising is also considerably more expensive than a public relations campaign, particularly when considered on a nationwide basis. A half-minute television commercial for the 2002 Academy Awards show cost over $2 million, and time during the Super Bowl was more expensive than that. True, there are other outlets, such as local stations, cable TV, print advertising, and radio, and even most regularly scheduled network programs are not nearly as costly as commercial time on a once-a-year event like the Oscars or the Super Bowl, but there is no denying the fact that conceiving, executing, and broadcasting an effective advertising campaign requires a huge amount of money in today's society.

In their essential book *The 22 Immutable Laws of Branding,* Al and Laura Ries list as fourth among Branding laws, "Once born, a brand needs advertising to stay healthy." They elaborate: "Publicity is a powerful tool, but sooner or later a brand outlives its publicity potential. . . . Leaders should not look on their advertising budgets as investments that will pay dividends. Instead leaders should look on their advertising budgets as insurance that will protect them against losses caused by competitive attacks."

Notice that the Rieses do not consider advertising an essential for launching a brand; they believe it is central to the concept of maintaining and advancing a brand, and mostly toward fending off attacks from competition.

A BRANDED WORLD

Advertising is expensive; it is reactive; it is defensive and not always specific to the brand. But it is a necessity. Indeed, without a strong advertising program, even discussing the idea of a national brand identity is foolhardy. The countless celebrities with whom I have worked over the years don't advertise themselves per se, but they are seen in television programs, feature films, and other projects that are advertised on television and radio and in newspapers and magazines. Some are seen advertising other products. Without advertising, there would be very little chance that anyone—not Julia Roberts, not Tom Cruise—could guarantee a strong opening for a film. Without ads that explain a new television series and include information on its broadcast date, time, and station, it is unlikely that a program like *The West Wing* could have become a huge hit. Yes, public relations plays an enormous—some would say a central—role in developing public interest and communicating a message, but sometimes the simple truth is that a direct message from the brand to the consumer is necessary merely to explain the product or to remind consumers how much they have enjoyed the product in the past.

Given that, an examination of the methods by which advertising introduces, establishes, explains, reinforces, and maintains a brand identity is called for. Why, for example, do brands like McDonald's, Coca-Cola, or Disney, known throughout the world, still spend countless millions on advertising? How can a brand like *Playboy,* established globally, continue on so phenomenally with very little direct advertising? How can a product become a brand through the use of advertising, and is it possible for every product to do so?

ANATOMY OF AN AD CAMPAIGN

One of the shrewdest things good Branding does is to psychologically pander to the appetite of its audience, without the audience knowing what is being done; but a real falsehood is absolutely out of bounds. In the Alfred Hitchcock classic *North by Northwest,* Cary Grant, playing a slick Madison Avenue advertising executive, tells his secretary that "In the world of advertising, there's no such thing as a lie; there is only the expedient exaggeration." That is a clever line, but it isn't true. There *is* such a thing as a lie, and it is the most dangerous thing an advertisement can contain.

An ad campaign is just that: a campaign. It is not a single television advertisement, nor is it a catchphrase, logo, or spokesperson. It is a coordinated effort on the part of all involved to create a unified whole, a single message delivered in a number of different ways through various media until the larger idea is not only clear but felt instinctively in the public's consciousness. And if that doesn't describe the effect of a superior Branding campaign, I don't know what would.

The first time you saw the Nike swoosh, did you know what it meant? Now when you see it, do you even have to consider for a split second what that emblem means? It's true that the difference between the two reactions is based largely on the repetition of the symbol, but the experience you've had in between these two events is crucial to the understanding of a strong brand identity.

When the Nike symbol was first unveiled, it was in essence meaningless. It was a swirl that held no inherent emotional signal; it didn't remind its viewer of another object, an activity, or even a feeling. But because Nike used that symbol in conjunction with a brilliant series of advertisements that explained (usually without words) the brand's identity, the swoosh became associated with that identity. Now, when people view the emblem, they talk about its built-in feeling of movement, of activity, even of determination or superior talent. And that is precisely what the advertising executives associated with Nike intended for the symbol at the company's onset.

"When you pair the Nike swoosh with Michael Jordan, you are taking a completely meaningless symbol and pairing it with one that elicits an emotional response," says Dr. Robert Epstein of *Psychology Today*. "That's part of brand management. Every single brand pairs its name or symbol over and over again with important emotional symbols. You take a meaningless stimulus and you pair it with a meaningful stimulus, and what happens is that some of the meaning transfers. That's what classical conditioning means. The success rubs off onto the swoosh and it makes you feel the way you would feel in your imagination if you were hanging out with Tiger Woods."

This takes into account both the power of an advertisement and the strength of association with an instantly recognizable company spokesperson. It may seem like a small gesture to have Michael Jordan wear Nikes, or for Tiger Woods to have the swoosh on his hat, but that image will immediately translate to something the consumer might not even notice on a conscious level, and will transfer the cachet of that successful spokesperson onto the brand identity itself. It is the ultimate example of the Tiffany Theory: Wrap your product in Tiger Woods, and you are well on the way to becoming a brand.

Epstein says there are three processes that enter into the psychology of advertising. The first is adaptation, which comes with frequent repetition of the message or the image so the consumer can recognize the message and then associate it with the product to develop awareness of a brand. Next comes classical conditioning. "This involves the pairing of two stimuli. You're going to pair a stimulus that's already powerful and familiar with one that is not as powerful," Epstein says. "That is widely used. It is deliberately and systematically used."

The merging of a strong, successful celebrity like Tiger Woods with the symbol of the company would be a potent example of classical conditioning. It's not something the consumer will necessarily notice, but it is something the consumer will very likely remember, and the association will be made on some subconscious level in the public's collective mind. It is as direct as it is effective, and in many cases, it can be the central image in a strong advertising campaign.

More subtle, and more associative, is the idea of operant conditioning, the third process in the trio, which Epstein describes as "the more common kind of conditioning that goes on. You go, 'aha, the next time I want to make a light go on, I'll flip a light switch.' It's how behavior is changed by consequences. If you do something and it's successful, you do it again."

How does that enter into an advertising campaign? The first, and most important, way is that an ad urges a consumer to sample a particular product. If that product does not perform up to the consumer's expectations (and, hopefully, exceed them), no amount of advertising is going to convince that consumer to sample the product again. So the product must be everything the advertisement claims it will be, thus eliminating the "expedient exaggeration" and making sure there is no lying going on in the advertising.

The second way that operant conditioning is used is more oblique. It is consistently used in television and radio ads especially, but is the cornerstone of almost every ad campaign every conceived. It is an association made between the use of the product and a benefit to the consumer.

"You show in an ad that when someone uses the product, something good happens," says Epstein. "You show that using the product has wonderful, amazing consequences. What you're showing is that if people use this product, there will be good consequences. And the consequences that are shown are usually so absurd and so ridiculous that they are things that would not happen in a million years. You give an example of operant conditioning and say, 'If you do this, good things will happen to you, too.' There's no magic to this."

Perhaps not, but there is a considerable amount of method. The old newspaper ads showing a "98-pound weakling" suddenly becoming the Incredible Hulk with the use of a particular exercise program or weight management product are no longer accepted as fact by a skeptical, Data Smog–ridden public. It is far more difficult to project a direct benefit for each product advertised, and sometimes that benefit is seen in the lifestyle the ad projects, the unstated promise coming through loud and clear: "Use this product (drive this car, invest with this firm, wear this suit), and this rich, lush lifestyle can be yours as well."

That promise is never stated directly in ads for Lexus, Paine Webber, or Men's Wearhouse, but it is implied with every camera movement, every view of the happy, successful people patronizing these brands, and every rich, intoning statement made by the satisfied-sounding narrator. The operant conditioning going on in these ads might even surprise the executives who conceived the campaign, but it will not be missed emotionally by the consumer, who is the ultimate judge of the success or failure of advertising. If sales go up, the campaign is a success. If sales don't increase, but the ads win awards, the campaign is a failure.

In fact, the secret ingredient behind many of the successful brands is the confidence and exuberance of a product or service that truly believes itself to be the best in its field. Arrogance is not helpful, but confidence is a true propellant. And that quality, above all, must be exhibited in advertising, particularly for a brand that has not been experienced before by the consuming public.

A recent television commercial for Mercedes-Benz illustrates this point: An aging Mercedes is lifted into a car crusher at the junkyard. As the car is compacted into something roughly the size of a briefcase, its "life" flashes before its "eyes," and we see all the images: graduations, birthdays, swerving away from hazards, some implied amour in the back seat. A bright light beckons, and at the other end of it a brand-new Mercedes rolls off the assembly line. Voice-over narrator Joe Mantegna tells us, "The shape may change, but the soul remains the same."

The implied messages here are myriad, but the key one is this: Everything you've always loved about your previous Mercedes-Benz is still here in the newest models. And in that message is the clear implication: "We know we're the best, and we know you're aware of that. Don't worry; we haven't changed anything you already loved."

If that statement were made with arrogance, rather than confidence, it would be presented less emotionally and would appeal more to our envy or desire to be envied than to our comfort with a superior product. We'd see a brand-new car being driven down the street, and people who aren't as good as us drooling over it. We'd see the car passing other, less prestigious automobiles in the street, and the frustrated drivers trying desperately to catch up. Instead, the confidence seen in this ad is an infinitely more powerful message for the target audience being courted by Mercedes-Benz.

In the case of Mercedes-Benz, clearly the advertising is intended to service an existing brand, and not to communicate the brand identity message to an unfamiliar public. That is calculated and well advised; advertising, as the Rieses point out, is at its best when reinforcing and expanding the consumer's views rather than creating a new impression. But sometimes there is no logical choice but to advertise at the onset of a business, when the public is not comfortably familiar with the brand being created. Is it possible, then, for advertising to carry the load of brand identity communication?

It's certainly not the first choice. No one discipline—not public relations, not marketing, and not advertising—should be asked to shoulder the responsibility for all aspects of a brand introduction. And advertising is perhaps the least well equipped to handle such a task. Because of the high cost involved with national advertising, the message must be kept extremely brief, and that means certain key points—identity traits that will endear the brand to the consuming public—must be eliminated from the message during initial campaigns. It's not that the public can't absorb more information; it's more that all the information would be impossible to compress into a 30-second television commercial.

When the average consumer watches a television ad, it is likely he or she remembers two things: the story line of the commercial (and every such ad has a story line) and the company the spot is advertising. It takes a number of repetitions before the consumer can be counted upon to remember the name of the product itself, and it is unlikely anyone will ever be able to recall every claim made about the product in the course of a 60-second ad—other than the people responsible for creating that ad.

Scott M. Davis is the author of *Brand Asset Management,* and managing director of the Chicago office of PROPHET Brand Strategy. He sees the big picture in terms of Branding, and notes that one of the great misconceptions in the field has been the tendency to mistake Branding for advertising alone. He knows it is not that simple. But he is heartened by signs that the situation is changing for the better.

"For the first time in the past 50 years, senior executives have awakened to the fact that a brand is much more than advertising, a tagline, a logo or a spokesperson, what I call 'marketing tactics,' " says Davis. "This has been fueled for a few different reasons: (1) There has been an incredible intensity over mergers and acquisitions in the past 12 years. A number of companies have bought brands that they really didn't know what to do with or how to manage. (2) The number of dot-com bombs over the past several years was a clear sign that you can't just pour money into an aspect of your company—advertising—and expect to get returns. Your brand is a much more holistic approach."

A brand is built from the ground up. If it is not infused into everyone, from the person who cleans the rest rooms in the corporate headquarters to the CEO, it will not be communicated effectively to the consumer and will not be maintained properly by the company that owns the brand. It has to be a philosophy, a religion, an obsession for every employee involved directly or indirectly, or it will not have a glimmer of hope of becoming a true brand.

Advertising serves part of the Branding function. And while it should be stressed that it is just one part, we also must not downplay advertising's role. Without it, something might be a very successful product, but it is unlikely to become a brand. The key is to design every advertising component. Every broadcast commercial on any television, radio, or cable station; every print ad in any magazine, newspaper, or flier; every billboard, in-store signage and other image-based advertising must be conceived and executed with the brand identity foremost in mind and with full knowledge of concurrent campaigns by public relations and marketing arms of the company. Communication internally and externally will be essential.

"If you do not link your brand with your business strategy, you will fail," Scott M. Davis says. "The majority of business organizations assume that Branding is something in marketing, and it's something pretty far down the marketing tube. When that assumption is made, Branding most likely will get treated as something that's not very important. If brand is not wrapped around the mission statement, the long-term strategy for the next five years, not only is it a disservice to the company, but any of the brand efforts that anybody in your company tries to push will fail."

Everything from the company's mission statement to the packaging of the product is important. Every customer service call must be handled in precisely the correct way to ensure a satisfied customer. You will never call L.L. Bean with a customer service question or complaint and not be satisfied when you hang up. Every employee of that company knows it, and every customer will find out about it if the situation arises. If Hollywood believes movies can be sold by word of mouth among satisfied audience members, you can bet that any other business can rely on the same kind of consumer-to-consumer communication to spread—with positive or negative comments—once the consumer and the brand come into direct contact.

Advertising can emphasize that. Advertising can present the unblemished record of a customer service system, and it can provide word of mouth. Perhaps the word coming from an advertising campaign isn't as credible as that coming from a close friend or family member, or even from a media source like the *Wall Street Journal* or *Nightline,* but what advertising does when it is executed properly is to provide sample word of mouth—the kind of thing you might consider saying to a friend about a product if you determine that the claim made by the advertiser is true. Advertising can't produce absolutely credible statements, but it can certainly offer suggestions and dare the consumer to test them in the field.

A FRIENDLY NUDGE

For Just the Best, our ad campaign must convey the brand identity while it provides one central piece of information: There is a new brand of ice cream that you really must try. If anything beyond that message is communicated in the ads, it will be strictly a bonus. Our aim is to introduce the brand and compel the consumer to try it as soon as possible.

The campaign will begin after the Election Day promotion, although there will naturally be television, radio, and print ads that support the initial brand launch event. Assuming that some consumers have opted not to participate in the promotion, and have not yet taken advantage of the free samples and coupons the brand has provided to sample the product, the advertising elements will be called upon to make Just the Best so enticing, so irresistible and exciting, that large numbers of consumers who have not yet done so will consider buying a quart of Just the Best and trying it for themselves. In other words, the goal is for consumers to decide whether or not they will accept our suggestion and provide positive word of mouth for the product to their friends and loved ones.

Where the Election Day promotion was frenetic and high-energy, the initial ad campaign should be somewhat more warm and friendly. There should not, however, be such a dramatic change in mood that the consumer becomes confused about the brand identity and loses interest in the product itself. Elements of the identity that seem to be contradictory—the idea of fun coupled with the warm, sweet feeling of nostalgia—have to be reconciled so they form a cohesive personality for the consumer to recognize, empathize with, and embrace thoroughly.

To capitalize on the nostalgic image we intend to convey, but at the same time to inject a sense of play into that image, we can start with the most iconic of American nostalgic images—the paintings of Norman Rockwell on the cover of *The Saturday Evening Post*. These well-known, heartwarming images are perfect for the Just the Best campaign, since they evoke the kind of feeling we're trying to encourage while remaining open to good-natured teasing.

Consider a view of the Rockwell painting "Soda Fountain," in which a young soda jerk, circa the 1950s, entrances a group of teenage girls (and their dog) while failing to attend to his duties. A television ad could begin with that original image, then dissolve to a live-action tableau of the scene with actors playing the roles depicted in the painting.

Here's how our ad might proceed:

[After a second or two, the actors move. The girls, as one, sigh in the direction of the soda jerk.]

First girl: Gosh, Jimmy, you're just the sweetest.
Second girl: And the coolest.
Third girl: And the smoothest.

[The dog barks; he's in on it, too.]

First girl: You're just . . . the best!

[The soda jerk smiles and shakes his head.]

Jimmy: Nah, girls, you're wrong. *This* is Just the Best.

[He produces a quart of ice cream from under the counter. He scoops out the ice cream, which looks delicious.]

Jimmy: It's the sweetest, the richest, the smoothest ice cream you've ever had. Vanilla, chocolate, or chocolate chip, made with the finest ingredients ever for the freshest taste. And the best part is, it's in your supermarket's freezer.

Marrying Public Relations and Advertising in Branding

[The girls sigh again, until the second girl absorbs what he just said.]

Second girl: Wait a second. You mean we can get Just the Best at the supermarket anytime we want?

Jimmy: That's right. It's in quarts in your supermarket's freezer.

[The other two girls wise up too.]

Third girl: Come on, girls! We don't have to flatter this loser to get Just the Best!

[They walk out, as Jimmy ponders where he might have gone wrong.]

Narrator: Just the Best. Ice cream parlor taste you can have at home. Anytime.

[Close-up of Jimmy]

Jimmy: Yeah. Thanks a lot.

[Fade out]

What does this ad accomplish, and how does it go about doing so? First and foremost, while it may not be the most artfully constructed piece of dramaturgy ever conceived, it does communicate basic, important information about the product, and, more than that, the brand identity that has been developed for Just the Best.

From this brief message, consumers can discover that there exists a new ice cream product called Just the Best, which is made from fresh ingredients, comes in three flavors, and is sold in quart-sized containers in supermarkets. That's the factual information the commercial offers.

But beyond that, the ad conveys a feeling, a mood that exemplifies the carefully crafted brand identity Just the Best is meant to exude. It begins with the familiar view of a Norman Rockwell painting; there are few things as iconic and easily identifiable in this culture. By starting with that image, Just the Best employs the Tiffany Theory, associating itself with something the consumer already knows and trusts, perhaps even subconsciously. It adds a certain cachet, and extra believability, to the ad that is about to begin.

A BRANDED WORLD

Once the live action starts, the nostalgic flavor is perpetuated again and again. The idea of a soda jerk standing behind a counter and dishing out ice cream is something that few people under 50 will remember clearly. But it is an idea that we all wish we remembered, something that calls to mind calmer, easier days and friendlier climates than those in which we live today.

Still, there is something just a little bit silly about that image, and the commercial exploits that to bring the brand identity into the twenty-first century. Since in the fifties few people went to the supermarket, there is an anachronistic tone to the mention of Just the Best's distribution stream, which signals the viewer that maybe this isn't going to be the most reverential commercial ever made. And immediately thereafter, the 1950's-era girls begin behaving in a very twenty-first-century manner, refusing to kowtow to the "dreamy" soda jerk once they find out they can buy the desirable ice cream product elsewhere.

The idea, beyond giving the audience a laugh, is that the brand identity of nostalgic association begins the ad, but the equally important trait of irreverence and playful fun closes the commercial. Both are present, and they are presented with equal weight, so that the satire that ends the ad does not seem to be contemptuous of the gauzy nostalgia that is the first image we see.

Keep in mind that the average consumer will remember only the basic story line of the ad and the brand name after a single viewing (the brand name is repeated five times in the course of a very brief commercial to reinforce that memory). So even if they forget the three flavors offered by the brand, or that it is distributed in quart containers, and even though the reasons for making only three flavors or selling in larger containers are never mentioned in the ad at all, we can safely assume that consumers will remember that there is an ice cream called Just the Best and they will recall seeing it in a funny commercial where the young girls give the soda jerk his comeuppance.

After repeated viewings, consumers might recall the three flavors offered, and other details about the brand. But the things that they remember immediately will reinforce the brand identity. They'll remember seeing that old-fashioned painting in the beginning, even if they can't recall (or never knew) the artist's name. They'll remember the teenage girls turning the tables on the arrogant young soda jerk, over an ice cream that looked delectable in its close-ups. And because the storyline is very clear about it, they might very well remember that this ice cream is sold only in supermarkets.

Those facts will translate in the consumer's mind into a sense of enjoyment over the humorous moment, as well as a subconscious association with a nostalgic time when the worst thing young girls had to worry about was a soda jerk who thought he was the cat's pajamas. The brand identity, while never stated directly, is the real point of this commercial, and is the most important message—other than the existence of the product itself—communicated through this advertising campaign.

Subsequent ads can begin with other Rockwell paintings (creating a visual signature for the brand) and send them up in similar fashion, always affectionately and always with the core information communicated. Remember, the key goal of advertising is to spark stronger sales of the product, and, in the context of the Branding process, to establish and reinforce the brand identity. These ads are designed to do exactly that for our fictitious ice cream product.

Once the brand has been established, of course, there is the ongoing business of maintaining the brand identity, which is the most important, most difficult part of the Branding process. Advertising will play its role, of course; but without marketing, without public relations, and without a very strong, well considered, and effective maintenance plan, there is no brand on this earth that can expect to succeed.

The next step, then, is to develop a very detailed, comprehensive maintenance plan for our brand.

CHAPTER SEVEN

BRAND MAINTENANCE IN THE PUBLIC EYE

Most people, even those involved in marketing and advertising, believe that brand maintenance is simply a matter of keeping the ball rolling—that a trained chimp with a computer keyboard and a Rolodex could keep strong publicity coming to a brand that is already established.

On the contrary, brand maintenance is the meat and potatoes of the Branding process. It is the continuing and constant reinforcement of the brand promise, the brand identity, and the brand integrity that will be absolutely essential if the brand is to survive in a hostile marketplace. And keep in mind that every marketplace is a hostile one.

While a launch campaign can last anywhere from a few weeks to a few months, brand maintenance must be open-ended, extending forward to infinity, because there can never be an end to the vigilance and the dedication of the effort that goes into Branding. Branding isn't something you do once; it's something you never stop doing.

There is no better way to grasp the importance of brand maintenance than to observe what happens when it is not done properly. Consider the cautionary tale of what happened to one of the most recognizable, most accepted, and most successful brands in history, McDonald's.

It is my contention that if Ray Kroc, the man who revolutionized the fast food industry in 1955 by taking a local hamburger stand and creating a worldwide marketing empire, were to be resurrected and walked into one of his 30,000 McDonald's restaurants today, he wouldn't last long.

There was a time when McDonald's was among the most trusted brands in the world. When they entered one of Kroc's restaurants, people could expect a clean atmosphere (especially the rest rooms), a wholesome product served fast, and prompt, friendly service from a staff that had been trained to provide all those things without question.

I walked into a McDonald's not long ago in the Los Angeles area where I live. The place was filthy, the rest rooms were worse, and when I asked the woman behind the counter for more ice in my drink, she couldn't comply—she didn't speak English.

This scenario, alas, is not unusual. According to the April 29, 2002 issue of *Fortune,* McDonald's is not delivering what the consuming public expects from it. "Among the gripes: Pictures in advertisements don't resemble the real food," the article contends. "Its overall satisfaction score of 62 in the 2001 survey puts (McDonald's) 10 points below Wendy's and 3 below Burger King. In terms of approval ratings, that's not far ahead of the IRS."

When your business is just a little bit more popular than the people who collect taxes, you have a serious public relations problem, and your brand is in a tremendous amount of jeopardy. It doesn't matter how the situation became so desperately serious; what matters now is what can be done to rejuvenate your brand. It should have been handled long before a situation this dire developed.

BRAND MAINTENANCE

"We talk about the need for products, no matter how old they are, to create relevance for their audience. Whether you have a brand that's just out of the box or something that's been around for 25 years, if you neglect it, it becomes like a garden that dies out. You have to watch out for all the elements no matter what you're working on."

—Karen Benezra, editor of *Brandweek*

Launching a successful brand is not enough; Branding is also the art and the craft of maintenance, the most difficult thing to sustain in business. Maintenance isn't just the chore of keeping a brand alive, it is also the core of the Branding process. With enough money and effort, anyone can launch a relatively successful brand; that is simply the product of attention, and attention is easy to attract if you employ simple public relations techniques. Maintenance implies an ongoing effort to keep the public informed about your brand—to continue public relations efforts that will reaffirm the brand identity with the consuming public and will remind consumers about which qualities they found attractive in your brand to begin with. Maintenance is not janitorial work. It is the care and feeding of the most precious asset you own: your brand.

The McDonald's example is the most dramatic one illustrating the basic miscalculation destroying more brands today than any other: the inability (or unwillingness) of a brand to live up to its promise.

At the same time, McDonald's was losing sight of its own brand promises and brand identity. "McDonald's probably has one of the more famous recent biggest flops on record with the Arch Deluxe sandwich," says *Brandweek* editor Karen Benezra. "They tried to roll it out in '95 or '96 and came out with what they called a 'sandwich for adults.' This was something they purported at first to have better ingredients and higher quality, a burger that the folks would like and the kids wouldn't like. They showed ads for it with kids with very disgruntled faces looking at this burger disdainfully and saying they would never eat it. McDonald's really violated one of its core tenets by saying, 'We're telling a portion of our audience: Don't eat this product.' By the time it did come out, adults went and tried it with a free coupon or they saw an ad, and what they got was a pretty mundane burger with iceberg lettuce and American cheese. McDonald's spent somewhere in the neighborhood of $200 million introducing this thing, and in eight or nine months, it had disappeared."

Brand identity is nothing if not a few basic promises made by the brand to the consumer. In McDonald's case, the promises were easy to understand: tasty food delivered quickly in a clean, friendly atmosphere. McDonald's didn't promise to deliver elegant cuisine in a sumptuous atmosphere with tuxedo-clad waiters. It didn't promise healthy, heart-friendly food served in a plant-laden setting. In the beginning, McDonald's knew exactly what its identity would be and which promises were central, unbreakable, essential tenets of the philosophy that identity would promise to its consumers. It delivered on those promises every day, every time, every store, every hamburger. Always, no exceptions.

Brand Maintenance in the Public Eye

As years wore on, however, two things happened that changed the way McDonald's did business, and not for the better. First, competition began springing up. Burger King, Wendy's, and other chains built restaurants based on the McDonald's model, but with subtle differences. Burger King's famous jingle and slogan "Have It Your Way" dramatized the new chain's system of cooking its burgers, which allowed for quick changes in condiments that McDonald's couldn't handle with its precooked system. People who didn't want mustard and ketchup on their hamburgers, and didn't want to have to wait an extra 10 minutes or so while their lunch was prepared, tried Burger King's product, and in many cases preferred it to the McDonald's original. McDonald's market share, while still very high, began to erode.

According to Bob Nelson, president of Nelson Motivation, Inc., "I've worked with McDonald's, and I find that brands breaking down are a combination of things. They have over 20,000 restaurants, and as you get farther from the store, it's a stretch. It's hard to do it when you're big. It's a challenge. I know McDonald's has good people who want to make it work well, but it's hard."

The second event that changed the McDonald's brand was the death of Ray Kroc in 1984. Many people believed that Kroc had been the overseer of the McDonald's brand and its integrity, and when he was no longer present, the public began to question McDonald's commitment to its basic promises. In urban restaurants especially, the cleanliness of the facility and the rest rooms was judged as less than acceptable by many consumers. *Fortune* reported in April, 2002 that "Burger King and Wendy's . . . have long scored higher in customer satisfaction surveys." The central promise stated by the McDonald's brand in all its publicity—and in some cases on signs in the restaurants themselves—has been broken. Whether this erosion—one example of the brand completely ignoring its initial pledge to the consumer—was already beginning before Kroc died or not, once his presence was gone from McDonald's, consumers began to look more closely and to notice that things were "not like they used to be" in the world's number one restaurant chain.

"Ray Kroc said their restaurants would be cleanest in class, and that's still one of the five parts of their brand promise on the front door of the

McDonald's University in Oak Brook, Illinois," says Duane Knapp, president of Brand Strategy Inc. and author of *The Brand Mindset*. "Brands without proper management don't have to go out of business, because people are willing to put up with a lot. They're not following their promise. No one calls people on their promise."

That promise is a sacred covenant made between the brand and the public, and it is much, much more than simple repetition of a brand name. According to Charlie Koones, publisher of *Daily Variety,* "I don't believe that a brand means only name recognition. Any brand it that is built on name recognition alone will fail. A brand needs to stand for the communication of a benefit."

Keep in mind that the University of Michigan's American Consumer Satisfaction Index, which many analysts consider the most credible such measure, has always listed McDonald's last among fast food restaurants. That means consumers, when questioned about their preferences in this area, have continually found the overwhelming market share leader lacking. But the university didn't start measuring such things until eight years after Ray Kroc died. By then, things had already declined very seriously from the company's heyday.

No one is crying crocodile tears for McDonald's; it is still an enormously successful brand that owns almost half the market share for its category and makes billions of dollars per year. But that market share is eroding, the stock price is dropping, and customer satisfaction—the most accurate and telling barometer for a brand's appeal—is in serious decline. And the fact is that, with proper brand maintenance, all that could have been avoided.

How bad is the McDonald's situation? Scott M. Davis of PROPHET says: "[Recently], the University of Michigan did a study on customer satisfaction, and they ranked 175 companies on a number of different attributes. Polling customers and customer satisfaction, McDonald's was rated 171 out of 175. The McDonald's brand empirically had a contract with all of us consumers. They broke it in every possible angle. They were actually able to quantify how much this terrible customer satisfaction perception is costing, and they quantified it at $175 million per year. McDonald's is an easy target."

Brand Maintenance in the Public Eye

To the consumer, brand maintenance is nothing short of reassurance—the continuing affirmation that everything is all right and that what has been will continue to be. Maintenance is not the same thing as damage control, which is a reaction to an existing situation that is not favorable to the brand. Instead, to maintain the brand is to protect the status quo of the brand identity at all costs.

Consider the classic example of a brand mistake: the introduction of New Coke. What could have been merely a brand extension, like the recent introduction of Vanilla Coke and other successful offshoots (most famously Diet Coke, which was an extremely savvy move on the part of the world's most famous brand), New Coke was a brand replacement, and that was the crucial mistake made in that notable debacle.

Dick Morris, the political consultant and pollster, says the introduction of New Coke was a reaction to a basic premise that Coke didn't want to admit, but knew was true: "I once talked to Coca-Cola's top advertising person, and he said, 'Our basic problem is that Pepsi tastes better than Coke.' You have two products here where everyone agrees that one is better than the other. So they have to sell their product based on things other than the product." The "things other than the product" were the brand identity and the way people felt about Coke, as opposed to the experience of drinking the soda itself.

Because the Coca-Cola Company had market research data suggesting that the average consumer preferred the taste of Pepsi to Coke, and because market share was starting to slip just a bit, in the 1980s the company had an infamous overreaction and decided to introduce a new product under the Coke banner that would taste more like Pepsi, thus increasing the satisfaction of the consumer while, the marketing executives believed, preserving the integrity of the Coca-Cola brand. That in itself was not necessarily a wrong move.

The problem came when Coke decided to discontinue its original brand, which had been beloved for decades, and use the new product as a replacement, rather than an extension. Where consumers might have been inclined to sample the New Coke and then decide if they wanted to continue with the original version, they were now being deprived of the choice, and it became evident very quickly that Coca-Cola had grossly

101

underestimated its own brand loyalty. The millions it spent on developing New Coke, tooling up factories to produce it, creating publicity for the move, making the product, and introducing it were wasted because consumers liked the brand identity they had known all their lives. Coca-Cola had done something far worse than ignoring its initial promise to consumers: It had made its core consuming demographic feel betrayed. That kind of bad feeling lasts a long time and is fundamentally difficult to overcome.

"What they were doing was diluting the brand," says Adam Christing of Clean Comedians. "In the end, Coca-Cola became stronger than ever when they went back to the original ABC of their brand."

Indeed, Coca-Cola decided, after enormous public consumer outcry, coverage on *Nightline* and other news media, protests, boycotts, and great teeth-gnashing in Coke's home office in Atlanta, to reinstate the original formula for Coca-Cola as "Coca-Cola Classic," while maintaining distribution of New Coke. Sales for the Classic version soared, the New version bombed, and eventually, New Coke became a collector's item and the print size for the word *Classic* on bottles of the original formula became smaller and smaller. Coke was Coke again.

Damage had been done to the brand's integrity, but after the smoke cleared (which took a few years), the brand was just as popular as it had ever been, and sales continued to rise. In fact, the reinstatement of the original Coke formula after weeks of vehement protest underlined how dear the Coca-Cola brand was to the heart of America. Every brand extension since that time has fed off the identity of the original brand and has associated itself with the original brand in an attempt to wrap Tiffany paper around the new product.

NEVER UNDERESTIMATE BRAND LOYALTY

The chief lesson to be learned from New Coke is that once a brand is well established, maintenance is necessary but loyalty to the brand identity is never to be underestimated. Branding is so misunderstood a concept that

Brand Maintenance in the Public Eye

even behemoths like Coca-Cola can fail to comprehend their own power, and in the process risk losing it.

McDonald's is a prime example of just that, but in a different context: By reneging on its promises to the consumer, McDonald's is relying on its brand loyalty to carry the day without delivering what built that loyalty to begin with. Lily Tomlin's Ernestine the telephone operator character once had a mock slogan for Bell Telephone: "We're the phone company; we don't have to care." McDonald's is exhibiting exactly the same attitude. It assumes an arrogant position that because it is the largest, most pervasive fast food brand in the world, consumers will be forced to buy its products whether McDonald's delivers what it promises or not. The company doesn't overestimate its brand loyalty, since consumers are still buying huge numbers of hamburgers at McDonald's, but it certainly takes that loyalty for granted and does not work hard enough at maintenance.

So how does McDonald's survive this level of dissatisfaction? Political consultant Dick Morris analyzes Branding and marketing plans, and he believes some of it is merely the momentum McDonald's has managed to gather in its 45-year existence. Sheer size also helps.

"The first way they sell it in the fast food example is that there are twice as many McDonald's as Burger King restaurants," Morris points out. "They have to pass a McDonald's to get to Burger King. You're not going to do that; you're hungry. Then, they make it a playground where kids feel really neat. . . . The hamburger is very far behind now as a selling point."

Where McDonald's failed was in brand maintenance, and brand maintenance is at its heart a public relations exercise. Advertising can do only so much, and marketing relies on research and development to create new and improved products for it to introduce. Public relations is on the front lines of consumer acceptance, the element from which brand loyalty arises. It must be the central component of a successful brand maintenance endeavor.

A PR campaign that aims at brand maintenance is different than one striving to introduce a brand. The goal here is to reinforce the information that has already been communicated in previous campaigns, but also to remind consumers of what it was they found attractive about the brand identity to begin with.

When I work with a celebrity who is already established in the public's mind, what I'm doing is brand maintenance. There's no point in trying to introduce the public to someone people already believe they know.

The first time I met with Charlton Heston, I presented him with a very detailed resume and explanation of the work I'd done with other stars and celebrities. After this elaborate presentation, Heston took a very long pause, then boomed in his best Moses-like baritone, "Well, Michael, you're obviously a very bright young man, but I don't believe you can make me more famous."

Of course, he was right. Charlton Heston had won an Academy Award and been the star of major motion pictures for decades before I met him. Everyone had an idea of who Charlton Heston was, and at that point in time, it was something other than a vital, exciting actor whom they'd just seen as the star of a movie. Charlton Heston was, to most younger moviegoers in the 1980s, a man who had starred in a lot of old movies, usually playing biblical characters. Some wondered if he was still alive.

"You're right," I told Heston. "I can't make you more famous. But I can make you more contemporary." This was not so much a case of brand maintenance as brand expansion, since Heston needed his image to be updated, not reinforced. The maintenance that I did with him was to remind people that Charlton Heston was more than someone who used to be an actor, he was still an actor and a very good one. The public needed to be gently nudged into remembering its original impression of Heston with a very detailed, well-constructed, and strategic campaign.

What Heston needed to do at that time was to remind the public of his initial promises, which are similar for each actor or performer: He promised to deliver an enjoyable performance and to behave in a relatively consistent manner. In other words, it would be frightening to see Charlton Heston starring in a role written for Adam Sandler, but seeing him tweak his Moses-on-the-mountain image a little would not be out of bounds. That is not breaking the promise.

I spent a good deal of time securing for Heston a spot hosting *Saturday Night Live*. When the producers agreed to the date, I excitedly called Heston with the news, and was met with that familiar voice that had spoken from Mt. Sinai in *The Ten Commandments*.

Brand Maintenance in the Public Eye

"What's *Saturday Night Live?*" Charlton Heston asked.

Convinced this would be an intelligent Branding move, Heston did, in fact, host *Saturday Night Live* twice, and gently tweaked his more famous roles in movies like *Ben-Hur, The Ten Commandments,* and *Planet of the Apes.* The stints as host were very successful, and expanded Heston's brand in the same way that making the film *Airplane!* had expanded the brand of Leslie Nielsen, who at the time was considered a very serious actor. *Saturday Night Live* proved that Charlton Heston could successfully play comedy, proved that he wasn't stuffy and intimidating, and, to some, proved that he was still a living, breathing actor.

It was a very successful brand expansion. While, as Heston pointed out, our public relations work was not able to make him more famous—he was already a very famous man—it did broaden the ways in which the public (as well as producers and directors) thought of him, and made him a brand which could now be seen in comedic roles, in friendlier roles, and not only as a stalwart defender of the people. He was able to be a versatile actor again.

Similarly, when the Beatles greatest hits CD *1* was released in 2000, it was a classic example of brand maintenance. Here was a brand the entire world knew intimately, presenting a product made up of ingredients everyone knew by heart and probably already owned. But by reinforcing the brand identity—through interviews with the surviving Beatles and a public relations campaign that tied to advertising and reminded consumers why they liked the Beatles in the first place—the public relations executives involved in the project clearly managed to remind the public of the promises made almost 40 years earlier and to convince consumers those promises where still vital and, best of all, available in a newly conceived and packaged form. Once again, the Beatles scored a number one album, 30 years after their last recordings were released. That is an example of brand maintenance that puts most other brands to shame.

A maintenance project for an existing brand is often an ongoing affair, not something that has a definitive beginning or end. It can consist of a number of press releases, distributed in sequence and at appropriate intervals, that mention the brand name and a news item. For instance: The brand is now sponsoring a scholarship for local youths; the brand was named one of the 10 best by a major publication; the president of the company was recently honored by a well-known national organization for service to the community or success in business. It is the kind of effort that doesn't aim at huge results all the time, but always has as its goal the placement of a positive news item about the brand in either local or national media.

SOUL BRANDING

"Target donates whatever percent it donates. Do you go to Target because you like them better, or because you think you're doing good for the world? When you look at Ben & Jerry's, or Häagen-Dazs, is there a reason to buy a premium ice cream and pay more than others based on taste alone? I don't think so. I think it's what their research shows about different populations. The Ben & Jerry's brand might mean no hormones to 15 percent of their buyers, where it might mean the feeling of the sixties for me. Their personality is complex, but you only have to pitch in to one piece of that."
—Grace Ascolese, president of Ascolese Associates

There are, however, many ways to build and maintain a powerful marketplace reputation. Some companies are better known for their brand identity than for their products. For example, companies like The Body Shop or Ben & Jerry's might be as famous for their charitable works and commitment to environmental issues as they are for cosmetics and ice cream.

There is a growing contingency of consumers who see their purchase decisions as equivalent to a voting record, and they are sometimes willing to change their buying habits or pay a bit more for a product if they believe they are helping a worthy cause by contributing to that kind of company. There are companies that make it a policy to emphasize these good works, and they make sure the public is aware that investing in their products will help the environment or other causes.

This concept, called *Soul Branding,* was pioneered by Elsie Maio, president of Maio & Co., Inc. Management Consultants in corporate positioning and brand strategy. Maio believes that companies that appeal to the soul will eventually be the rule, rather than the exception, as the public increasingly demands moral and community responsibility from the brands its patronizes.

As Maio says, "Ethics and morals will become integrated into the decision making at every level within the organization because authenticity will be required to establish trust. Trust is essential, and trust has been shattered. The dot-com incidents in the investment community and Enron have made the cynicism levels rise significantly. The other aspect to this is that when the companies sit back and wait for regulations to fill in this void, it's smart business to anticipate the requirements of your constituents. If you don't, you'll find yourself subjected to a reactionary backlash of regulations. It could hamstring you and severely limit your operating position."

Public relations is integral to Soul Branding. If a company does good works and doesn't tell anyone about them, the good works are still done (although it could be argued that more good works would be done by others with the proper example set). But that is not Branding; it is simply charity. If the goal is to do good works *and* position the company as one with the right ideas and the public's interest at heart, public relations is central to the concept. Soul Branding does not take place in the dark; it must be well publicized to do the most good for the brand and the causes that brand supports.

As Maio says, "Public relations gets redefined in the Soul Branding concept to its literal meaning. Public relations has been about directing messages out. Public relations in the Soul Branding concept will be a permeable gateway through which changing values and preferences come into the corporation, get processed, and flow out in responsive and anticipatory initiatives from the company. So public relations takes on a much broader strategic role in terms of its interface with the public."

Not every company has embraced the concept of Soul Branding yet. In fact, it's difficult to find a CEO who can give you a strong working definition of Soul Branding (the majority don't always have a working definition of Branding at all), but Maio's company has been working with a good number of Fortune 100 corporations on their social responsibility, and the definition of Soul Branding is starting to become more universally understood.

"Soul Branding is the process of aligning corporate behaviors with the higher social values," Maio says. "You will have noticed in running your business over the past 10 years or so an increasing requirement for something other than providing the best product at the best price. You will notice there is increasing attention being paid to who you are as an organization and how you behave as an organization in terms of where you sort your priorities. For example, if you are private labeling and engaging factories in the Third World to help you manufacture your private-label brands, you'll notice that you have come under scrutiny by organizations known as NGOs [nongovernmental organizations] that are keeping track to see if, for example, the standards that are applied in your home country to fair labor practices are being applied to the manufacture of your products outside of your country."

One of the key examples of the impact of Soul Branding came when the Kathie Lee line of clothing, sold through Kmart, was discovered to be constructed in offshore sweatshops. This became a public relations disaster not just for the clothing line, but also for the celebrity who had lent her name to it. Maio now calls this kind of horrible miscalculation the "Kathie Lee Syndrome."

But is Soul Branding a realistic concept? Does the average teenager scoping out a new pair of jeans at the mall care whether those pants were assembled by a badly mistreated worker in a country halfway across the globe, or does it matter more that Julia Roberts wore them in her last movie?

Both, Maio says. "The vast majority of consumers are looking for price value, and value in terms of teenagers is largely driven by cool. Cool is often defined by celebrity association, celebrity brands. Now, celebrities are not shy about talking about what social causes they espouse, and environmental issues in particular. So there's an influence there, even on that end of it." Meaning that if Julia Roberts exercises her social conscience by refusing to wear sweatshop-assembled jeans in a film, it is a reasonable assumption that a percentage of her many fans will follow suit, even if they don't know why they're buying one brand of pants over another.

The current problem with Soul Branding is that those companies that have been vociferous about their social consciences have not been such enormous success stories that all other companies are inspired to follow their lead. Yes, says Maio, Ben & Jerry's and The Body Shop have both been shining examples in their social practices, but both companies have had trouble showing the kind of profit margins that spur wild enthusiasm on Wall Street.

Maio explains: "Ben & Jerry's, like some others, have addressed pieces of this puzzle. The reason we call it Soul Branding is because it's a process. To be a successful business in our world today has required a certain arm's length with these issues. How can you satisfy Wall Street and its requirements for short-term profit and also have the long-term strategy to be compassionate and cooperative, to have a sense of equity and fairness in your practices? Those issues have largely been incompatible. They've been pioneers, but they have not been wholly successful in a traditional business sense, and therefore they're not proving the case. They've led on the compassion side and the social responsibility side."

Still, Maio believes the possibility for enormous profits coupled with socially responsible practices exists, and is only a matter of time. And not much time at that. "I'm an optimist as it relates to America and corporate America for the next 10 years," she says. "I think [Soul Branding] is absolutely essential. Take a look at one of the primary stakeholder groups—employees. We've evolved into a knowledge-based economy. The knowledge worker is a worker who is highly educated, highly motivated, and increasingly demanding quality of life. If an organization cannot relate to that, in a manner that is responsive and receptive, that organization is not going to attract and retain that talent. That's not good business."

Not everyone agrees that Soul Branding will eventually be the rule. Even the success that Ben & Jerry's has enjoyed (while not overwhelming, it is still a very successful company) is not necessarily tied to its corporate policies of environmentalism and activism, according to Cable Neuhaus. "I don't think the success has been based very much on the fact that they're a do-gooder company," he says. "Not everyone agrees with their fairly liberal social policies."

Soul Branding does, however, represent a terrific type of brand maintenance, as it offers wide opportunities for public relations exposure when a company helps save a portion of the rain forest or expresses its opposition to bovine growth hormone use in dairy products. Shallow gestures meant only to generate publicity, however, will be discovered by the media and used against companies if they are not sincere, Maio contends.

"Gestures are valuable in the Soul Branding concept only when they reference a much larger commitment," she says. "Authenticity is so crucial going forward that things like cause-related marketing—Revlon sponsoring Breast Cancer Awareness Week and Philip Morris pumping out lots of advertising related to its contributions to protecting battered women—are very dangerous tactics. They don't connect directly to the core values of the company. You must be able to show your constituents how your behaviors relate to your heart and soul. If it is a part of the heart and soul of your company to be compassionate, it's conceivable that you would reach out to underprivileged or disadvantaged individuals. But if it is perceived as the heart and soul of your company—as with Philip Morris—to obfuscate the truth at the expense of people's health, then gestures like that can only hurt you."

For example, when Anheuser-Busch provided canned drinking water to flood victims in Kentucky in 2002, it made sure people knew about the deed. That didn't diminish the beer manufacturer's good deed, and did provide a serious public relations boost at the same time.

Brand maintenance is the ongoing process of reinforcing the promises the brand made at its onset. If those promises are contrary to a gesture being made later in the Branding cycle, they are not going to be helpful. Insincerity in public relations, or outright lying at any part of the process, is always a mistake and will always be discovered, exposed, and turned against the brand.

But maintenance alone does not encompass what must be done after a brand launches. Possibly more important is the concept of brand expansion, which is a more delicate and somewhat riskier proposition. Expansion will take the concepts of brand introduction and maintenance and increase the intensity while combining aspects of both. Massive prior planning and meticulous forethought are required before it should even be attempted.

CHAPTER EIGHT

BRAND EXPANSION

"There is an analogy that Hef uses all the time. He talks about 'Schlitzing up the brand.' The story is this: Schlitz beer was the beer in this country before Bud, making a ton of money. Somebody at Schlitz decided that they could actually make a little more money, and what they did was tinker with the product. The beer drinkers recognized it, and from that day on that company went right downhill."

—DICK ROSENZWEIG, EXECUTIVE VICE PRESIDENT OF PLAYBOY, INC.

In May 2002, the Coca-Cola Company introduced a new product to its world-famous brand. This drink, Vanilla Coke, did not cause the same public relations nightmare that the New Coke introduction did in 1985, because Coca-Cola had learned its lesson during that fiasco.

This time, Coke was expanding its brand, not replacing something the public saw as sacred. Vanilla Coke did not displace any other Coke brand. As of this writing, it seems to be a success, but it is too early to say. Vanilla Coke will succeed or fail one based on its own merits. In other words, the product's taste will determine its success or failure. The Coke name on the can won't guarantee success, as New Coke illustrated.

That does not mean Vanilla Coke is going into the marketplace without any Branding plan, or without public relations campaigns well in place before the introduction. On the contrary, the day the product was introduced, it appeared on *Today, Good Morning America,* and *The Daily Show with Jon Stewart,* among others. Clearly, a great deal of work had been done.

Brand expansion is the step a successful brand can take after it has been well established in the consumer's mind and its identity is never in question. Given the speed with which messages are sent and absorbed in today's society, this doesn't have to take an extremely long time, as can be witnessed through the expansion of a brand like Amazon.com. Initially an online bookstore, Amazon.com has successfully expanded into music, movies, clothing, electronics, toys, and many other product lines without diluting its brand or ever jeopardizing its brand integrity. Indeed, Amazon .com is one of the most trusted brands in the country overall, and clearly the most trusted online retailer in the world.

There is a good deal of danger involved in brand expansion. In *The 22 Immutable Laws of Branding,* Al and Laura Ries cite a number of examples of brands that expanded their product lines to the point that their identities were no longer definable, causing the companies to lose market share. The Rieses' conclusion: "The power of a brand is inversely proportional to its scope."

If Just the Best ice cream is to expand as a brand, it must also be extended as a brand. The public must be made to understand that the original three flavors of Just the Best are meant to be a starting point, a source of pride and accomplishment, but not the complete brand. There will be more at some point, and public relations will have to pave the way. If not, the consequences may be dire.

Perhaps the best example in recent years is the decline and fall of Kmart. The general merchandise chain, which had commanded a huge market share and brought in billions yearly in sales, filed for bankruptcy protection in 2001 and is currently reorganizing in a desperate attempt to stay in business. Kmart's problem? It tried to be all things to all people—it expanded its brand too much—and ended up being nothing the consumer could recognize.

Of course, stiff competition from such chains as Wal-Mart and Target contributed to the Kmart woes, but both those chains managed to stay afloat quite nicely at the same time Kmart was foundering, chiefly because they stayed true to their initial promises to the consumer. Kmart, as the competition grew, attempted to broaden its consumer base by offering higher-end merchandise, adding celebrity endorsements, and not sticking to its promises—to have the lowest prices. Wider selections of merchandise appear to be a desirable quality in a mass merchant, but adding high-end clothing lines that the average Kmart shopper will probably not consider won't bring new customers into the store in numbers large enough to make a difference. People who really do shop at Tiffany's don't need to worry about the price, and they won't care if Kmart offers the same merchandise for a little less. The brand identity of Kmart is completely devoid of snob appeal; the shoppers the chain was trying to attract with its brand expansion had no intention of ever setting foot in one of the mass merchant's stores.

On the other hand, Target, which entered the market with a promise to offer the same types of merchandise as its competitors, but to offer faster service, has not strayed from that pledge—and its business has grown as Kmart's declined. The moral of the story could not be more clear.

If there is one grand commandment in the Branding process, it is this: Never, ever lose sight of your brand identity. And your brand identity is merely the promises you make to the consumer.

"Target has done an exceptional job, because their promise from their chairman on down is that they're going to be fast," says Duane Knapp, author of *The Brand Mindset*. "They are possessed and obsessed with fast. When you fill out their customer survey, which they do in every store twice a year, four of the eight questions are about time. That's a small piece, but they are possessed, and they are very distinctive, because they're not the same as Kmart, not the same as Wal-Mart, but they are a discount department store."

Notice the words *obsessed* and *possessed*. Without a tunnel-visioned, completely dedicated devotion to the brand promise, no brand will ever manage to transcend its product identity and become a brand.

A product identity is just that: The consumer relates to the product and not the brand. Nobody today goes to a particular movie just because it is being released by Warner Bros. (although in the 1940s, each studio had a brand identity). Studios today are distribution arms of large corporations, and each film lives or dies based on its own merits. *Star Wars* would have been a huge hit if it were released by Paramount, Disney, or Warner; as it happened, it was released by Fox. And not one ticket buyer went to see it saying, "I can't wait! It's a film from Fox! What's it about, again?"

The difference between product identity and brand identity can be seen in any number of consumer areas. When given a selection, moviegoers may see a film at a favorite theater, but in most cases, market research shows the consumer will go to the theater closest to home; convenience is more important than real butter on the popcorn. The movie theater industry has multiplexed itself into a cookie-cutter mentality, and consumers rarely know the name of the theater at which they saw a particular film. The product being sold is the film itself, and location rather than brand identity will draw more patrons to one outlet and not another. Theaters have no brand identity, or at least none strong enough to influence a consumer's purchasing decision, and that is all that matters in the Branding world.

By the same token, Coca-Cola could have had merely a product identity when it started, and in all likelihood the company would have been acquired by a larger corporation or gone out of business by now. If the drink alone were what people were buying, research would indicate that Pepsi would have taken over the market. But as the New Coke period illustrated, consumers are not simply buying a cold drink when they reach for a Coke; they're buying an identity, a personality, something that makes them feel something or remember an experience they've had that they want to revisit. It reaffirms a piece of the consumer's view of him- or herself, and that can't be accomplished merely with a product; a brand identity is required for such rabid, unadulterated loyalty.

EXPAND AT YOUR OWN RISK

With all that said, should a brand never expand? Should every company take the Rieses' law about expansion literally and never try to move in a slightly different direction? Of course not. There never would have been Diet Coke if Coca-Cola hadn't been willing to expand, and that product now rivals the original in terms of overall sales and market share.

Without brand expansion, Frito-Lay would never have added Doritos, Chevrolet wouldn't have designed the Corvette, *Time* would never have spun off *People* from its pages, and the Walt Disney Company would still be making seven-minute short cartoons in black and white. Expansion is necessary to brand survival in some cases, but it must never be taken lightly and should not be entered into rashly.

Businesses that refuse to pay careful attention to the power of Branding will quickly attenuate the long-term value of their enterprises. On the other hand, expansion is not a total panacea solving every business problem ever created. A proper brand expansion—which should not be confused with a brand extension—is the addition of a product that takes the brand into a new category while preserving the brand integrity. For example, once Doritos was established as a brand, Cool Ranch Doritos was a brand extension, a variation on the same product that would hopefully attract more consumers while not diminishing sales of the initial product. But Wow! the low-fat version of Doritos, was a brand expansion, bringing the brand into an area (low-fat snacks) it had never been before, and beginning a broadening of the brand that would continue with other low-fat, health-conscious products.

Another danger in extension and expansion comes with the spending of funds on advertising and public relations. While a brand expansion must be introduced to the consuming public—and given the fact that such a campaign will not be inexpensive—draining funds from the core brand to service the extension or expansion of the brand can do damage on both ends, and the company might end up with a failed expansion and a diminished core brand.

John O'Brien, former vice president of marketing for the Sherwin-Williams paint company, has been involved in many brand extensions and knows both expansion and Branding very well. He recalls the time a very successful brand attempted to extend itself into new territory, and in the process managed to overlook the product that had gotten the brand on the map to begin with.

"A tremendous brand, STP automotive products, known for oil additives and gas additives, had a tremendous following equity image for racing performance," O'Brien recalls. "It introduced a line extension to its core oil treatment, which was the cornerstone product. (The new product) was a high-end engine treatment, which was the same thing with a different name. (The company) put a tremendous amount of resources against this new item. A sufficient amount of homework wasn't done behind it. All the resources were put against this high-end item, and it failed for a number of reasons. If we spent $10 on this new product, the damage done was not just the $10 that was spent, but the $10 that wasn't spent against the core, and we lost time. The lesson learned could be summed up as: With a failed line extension of the core brand, you're not out the money you spend on it; you're out the intangibles of supporting what you currently had."

Protection of the core brand, or the product that holds the brand together, is paramount. When Coca-Cola decided to expand its brand with New Coke, it made the deadly error of not protecting its core product, and enormous damage was done. But when General Motors created the Saturn division, it was decided to keep the new brand absolutely separate from the core products: Chevrolet, Pontiac, Buick, Oldsmobile, and Cadillac. By isolating Saturn, GM managed not only to create the impression of an independent car manufacturer that would be slavishly devoted to its customers (in fact, many people to this day don't realize that Saturn is a General Motors car) and also to insulate the five core brands from any fallout should Saturn have been a dismal failure (which it certainly was not).

Budgeting must be done with this in mind; a brand extension can't be funded at the expense of the brand's core product, or both will suffer. Therefore, public relations, because it is less expensive in both the short and long term than advertising, can be extremely useful in the introduction of a new brand extension or expansion.

In fact, public relations plays a central role in brand extension and expansion. While an extension can rely chiefly on advertising to communicate to the consumer, it is a mistake to exclude public relations entirely. A brand expansion should be introduced and explained to the consumer mostly through public relations and not advertising, just as a brand introduction is handled more with publicity tactics than with splashy ad campaigns.

BRAND EXTENSION

Brand extension is a simple concept: It takes an established brand and adds a product (or products) to that brand. It does not move the brand into another marketing direction overall, and it does not jeopardize in any way the integrity, identity, or promise of the established brand.

In his book *Brand Asset Management,* Scott M. Davis of PROPHET equates brand extension with "brand-based innovations," breaking new ground with new products that tie in with the original brand. Brand extension is an addition to the brand, not a broadening of the brand. It might move into heretofore unexplored areas for the brand, but it will not change the brand's positioning in any way.

If Just the Best adds strawberry ice cream to its line after introducing the brand with chocolate, vanilla, and chocolate chip, that will be a brand extension. It gives the consumer another choice within the parameters of the existing brand while maintaining everything about the brand identity that has been established, other than the stated obsession with three flavors to keep the product of high quality and purity.

From a public relations standpoint, this situation needs to be handled delicately, but it is not terribly difficult. Introducing a new flavor to an existing roster does not violate the promise the brand made initially that it would be devoted to the highest quality and provide pure flavors without any of the "frills" added by other brands, which tend to confuse consumers.

Assuming that we decide we will add the strawberry flavor as a brand extension, public relations will begin by sending out press releases to all industry media outlets (trade magazines and newsletters, for example) slightly in advance of the press kits we will be making available to the consumer press (newspapers, magazines, television, and radio news outlets). While the press release will not directly address the seeming contradiction in adding a new flavor, it will make sure the message gets through loud and clear:

FOR IMMEDIATE RELEASE
For further information, contact:
Michael Levine, 310-555-5555

LOS ANGELES, CA—Just the Best, the ice cream brand that has become one of America's favorite brands in only a few months, today announced the first addition to its product line, Just the Best Strawberry ice cream.

Using only fresh strawberries and the best-quality cream and natural flavors, Just the Best Strawberry delivers pure ice cream parlor taste in a supermarket product. It represents the first time Just the Best has added a flavor to its product line, joining Just the Best

Chocolate, Just the Best Vanilla, and Just the Best Chocolate Chip in grocers' freezers.

"We didn't want to add something to the line until we were sure it was the best it could possibly be," said National Brand Manager Thomas Warden. "Strawberry has long been one of America's favorite ice cream flavors, but we wouldn't market a flavor until such time as we knew it would be Just the Best Strawberry."

Distribution of Just the Best Strawberry will begin in two weeks, with quart-sized containers available in supermarkets nationwide. To help consumers sample the product for the first time, Sunday newspaper supplements will include $1-off coupons that can be redeemed only on Just the Best Strawberry.

For fans of Just the Best Chocolate, Just the Best Vanilla, and Just the Best Chocolate Chip, 50¢ coupons will be available for any Just the Best flavor other than Just the Best Strawberry.

Just the Best is a nationwide manufacturer of super-premium ice cream that delivers just the best ice cream available in (now) four flavors. Its extremely successful introduction was made with the help of an "Election Day" promotion last October.

This press release makes the point that Just the Best has added a new flavor, describes the new product as of the highest quality, and explains how it will be introduced with consumer incentives. It also includes information about the company itself and mentions each product in the existing product line by name twice.

It does not say, "Despite its previous declarations that it would concentrate only on three flavors, Just the Best today went back on its word and introduced Strawberry." Clearly, this would be a public relations faux pas of unprecedented stupidity, but what the press release does say is all true. In fact, it goes out of its way to explain that the new product would not have been added to the line if it were not of the highest possible quality and therefore worthy to join the three flavors the country has taken to its heart already.

This smoothes the way for the brand extension, introduces it to the public (through the press) and provides an incentive to sample the new product—Sunday supplement coupons. The campaign also provides coupons for the existing flavors (albeit smaller-value coupons) to reinforce the brand while the new product is extending it—and keeping the protection of the core products as our top priority.

BRAND EXPANSION

Expansion is a completely different concept than extension. With this idea, the core existing brand is moving into new territory it has not ventured into before with something other than a variation on its original core product. If Sony adds a new TV to its product line, that is an extension. If Sony adds refrigerators to its product line, that is a brand expansion.

In many ways, expansion is a more complicated public relations problem than extension. It resembles an introduction in that it brings the brand into an area that is new and untested. But an expansion is much more dangerous from a public relations point of view, because now the brand has a strong reputation to lose, whereas an introduction does not stand or fall in the public's estimation; it's still building the core product and the brand identity that will be in jeopardy when an expansion is made.

In order to protect all the good work that has been done in building the brand and the identity that has built the brand to the point that an expansion is possible, very careful planning must be done by public relations professionals before the expansion is ever mentioned in public. First it must be determined how the expansion continues concepts in the original brand identity and in what ways the expansion will differ from the established brand. Any potential contradictions in the identity must be dealt with before the trade or consumer press—and especially before any consumer—hears about the coming brand extension.

If, for example, Just the Best were to enter into ice cream novelties (ice cream sandwiches, pops, and other preportioned specialty items) the questions would have to be asked: How is this a continuation of the brand identity, and how will this expansion be different than the line already on the market?

Clearly, the similarities are that the product is an ice cream treat and that it will be produced with the same attention to high quality as the core product. In terms of brand identity, the novelties will exude the same type

119

of nostalgic, friendly, slightly off-center qualities exhibited by the three original Just the Best flavors. The product choices will be limited to those that are best remembered from childhood: an ice cream sandwich and a prepackaged ice cream cone, perhaps. Not something that shouts of its New Millennium introduction, like pops in the shape of a computer mouse or Spongebob Squarepants.

The differences will be more problematic, of course. Again, we have the appearance of contradicting the initial promises made by the brand. The purity of the original core product was supposed to lie in its simplicity; making fancier ice cream products will once again seem to be a reneging of that initial promise, and possibly a source of damage to the brand identity.

In sidestepping these contradictions, we must reassure consumers who have taken the brand identity to their hearts that nothing is changing about the core products, and that this does not mark a change in the direction of the brand as a whole. By the same token, since the intention of a brand expansion is to create new excitement about the brand overall, it will be necessary for consumers to feel that these new products will be a continuation of the original brand, a "more of the same, but better" approach that fans of the core products will be asked to embrace wholeheartedly.

Naturally, the new products will carry the Just the Best logo and slogan on their packaging. In order to make sure that this is a Diet Coke and not a New Coke scenario, the initial public relations campaign should strive to reaffirm the core brand and make sure the public knows it will remain available, while introducing the brand expansion.

At the same time, effort should be made to create excitement around the expansion products and not to "sneak them out" in an effort to protect what already exists on the market. There is such a thing as being too cautious, and the intelligent brander never enters into that realm. Branding depends on the inclusion of drama, a somewhat histrionic exchange between buyer and seller.

How does an expansion product create drama? It may not be overtly stated, but most brands are trying to bring about a feeling of ecstasy. And if such a feeling is not created by the product itself, the brand identity—

the personality assigned to the brand through meticulous planning and invention—should aim at that emotion. Drama is a natural by-product of enthusiasm and confidence. Ecstasy, or something approaching it, should be the result of drama.

It might appear to be an overstatement to suggest that an ice cream product can evoke ecstasy in the average adult consumer. What is important in the public relations realm is that the consumer be provided with the *impression* that he or she is ecstatic over the experience of eating this product. More than an illusion and in all likelihood less than the true realization of ecstasy, the impression being created is one of the ultimate possible expression of this experience—or, put more plainly, the best you can feel as a result of eating ice cream.

The press release that would be circulated to trade and consumer publications, and to broadcast and Web media, to introduce Just the Best ice cream novelties would once again emphasize the excitement of the new product while reinforcing the original core brand. It would, as with the brand extension press release, correct the mistaken impression that the brand is reneging on a core promise. But the difference between the two statements is that this is the introduction of a brand expansion, so it should emphasize the move into a whole new direction rather than an addition to the existing core brand.

FOR IMMEDIATE RELEASE
For further information, contact:
Michael Levine, 310-555-5555

LOS ANGELES, CA—Just the Best, the ice cream brand that has become one of America's favorite brands in only a few months, today announced a major brand expansion with the introduction of Just the Best ice cream novelties.

Three new products—Just the Best Ice Cream Sandwiches, Just the Best Ice Cream Cones, and Just the Best Ice Cream Pops—are being introduced by the brand as they are distributed nationwide. Packages of eight novelties each will be appearing in supermarkets two weeks from today.

A BRANDED WORLD

"This is something the company has been anticipating since it began," said National Brand Manager Thomas Warden. "Consumers have a very good feeling about an ice cream cone, an ice cream sandwich, or a vanilla pop covered in chocolate. We have always intended to provide them with Just the Best possible examples of those familiar treats, but we had to wait until we could provide novelties worthy of the Just the Best name."

In fact, before Just the Best introduced its novelty packs to stores, the company had been deluged with requests for such products from consumers. Warden and Just the Best President Martin Carter both said at a news conference today that the company had received over 16,000 letters in the past six months asking for novelties with Just the Best quality.

The three varieties, Just the Best Ice Cream Sandwiches, Just the Best Ice Cream Cones, and Just the Best Ice Cream Pops, were developed in direct response to those queries, after the company determined that these three novelties were those most desired by consumers. While selling ice cream cones in supermarket freezers has always been a problem because the cones, being frozen for so long, become either too hard or too soft, Just the Best has solved this problem by packaging the scoops of ice cream in a separate plastic container and the cones in the other half of the package, in a microwavable box with explicit instructions on how long and at what power level to prepare the cones. Carter emphasized that this brand expansion was meant to bring the quality of the popular Just the Best Ice Cream flavors (Just the Best Chocolate, Just the Best Vanilla, and Just the Best Chocolate Chip) to the novelty products consumers had requested.

"People have been so enthusiastic about our Just the Best flavors that we were reluctant at first to add more products," he admitted. "But with the overwhelming number of requests we received, and the unprecedented quality of the varieties we developed, it was clearly time for Just the Best novelties. They take the purity and quality of our core products and expand them into an exciting new direction."

To help consumers sample the product for the first time, Sunday newspaper supplements will include $1-off coupons that can be redeemed only on Just the Best novelties.

Brand Expansion

For fans of Just the Best Chocolate, Just the Best Vanilla, and Just the Best Chocolate Chip, 50¢ coupons will be available for any Just the Best quart.

Just the Best is a nationwide manufacturer of super-premium ice cream that delivers just the best ice cream available in three flavors (and now in three novelty packs). Its extremely successful introduction was made with the help of an "Election Day" promotion last October.

While this press release follows roughly the same format and has the same structure as the one announcing a brand extension, the emphasis here is on the way things are different, rather than assurances that things are the same. There are references to the core products, to remind consumers that they are still available, but the gist of the statement is about how consumers requested the new products and how the company is delivering what has been requested.

The first statement by a company official, that this product is something that was always in the company's plans, is meant to deflect any criticism of the expansion based on the idea that the original three products were introduced with purity and simplicity in mind, and that these new products somehow dilute or contradict that promise.

In addition, the core products are mentioned more than once, to emphasize their continued presence in the marketplace. And the information about sales promotions, coupons, and distribution is virtually identical. The identification of the company (the last paragraph in both releases) is boilerplate, included on all press materials, to provide the company's description of itself in the event a media outlet wants to identify Just the Best.

It is also significant that statements made by both company officials in the release repeatedly drive home the idea of reluctance to stray from the original formula, with immediate assurances that the demand for and quality of these products made the choice to expand the brand absolutely unavoidable. This is meant to assuage any unease on the part of consumers who feel their favorite product might be changing in some unfamiliar, undesirable way. If the company felt the way they do, and still went ahead with these new products, the brand expansion must be something of which the consumer will approve, too.

PLANNED CONTRACTION

Should a brand expansion fail, the company must be willing and prepared to reverse it after all efforts to revive the expansion prove unsuccessful. Even in the biggest Branding blunder in history, Coca-Cola managed to save face (and in some people's opinion, score a public relations coup) by reversing its direction and reintroducing its original formula as Classic Coke, then phasing out New Coke.

Expansion is not a step to be made rashly or prematurely. Expansions don't always catch on with the public immediately, nor should they be expected to. Consumers are loyal to favorite brands but wary of interlopers and changelings. They might take a while to sample something new from a familiar brand, and it can take much longer for the new product to assume the status of a trusted friend. Consumers have to be reassured that their loyalty is being reciprocated; they don't want to feel fickle, and a smart brander does not under any circumstances want to make loyal consumers feel that their brand is deserting them.

In fact, the only time a brand expansion should be scaled back or eliminated is when it has been given a strong introduction and time to grow, but still fails to show any sign of building a base with consumers. When months have gone by and sales, coupled with market research data, indicate that the expansion is not gaining strength and is unlikely to do so anytime soon, in some cases it might be best to put the expansion out of its misery before the core brand or the brand identity itself begins to suffer.

This becomes more difficult, of course, when the core product is not a commodity but a personality. In entertainment or politics, people have become brands unto themselves, and while brand expansion is possible, it is very difficult to scale back when you are the brand. There are specific benefits and deficits to branding a person, which are discussed in the next chapter.

CHAPTER NINE

THE CELEBRITY BRAND

"Just because people know your name doesn't make you a brand. You have to stand for something, preferably something positive. All these celebrity brands are built by PR. No one says, 'OK, we're going to launch our band by doing an advertising campaign.' Any noun that exists in the mind is a brand. Los Angeles is a brand. Chicago is a brand. United States is a brand. Madonna is a brand. People are brands."

—AL RIES, AUTHOR OF *THE FALL OF ADVERTISING AND THE RISE OF P.R.*

Think of the people you went to high school with: Each of them had one particular personality trait that you remember most vividly to this day. The girl all the boys wanted to date, the boy who was the A/V nerd, the math whiz, the football player, whatever. Each of those traits represents the brand that person wanted you to perceive (or in some cases, the brand with which the person was stuck by others), and that impression was made strongly enough that no matter how many years it has been since you graduated from high school, you can still remember that person in that way.

The exact same thing is true in my business. Helping an entertainment personality create and maintain an image is the precise definition of Branding in perhaps its purest form. We all know what a human being is like, because we're all human beings. Assigning specific traits to a person to create a brand identity that resonates with the public in unprecedented ways and helps to elevate that particular human being into someone who is admired (in some cases, revered) is what Branding is all about.

There is a difference, however: Whatever personality traits you might associate with a personal acquaintance are those you have observed first-hand. Even if the prom queen in your high school wanted you to think of her in a specific way, and went out of her way to project the qualities she felt were especially attractive or appropriate, they were qualities she possessed and that you observed independently; they weren't elaborately orchestrated or planned months in advance.

When I work with an entertainment figure like Fleetwood Mac or Janet Jackson, everything you see has been meticulously prepared, calculated to maximum effect, and, in some cases, scripted. Any personality trait you detect is the result of the public relations planning and execution that is designed specifically to lead you to that conclusion.

In some cases, an actor or actress can be so closely associated with a role they happen to play that it becomes their personality in the minds of the public. Harrison Ford may or may not have heroic qualities, but once he was cast as Indiana Jones, he was assigned those traits by the public. Years later, when he assisted in a rescue effort in the mountains near his home by flying his helicopter to spot lost or injured climbers, the headlines read, "Indiana Jones Performs a Real-Life Rescue." Now, that incident certainly wasn't planned or orchestrated by Ford's publicists, but his participation did receive considerable media attention, and his role as a heroic personality was cemented still further in the collective mind of the moviegoing public.

Branding a human being's personality is not the same as branding a consumer product. For one thing, the person will have some characteristics, emotions, and feelings before the Branding process begins, unlike a can of soda or a wireless telephone service. Also, even though there is a considerable amount of crafting done on a celebrity's brand before the public ever gets to see that person in an interview, a personal appearance, or a film or TV role, there is no way to totally control the brand. The human being will have a life outside the context of the brand. Ask Dick Morris, the political consultant who handled Bill Clinton.

Morris says: "Branding implies trust. The whole concept of Branding is that you associate a given quality with a given company. You expect a product to repeatedly behave in that way. But trust at all levels is breaking down. Increasingly, nobody trusts anybody about anything. As we go through Enrons and Lewinskys and things like that, we become less trusting generically. So the concept of trusting begins to break down."

That is the difficulty of personal Branding: A consumer product, an inanimate object, will behave the same way repeatedly unless something has gone very wrong. But a person—particularly one with money and power—will often behave in one way when the cameras are rolling and another when they are not. That leads to the breakdown of trust that Dick Morris refers to, and the erosion of the brand in general.

In my experience, it is more difficult to brand a person than a product. Products don't balk at being asked to behave in a certain manner; they don't get themselves into trouble with the media or commit a faux pas when being interviewed, the way people occasionally will. A bag of potato chips won't be forced into a stay at a rehab clinic, and a new television set will not make a statement that might be offensive to people of a particular ethnicity or religion.

Yet the power of a personal brand can't be denied. Al Ries says, "We have Tina Brown, the most famous magazine editor in the world, funded with $50 million to launch a new publication called *Talk,* and she's an expert. *Talk* folds, while Oprah's magazine *O* is doing fantastically well. Why is that? Because Oprah is a brand and Tina Brown is not."

Demi Moore was a moderately successful soap opera actress when we first met, and she did not have an overwhelming public persona that would immediately identify her. She was not yet a brand. It wasn't until she was ready to make the move onto a larger stage that Branding was possible, and the same is true for politicians. Nobody is a household brand when they're running for a seat on the Milltown, New Jersey, Board of Education.

"The process whereby you become branded is fascinating, and it's a process that every well-known person has been through," says Dick Morris. "It's the only thing they all have in common. Adolf Hitler went through it and Mother Teresa went through it. It's like watching a portrait become a caricature. Maybe Mike Tyson loves little children; maybe he adores puppies, but it's not part of his brand. You have to accept that at some point, large parts of you are left out, and large parts of you are overemphasized."

It may not be the same thing to brand a political candidate (who might become a world leader) and a pair of sneakers, but the process is similar; the steps are the same. The differences lie mostly in moral and technical questions: The president isn't a running shoe.

A BRANDED WORLD

When Branding begins for a political candidate, there are long- and short-term decisions to be made. First, in most cases, the short-term goal is to win the upcoming election for whichever office the candidate happens to be running. But the savvy brander is also thinking a few steps ahead, to the next (and usually higher) office to which the candidate might eventually aspire. Bill Clinton wasn't thinking only of Little Rock when he ran for governor of Arkansas; the White House was always the eventual goal.

One of the first steps in the short term is to consider and develop the candidate's brand identity—which candidate will he or she be for this election? Political consultant and taxpayer advocate Joel Fox says it's important to know the answer in the context of the current election, but also for future contests that might loom in the distance. "If you can touch the nerve of the voter with a short saying, you can get your message across and upturn the experts," he says.

A strong personality is always a plus for a public figure. Al Gore was seen in the 2000 election as the bland, boring candidate, and George W. Bush was branded by his handlers as the man of the people. Bush made up a good deal of ground in the polls during that campaign, chiefly on the strength of his brand being more palatable than Gore's was.

In Hollywood, where I work, personality is an even more central and important factor. In essence, it is the personality of the celebrity that is being branded, because a career in entertainment can be sparked, but not maintained, on the strength of one performance. If the public admires your work but doesn't particularly like you, it's possible you'll be able to have a very healthy career as a character actor; but to be a star, your personality—the brand that is projected from you into the minds of the public—must be accepted and seen as positive by the people who pay at the box office or watch on their screens at home.

Public relations and personal Branding are very closely related, particularly in the entertainment and political fields. Because the brand being created and maintained is a person, the public's perception of that person—the brand being the public persona—is essentially the entire product. The public can't literally take that person home to live with them (although there are those who would try), but they can take home the brand, meaning the performance or the aura that public person exudes. Without public relations—

without the careful crafting of the brand's promise and presentation—the person in question would not be defined for the public, and the public is not usually enamored of what it does not recognize or understand.

Once a reputation has been established, it is a very difficult thing to overcome. Even in positive cases, when the public has taken a celebrity to its bosom and embraced him, the imprint made by a single role or too strong a brand identity can haunt the actor forever.

Manager/Producer Larry Thompson has handled many such cases, but perhaps his best-known client, William Shatner, was the template for celebrities trapped in a role. After three seasons on a failing science fiction TV series, Shatner was so identified with Captain James T. Kirk of *Star Trek* that by the midseventies he was having trouble finding work in other projects. In the collective mind of the public, Shatner was Kirk, and he could rarely manage to be anything else.

Thompson devised a plan by which Shatner could manage to tweak his image a bit without insulting the role or the public which had embraced it so dearly. He arranged for Shatner to host *Saturday Night Live,* on a memorable night in which the good captain was seen in a sketch that took place at a *Star Trek* convention, imploring his fans to "get a life!" and then being forced to apologize for his behavior.

"We first realized that he was a brand," Thompson explains. "A lot of people become brands and don't know it, so they don't treat it with the kind of reverence that they should, perhaps. He was on a particular series that established him as a brand. Over the years, sometimes he was so established as a brand that no serious director would want to put him in any serious piece of work because his brand would get in the way of their brand. He had to play against the brand. We were able to respect it, but have fun with it. Part of Shatner's success was that he could have fun with himself as the brand. He could make fun of the brand. There are some people who become icons for various reasons but take themselves so seriously that they can stay successful as long as they are viable as that brand alone. What we've been able to do is transcend the brand, or expand the brand by always paying tribute to it but having fun with it."

I had to help recreate a brand when the legendary producer Robert Evans, who had run Paramount Pictures, overseen *The Godfather,* and produced such films as *Chinatown, Marathon Man,* and *Black Sunday,* was trying to resurrect his career in 2002. Evans' autobiography, *The Kid Stays in the Picture,* had been turned into a documentary feature, and it was time to remind the public—through the media—that he is a vital, current participant, not a spectator, in Hollywood.

Evans, who admits that some people in Hollywood thought he was dead, narrates the film *The Kid Stays in the Picture,* and we made him available for interviews. He appeared in the *New York Times* and *Time* and on many television talk shows in connection with the movie, which got extremely good reviews. He arrived at the premiere in style, showed off his irrepressible personality and ability to tell it like it is, and, through the power of Branding and public relations, made himself relevant in the movie business again. Evans is producing a film as of this writing.

BRAND CONFUSION

One of the pitfalls of branding a personality is that one characteristic can be seen as the definition of the performer's (or politician's) character. Particularly in politics, advocating one specific position on a law can paint the candidate's views on other issues. While most office-seekers and office-holders tend to vote consistently in a conservative or liberal manner, they do not all do so exclusively; some centrists tend to "switch sides" on issues, while other candidates deal with issues one at a time, rather than as a block. If the candidate is branded based on one issue, it's possible the voter will be missing the big picture, and that can work against the candidate. Public relations people and political consultants have to work very hard to brand the candidate correctly.

Joel Fox says Branding "is a process to find a short handle for what the candidate means to voters, as quickly as possible, as succinctly as possible. In my business, if you want people to know that someone tends to be on the conservative side, you might want to get that identification as a tax cutter. People will naturally think that if they're advocating lower taxes, they're probably also for a traditional conservative agenda. Now, that's not necessarily true. But it occurs."

He notes that in a primary debate for the governorship of California,

The Celebrity Brand

Richard Riordan (who did not win the primary election) took a stance on the explosive issue of abortion while trying to illustrate a difference between himself and his opponents. "Riordan is pro-choice, the other two [Bill Simon and Bill Jones] are pro-life," Fox recalls. "Riordan indicated in one section of the debate that if you're pro-choice, that indicates to women that you're also pro-afterschool programs, pro-education. He felt that one brand connoted a lot of other positions beyond abortion. The other candidates took offense to that. They said, 'We are not anti-children; don't try to put us in that place.' This has become shorthand to a lot of female voters in the state of California."

In this case, the attempt by one candidate to brand his opponents on the basis of one issue did not prove successful; Bill Simon won the Republican nomination for governor. But the idea that female voters might associate an anti-abortion platform with positions on seemingly related issues that would make the candidates unattractive even to voters who agreed with them on abortion is intriguing. It presumes that the voter will not further research the candidate's position, and take the word of his opponent; but tactics like attack ads make that assumption on a regular basis, and, while they might not be the most morally upright campaign tactics, they certainly have been known to be effective.

The problem is one of brand confusion. Here, competition attempts to take the image, the identity of an established brand, and cloud it enough that it becomes a distorted version of itself that might not be true and that is definitely less attractive than the original branders intended it to be.

Brand confusion is common in advertising and public relations campaigns. It strives to make the competing brand (or, in politics, the competing candidate) seem more attractive by denigrating the established brand. Virtually every political campaign run against an incumbent candidate attempts some brand confusion. In some cases it can be extremely successful; in others it will explode in the face of the competing brand, exposing its weaknesses instead of emphasizing its strengths.

For example, when Bob Dole was running for president against Bill Clinton in 1996, he attempted to emphasize Clinton's well-publicized personal failings and vowed to "bring integrity back to the White House." The references did not help Dole overcome the extraordinary popularity of the incumbent President, and he did not come close to winning the election. His attempt to elevate his own brand at the expense of his competition had not succeeded, because the public was too enamored of the other brand. Trying to taint that brand, rather than to promote his own, doomed Dole's chances.

In that case, brand confusion did not succeed, and it failed based on the impenetrability of the established brand. If Snapple tries to outsell Coca-Cola based on a campaign that says, "Snapple is made from pure ingredients and is better for you," it might not succeed, but it would at least be operating from a position of strength against a wildly successful brand. If, however, Snapple decides to attack Coca-Cola on its own terms, saying, "Coca-Cola tastes bad; drink Snapple," it will almost certainly fail. The public's attachment to Coke is far too well documented, and far too strong, to support a brand confusion on that scale.

PERSONAL BRANDING IN THE CORPORATE WORLD

In many ways, any entrepreneur who starts a new business is branding him- or herself. The founder often becomes the chief spokesperson for the company, and the personality traits he or she exhibits will become associated with that company. Think of Colonel Harland Sanders and his Kentucky Fried Chicken. Sanders (the title *Colonel* was honorary) was such a high-profile owner that he and the product became one in the mind of the public. Today, decades after Sanders's death, his face is still on every KFC box or bag, and his image, now in animated form, is still used in the company's advertising. The same could be said of Dave Thomas, the founder of Wendy's. Even after Thomas's death, his image was so strong with the public that new advertising campaigns had to be devised, reassuring consumers that Wendy's was still making its food "Dave's way."

Particularly at the outset of a business, the founder will be an important asset or a devastating detriment to the product and the brand. Creating a brand identity for the person who starts the business is similar to branding a public personality or a political figure. Of course, the personality should be compatible with the brand identity being developed, which will probably not be a problem given that the founder of the company should have dictated the original brand identity to begin with.

Colonel Sanders's brand identity meshed with that of his product, which was supposed to hearken back to days of Southern hospitality and gentility. The fact that he was called "Colonel" (and in many cases, no other name was used) added to the mystique, and the slow-speaking, avuncular persona Sanders affected—which by some accounts was not all that similar to his personality in private—was precisely what was needed to take a local business and expand it beyond the state.

Not every company needs a colorful founder, of course. Such huge brands as Coca-Cola, AT&T, and Burger King have managed quite nicely without a founding CEO whom the public can embrace. Those brands are more product- or service-oriented. Others, however, from Microsoft to Nike, have prospered on the strength of their founders' personalities, and none has done so as well as the Walt Disney Company, which began as the vision of one man and has grown to an omnipresent force of truly global proportions. It is estimated that the Mickey Mouse ears logo is more recognized than any symbol on the planet, with the possible exception of the distinct shape of the Coca-Cola bottle.

All this sprang from the image—the brand identity—of the company's founder, who was among the first to recognize the enormous power of Branding. Walt Disney was always cognizant of the way he and his company were viewed by the public, and he controlled every aspect of his business, from the design of the animated characters to the grooming habits of the employees at his theme parks (male employees could not have facial hair, despite Walt's own mustache). Everything had to be family-oriented and keep the Disney image intact, or it would not bear the Disney name. While there has been some variation on the formula since Disney's death, his vision and his principles remain the cornerstones of the company to this day, and his nephew—who bears a striking resemblance to Walt himself—is on hand to make sure that the things upon which "Uncle Walt" would insist are never questioned.

All of this is well reported in the press, and the public is constantly being kept aware of the lengths to which Disney will go to maintain its integrity. As I mentioned earlier, when rumors that some Disney animated films contained three frames—the equivalent of ⅛ of a second on the screen—of obscene images, Disney immediately released information about the incidents, pointed out where mistakes had been made, and then cut the offending frames (which did not contain obscene images) out anyway. The branding of Walt became the branding of the Disney Company, and it has been as dramatic and overwhelming a success story as the country has ever seen.

ARE YOU A BRAND?

In their book *Be Your Own Brand: A Breakthrough Formula for Standing Out from the Crowd,* David McNally and Karl D. Speak put forth the theory that even in our own interpersonal relationships, we are branding ourselves. "A brand is a relationship," they write. "It is not a statement. It is not a matter of contrived image, or colorful packaging, or snappy slogans, or adding an artificial veneer to disguise the true nature of what's within. In fact, a 'branded' relationship is a special type of relationship—one that involves the kind of trust that only happens when two people believe there is a direct connection between their value systems."

Perhaps a brand is a relationship, as they say, but it is also a statement. What you choose to project is what the rest of the world will see of you. Perhaps the image you give off is not contrived, but it certainly is considered, and while I do agree with McNally and Speak that adding an "artificial veneer" or anything artificial to your image will cheapen and weaken it, it's also important to note that the image you project can be developed and honed to be the exact version of yourself you want the rest of the world to see.

You are a brand. So am I. We can't avoid being brands; it's part of living in society among other human beings. There's nothing wrong with being a brand, since society will observe and judge the qualities we project whether they're intentional or not. It's better to have considered them ahead of time and have made sure they are true and what we intend to communicate to the world. That's not artificial, and it's not a lie; it's simply a question of quality control. Each one of us, in branding our image, makes a promise to the people we meet that is the same as the promise a product makes to its consumers: This is what I'm going to be, and I will always be this, under all sets of circumstances. So it is better to make that promise based on what we really are, rather than what we would like to be, because a lie is much too difficult to maintain, especially under stress.

Naturally, it is possible to expand and extend your own brand, just as it is for a corporate brand. Your promise can be always to be the funny guy in the group, but that's not appropriate at a funeral, for example. So you show another side of yourself under that set of circumstances, and you have expanded your personal brand: You're the funny guy, but you also have deep feelings. Perhaps you want to use your quick wit to move a relationship from a friendly context to a romantic one. Saying the right things at the right times can become a brand extension: You're funny, but in a romantic way.

Personal Branding becomes a question of degree. If you begin with personal qualities that truly are your own, and you express those to the world in general, they become your brand. But when that brand represents only part of what you truly are, you run the risk of becoming a caricature of yourself—a brand with no person inside. It's a difficult line to walk, but with careful consideration, and remaining cognizant of the danger, it is possible to brand yourself properly, to your greatest advantage personally and professionally, and without becoming a lie.

CHAPTER TEN

STUDYING THE BRAND LEADERS

One magnificent way to find the correct path is to follow someone who has traveled that route year after year and knows every pebble in the road by its first name. That's why anyone who attempts to scale Mount Everest wouldn't consider taking a step up the first rolling hill without the aid of a Sherpa guide. These people, who live in the Everest area of Tibet and act as priests of the mountain, are familiar with every possible danger in the extremely hazardous enterprise. If you're going to climb a mountain "because it is there," enlist the help of the people for whom it is "here."

The argument could be made, however, that it is just as advantageous to note the errors made by those who tried to scale Everest and lost their lives. Knowing what the mistakes are and how to avoid them is at least as valuable as knowing where the shortcuts are and how to increase your odds of achieving your goal.

So it is with Branding. Studying examples of those who have done it exceptionally well, or those who have made colossal miscalculations, can help mark out a territory and identify a path. By the same token, knowing which path *not* to take can be equally, if not more, valuable. "You can observe a lot just by watching," said Yogi Berra, and he was right.

There have also been examples of brands that started out as huge successes and then made a fatal misstep somewhere along the way. Some made missteps that could have been fatal, but found a way to right the ship—often through creative public relations—before it went down for the third time.

CASE STUDY #1: NIKE

There are few Branding tales as epic and impressive as that of Nike. Before Phil Knight made the swoosh a universally known symbol, a soft shoe you wore to play sports or run in was called a sneaker. There weren't separate sneakers for basketball, running, walking, cross-training and tennis; there were just sneakers. They were made by companies like Keds and PF Fliers, and they were usually worn by children. Professional athletes wore shoes made for their individual sports, which were either not available to the general public or were not identifiable by brand. A few companies, like Adidas, were making "tennis shoes," which adults wore when they played a sport on the weekends.

Now, there are "athletic shoes." They are very specific to their tasks, and can be found in stores like Foot Locker and Sports Authority, classified by usage: Cross-trainers are not the same as shoes for walking, which are different from running shoes, which are not to be confused with basketball shoes. And much of that distinction can be attributed to Nike and the awe-inspiring job it has done in defining not only its own brand, but the very category of product the brand helped to create.

"The way you build a brand is by creating a new category you can be first in," says Branding guru Al Ries. "I have yet to hear anybody ever refer to Nike as a sneaker. It's only the older people who used to buy Keds who refer to Nike as a sneaker. There is an enormous difference between an athletic shoe and a sneaker. You can look at the two and say, they look alike, they smell alike, they sound alike. I say no: Your typical inner-city kid isn't going to wear Keds and call it a sneaker. They want a Nike; it's a different deal."

How did Nike transform the category of sports footwear into the massive $14 billion business it is today? And how did it manage to grab an astounding 45 percent of the market by the year 2000? Was it just such an obviously superior product that the public couldn't help but notice and respond? Or was the Branding of Nike so well-considered and crafty that it outshone all the rest of the brands in its category, using every possible Branding tactic almost perfectly?

I am inclined to state that the latter was the prevailing condition. Nike took what was, for its category, a revolutionary product (the waffle sole) and transformed what could have been a niche product into something that every kid in the street playing basketball had to have. Beyond that, however, Nike expanded its brand into other market segments, appealing to adults, to women, to non-athletes. And it extended its brand into products other than shoes: apparel, signature hats, shirts, and shorts, and many other products that bore the suddenly familiar Nike symbol.

"[Nike] figured out a very simple brand visually, and they didn't deviate from it at all. They kept that message very well defined," says Howard Rubenstein, president of Rubenstein Associates, a New York publicity firm. "If you just glance at [Nike's] logo, you know what the message is."

The swoosh, Nike's squiggly symbol, has no intrinsic meaning in our lexicon; before the company developed it, it did not exist as a symbol communicating anything. But once it was associated with the active, aggressive, powerful brand identity Nike had assigned itself, the swoosh became an incredibly articulate mark, communicating the continued thrust forward of anyone who had the wherewithal to don a piece of apparel that bore the symbol.

Still, the swoosh wasn't the only way that Nike differentiated itself from other athletic shoe companies, and it certainly wasn't the main tool in developing that brand's identity. More than anything else, the company was probably best known in its early years for its associations with well-known sports celebrities, who never, ever appeared in public without a swoosh on at least one visible article of clothing.

Tiger Woods, Derek Jeter, and especially Michael Jordan were routinely seen wearing the Nike logo, and, while they never necessarily said a word in a Nike advertisement, it was clear their endorsement was meant to relay a message to consumers: "Be like (fill in the extremely famous sports celebrity). Wear Nike." The copy might have read "Just Do It," but the message was loud and clear.

"Nike was successful in making that swish synonymous with performance," says *Variety* Publisher Charlie Koones. "Not just the performance of their shoe, but performance on a larger scale. By allying themselves with great athletes, by building a bit of a jock attitude. It's interesting to ask yourself what is the feeling that comes out of your brand promise."

Studying the Brand Leaders

The road for Nike has not been entirely bump-free, however. Allegations that the company's products were manufactured overseas in sweatshops have dogged the brand, and there have been declines in the athletic shoe market generally in the past few years. But Nike continues on, and even if its brand is a tiny bit diminished, it is still head and shoulders above the rest of the industry.

"At one time, I think Nike truly was a genuine brand," says Duane Knapp, author of *The Brand Mindset*. "In other words, they were perceived by the customer as one of a kind. Maybe in some customers' minds, that's true today. They're not perfect. At this point in time, you'd have to ask their customers what's the difference between Nike and Adidas. It really doesn't matter what the executives think; it matters what the customers think. When Phil Knight invented the waffle sole, they were a genuine brand. Now that they've gotten into different things, my feeling is they've probably moved from right to left on that continuum in the customer's mind. They are not a one-of-a-kind brand anymore. That doesn't mean they're a bad brand. But every brand is moving toward being a commodity unless the company does something continually, every single day, and that is where public relations comes in."

Nike's position in the athletic shoe and apparel industry is without peer, but it is true that the brand is not as strong as it once was, partially due to increased competition and partially because nothing could stay *that* hot. Allegations that the company used overseas sweatshops to assemble $120 athletic shoes didn't help.

Through it all, Nike's public relations professionals emphasized that the company was doing its best to improve conditions in its worldwide facilities, and, as it addressed the problem, continued to thrive. While the situation is not yet completely resolved, it has not crippled Nike by any stretch of the imagination.

Knapp brings up two important points: First, the company has to have a strong sense of its identity from the consumer's point of view. The image company executives have is irrelevant if the consumer sees the product and the brand in a different light. Second, the brand identity and brand integrity must be reinforced in the consumer's mind every day. Not once a week, not whenever there's a sales downturn: every day. If the mission of the company is not to satisfy the customer's expectations and exceed them every time, the brand might never become a true household name, and it certainly won't last for decades like Coca-Cola, Disney, and McDonald's—and even those brands have had major stumbling points.

CASE STUDY #2: MADONNA

For the past 20 years, which entertainer has been the most successful in establishing and maintaining a brand? Not Michael Jackson, not Steven Spielberg, not Paul McCartney and not J. Lo. It's been two decades, and the undisputed champion of Branding doesn't even need a last name to identify herself: It's just plain old Madonna.

Establishing herself as something different right from the start, Madonna has bucked every trend and every rule of Branding and still managed to become the most well-known, well-considered brand in the entertainment business since Eminem was in grade school.

One of the first rules in Branding is consistency: The product should be the same and offer the same experience every time it is exposed to the public. Madonna has made a career of never doing the same thing twice, starting as a downtown New York performer with an edge and moving through phases of film actress, material girl, cowgirl, stage actress, and boy toy, among a host of others.

Branding also assumes an identity that invites the target demographic to feel familiar and comfortable with the identity. Madonna does anything but that, constantly pushing the envelope of good taste and acceptability, and always managing to do so in a way that increases, instead of diminishing, her popularity. The public, far from being alienated, responds to every antic, every change in persona, without a blink, and continues to buy the records and sell out the concerts.

What seems contradictory is actually a clever circumventing of the traditional rules. Madonna does not so much fly in the face of Branding as create a new definition for her brand every time she makes an appearance. As a singer, there might be some you find more talented or appealing, but as a personality, as a brand, there isn't anyone to compare with Madonna.

From a public relations standpoint, this is both a dream and a nightmare.

Madonna manages to create a great deal of media attention with each new incarnation, but that amount of attention is necessary in order to reacquaint the public with the new version of the persona they thought they knew before. It's a double-edged sword, but one that Madonna has managed to wield successfully for a long time without any serious missteps.

While her brand integrity might seem suspect, the brand by which Madonna has become defined is the very changes she makes. In other words, the consuming public expects Madonna to be different each time she records an album or appears in a film, and so her fans are not in the least put off by her chameleon-like changes. The brand integrity remains intact because the brand identity hinges on the constant reinvention. It's truly an awesome public relations feat.

CASE STUDY #3: MILK

In 1994, the California Milk Processor Board began running television ads aimed at increasing consumption of milk, which had slipped from a 1976 high of 28.7 gallons per capita every year to 24.7 gallons. To remind people why they liked the brand milk to begin with, the ads very cleverly set up situations that screamed for a drink of milk, such as a package of chocolate chip cookies or a slice of rich chocolate cake, and then deprived the character in the commercial of the milk. The catch phrase, "got milk?" became universal enough that the national dairy farmers' group Dairy Management began to air the spots nationally not long after.

By January 1995, print ads bearing the "got milk?" tag line began to appear, and celebrities were starting to line up to be photographed with the "milk mustache" (which is really not milk at all, but looks like it) to promote the brand. Everyone from Cookie Monster to Britney Spears has been the subject of a "got milk?" print ad.

While the ads have undoubtedly raised the awareness of milk (by 1996, awareness of the ads was measured at an astounding 91 percent), their effect on milk sales is somewhat more controversial. In 1999, *USA Today* reported that the campaign had not "significantly [raised] milk sales, despite [the board] spending $85.5 million on ads last year. Sales dropped 0.4 percent." But the same article quoted Kurt Graetzer, CEO of the

National Fluid Milk Processor Promotion Board, as saying that milk consumption hadn't grown, but that the decline had slowed considerably since the ad campaign began. "It's not plummeting to the degree it was before the campaign broke," Graetzer said, noting also that milk prices had risen 10 to 15 percent the year before.

There is no question that the "got milk?" campaign, which also included selling merchandise with the campaign's logo emblazoned on it and licensing it to other manufacturers, made the public more aware of milk in a different context than previous campaigns had striven to do. But was it a successful brand revival?

" 'Got milk?' is an example of a great, memorable ad," says Merrie Spaeth of Spaeth Communications. "Milk sales have not moved. Most people who create advertising want to win awards. They ought to be using advertising to accomplish some business purpose. If milk sales haven't moved and the population is expanding, that means fewer people are drinking milk. It's a brilliant campaign, but it's art, not advertising."

Perhaps what the milk brand needed was less advertising and more public relations. In placing so much faith in the ad campaign, even though it was memorable beyond all logical hope, the dairy industry did generate a very good amount of press coverage. The problem? The coverage was about the ad campaign, not the brand. So people who were aware of the advertisements were now aware that they were extraordinarily popular, but hadn't learned anything new about milk; nor had they been given even the level of information that was in the print ads, which spoke of health benefits from drinking milk and the new, "cool" image of the brand.

It is possible to create a very successful, consciousness-raising advertising campaign, but not do your brand a comparable amount of good. It's hard to say that "got milk?" is a failure, as it has become as much a household phrase as "Where's the Beef?" was in the 1980s. And the decline in milk sales has slowed, even as the price has increased. But in light of the wild success the campaign should have had given its popularity, it is equally hard to call it a success in proportion to the impact it has had on popular culture. In the end, "got milk?" could be considered a qualified success that had potential to be an amazing one but never, for some reason, ignited the way it should.

CASE STUDY #4: RED BULL

In the late 1980s, Dietrich Mateschitz, an Austrian traveling extensively in Asia on business, came across several brands of "energy drinks" which he thought would define a significant product category in Europe. In 1987, he launched Red Bull, and sold 1 million cans that year.

By 2001, Red Bull was available in many European countries, as well as the United States, Canada, and parts of South America. Mateschitz, now general partner of the company, currently sells over 1 billion cans of the product each year. He hasn't just started a new product category; he has created a dominant brand.

With public relations know-how and amusing advertising campaigns, Red Bull became, in the minds of many Europeans and Americans, the only brand in the energy drink market, although it was in fact only the first brand in those markets, and far from first in Asia. It was the global thinking of Mateschitz that created the Red Bull mystique, and not thinking small has paid off handsomely for the brand.

"Powerful brands are brands that are not just confined to one country," says Al Ries. "If you want to build a brand today, you think global. Why should you confine yourself to the United States, which represents only 5 percent of the population of the world? Some of the big brands recently don't even think about being confined to a country. Red Bull, for example, the first energy drink, was actually introduced in Austria. [Mateschitz] borrowed the idea from a drink he found over in Thailand and when he introduced the brand in Austria, he didn't give it a German name. Why? Because if he had, then the brand could not have become a global brand. And now Red Bull does a billion dollars worldwide."

Like most successful brands, however, Red Bull has had to deal with unsubstantiated rumors about its product. Stories began circulating that the drink had been banned in certain countries, and that it had been found to be harmful, rather than beneficial (as the product claimed) to the health. On its Web site, Red Bull goes to great lengths to dispel these rumors.

"Red Bull has never been banned, though sometimes it hasn't been authorized," the Web information reads. "It takes a lot of time to get a completely new product, with special ingredients in a complex composition, through all the official channels. However, no authority in the world has ever discovered or proven an unhealthy effect in or from Red Bull."

It goes on to say that many foods containing certain vitamins, minerals, and amino acids are often restricted in countries with very stringent importation policies. "Not only Red Bull Energy Drink, but also cereals, sweets and other foodstuff producers encounter difficulties in marketing their products in these countries. Therefore, sweets from Germany may not be imported to France as well as some cereals such as Kellogg's may not be imported into Norway. Therefore, the marketing restrictions that Red Bull Energy Drink encounters in these countries are of a regulatory nature and do not indicate or imply that there is any health and safety concern."

Having aligned its brand with products from many of the countries it currently services, as well as a famous American name brand, the Red Bull information goes further to dispel any ideas that its product is harmful: "Scientists and doctors in the fields of toxicology, internal medicine, psychiatry and neurology as well as notable sports doctors and other health authorities of various jurisdictions have checked the ingredients of Red Bull Energy Drink and have concluded that the product and its ingredients are safe for human consumption. Consequently the marketing of Red Bull Energy Drink has been permitted and Red Bull Energy Drink is currently sold in more than 50 countries worldwide, including Europe, the United States and Australia."

The Red Bull strategy is to provide as much information as possible that refutes the rumors, and to provide them free to anyone who might find the rumors distressing. This is an excellent use of a Web site for public relations damage control, and as a result, the rumors don't seem to have hurt Red Bull's sales figures in the least.

CASE STUDY #5: GEORGE CLOONEY VERSUS DAVID CARUSO

Brand expansion can be a tricky proposition, as the Coca-Cola Company has discovered. When the brand is a personality, particularly in the entertainment business, that proposition grows fangs.

Studying the Brand Leaders

Two actors best known for their television roles, George Clooney (*ER*) and David Caruso (*NYPD Blue*), left their successful drama series in order to pursue film roles and, in effect, to expand their brands into the world of feature films. But their film experiences have been very different, and while Clooney is now a very well-respected film actor whose movies have done well at the box office, Caruso has returned to series television after finding very limited success on the big screen.

This is not meant as an estimation of either man's talents; I think they are both very good actors. But their appeal and their brand identities have not taken the same path, and an examination of their methods and their choices might very well determine why that has happened. First, let's look at the circumstances under which each rose to prominence and then decided to make the jump from series television to feature film leading roles.

David Caruso had played supporting roles and guest roles on television and in films before *NYPD Blue* premiered in 1993. In fact, he had already filmed *Mad Dog and Glory* with Robert DeNiro, Bill Murray, and Uma Thurman before the series began, and when the film premiered, Caruso got very good reviews and seemed to be a rising star.

He was anxious to move into films based on that experience, and left *NYPD Blue* shortly after it started its second season on the air. Caruso starred in a few films that were not well received by critics or audiences, and was relegated to lower-budget films by the time he returned to series television in 1997, in a series that did not last beyond that season. He has taken the lead in *CSI: Miami*, a hit series that began in the fall of 2002.

George Clooney had been a working actor, but not a star, in films and television before *ER* went on the air in 1994. He had, in fact, played a supporting role on a forgotten situation comedy series called *E/R*, starring Elliot Gould, in 1984.

When the drama series *ER* became a huge hit upon its premiere, Clooney was clearly the breakout star. But he remained committed to *ER* for six seasons, and worked on films during breaks from the series. Movies like *From Dusk till Dawn* showed potential, and then Clooney expanded his brand further by attaching himself to an already established mega-brand when he played the role of Bruce Wayne in *Batman and Robin*. Even though the film was possibly the least well-reviewed of the series, *Batman* was a huge franchise, and by playing the role, Clooney used the cachet of the enormous brand to expand his own, making him a bona fide action hero and leading man. By the time he left *ER* in 1999, he was a well-known movie star, and subsequent projects like *Three Kings, O Brother, Where Art Thou* and *Ocean's Eleven* have borne out his decision. When he returned, very briefly, to *ER* in 2001, he brought the already top-rated program its highest ratings of the year.

The difference could very well be found in the perceived personalities of the two actors, as such things are impossible to measure. Audience reactions are not predictable, nor are they necessarily logical; they are visceral things best left to analysis rather than anticipation. But the two men took divergent paths in expanding their brands—Caruso leaving his "core brand" before it could be well entrenched; Clooney working as a film actor while still servicing his core product, *ER*. These decisions are classic Branding tactics, and the history bears out the decision Clooney made. Expanding too quickly can confuse and alienate the core consumer. It's best to expand the brand only when the core product is so well established that the expansion will not damage its brand integrity.

CASE STUDY #6: TARGET VERSUS KMART

At first glance, a discount store is a discount store. Wal-Mart, Kmart, and Target all appear to be roughly the same: They sell the same kind of merchandise, they all claim to have the lowest prices, and the stores are even somewhat similar in appearance.

But the tales of Kmart and Target, as of this writing, could hardly be more different. Kmart has filed for Chapter XI protection from its creditors, while Target continues to thrive, to grow into new geographic areas, and to ring up sales on the order of 15 percent per-share growth for the company's investors. Target also owns the Chicago-based Marshall Field's department stores and other chains.

What happened? How did such a mighty company as Kmart fall on hard times, while an upstart competitor has managed to grow and expand its market share? Branding is at the root of both companies' fortunes, and the way each handled its brand will tell a good deal about how each has fared and why.

Kmart decided in the late 1990s to extend its brand identity by incorporating higher-end merchandise into its already well-stocked stores. In this way, the company believed it could increase its brand awareness among more upscale consumers, attract them in to buy the new products, and perhaps interest them in some more traditional Kmart fare while they were in the store. Jewelry and higher-end clothing began showing up on Kmart shelves and racks.

The problem was that upscale consumers were not interested in shopping at Kmart, for the same reason no one buys a BMW from a guy named Ed in a small lot behind the Public Works building. Part of the allure of high-end merchandise is that it *is* high-end merchandise, and the snob appeal of those brand names is diminished, not enhanced, when it is sold at a discount. You'll never see a Jaguar dealer advertising great low prices, but you will hear all about the luxury and performance associated with such a fine handcrafted automobile.

At the same time, Kmart's attempt to elevate its brand cachet resulted in two conditions for its core consumers: tighter shelf space for traditional Kmart merchandise and an alienation of the traditional Kmart shopper, who wasn't interested in buying higher-quality jewelry or brand-name clothing at a general merchandise superstore. They wanted lower prices on the staple items that had been Kmart's domain for years, and if they couldn't get what they wanted at Kmart, they'd go elsewhere.

Target stores were elsewhere. Making a clear promise to the consumer that it would deliver everything its competitors delivered, only faster, Target management made sure the stores could deliver on the promise. Consumer surveys and market research showed an absolute obsession with speed, as the company had determined that consumers did not want to spend a lot of time on the checkout line. If a Target store had too many people on one line, another line opened in the blink of an eye, and consumers noticed.

At the same time, building the Target brand meant that consumers' priorities were shifting, and their loyalties were moving from the products the store sold to the store itself.

"The retailers are getting bigger and they're getting better at their Branding," says former Sherwin-Williams marketing executive John O'Brien. "Target has done a tremendous job recently of building their retail brand as a destination. So it's not, 'I want to go buy Levi's,' but, 'I'm going to go to Target to buy jeans, and if they have Levi's that's fine, I recognize the brand. If they don't have Arizona jeans at Target, that's OK. If it's good enough for Target, it's good enough for me.' "

Clearly, for consumers, Target is good enough for them.

CASE STUDY #7:
CHARLTON HESTON

As I discussed previously, my work with the Academy Award-winning actor Charlton Heston began in the early 1980s and lasted almost 20 years. We managed to revitalize and expand Heston's brand image, and brought him to the attention of a new audience he had not reached before. Unfortunately, the story doesn't end there.

I stopped representing Heston around the time he began to fall under what I saw as the cultlike influence of the National Rifle Association. Now, I am not an opponent of the right to bear arms, but in my view, what Heston was doing was extending his brand into an area that couldn't possibly be beneficial to him, and which was moving in extreme, radical directions that mainstream Americans—even the majority that support what they see as the right to bear arms—would find disturbing and offputting.

These public appearances, his office-holding in the NRA, and in particular an often-seen film clip of Heston at an NRA event holding a rifle aloft and proclaiming that it could only be torn "from my cold, dead hands," were not the stuff of brand expansion, but more the type of thing that was tantamount to brand suicide.

At one time, the first paragraph in Charlton Heston's obituary would have included phrases like "Academy Award winner," "respected actor," "icon known for his biblical roles," but now, the first or second paragraph would have to mention phrases on the order of "controversial political views," "radical proponent of the NRA," and so on. It wasn't just failing to expand the Heston brand; it was deteriorating what had existed to begin with.

Dismayed, I resigned the account, and we parted ways. We didn't have a political disagreement so much as a difference in Branding philosophies. I did not see Heston extending or expanding his brand through his political activities, particularly in what I considered to be extreme methods for an organization that had an agenda beyond the good work Heston saw himself doing.

To argue that Heston was expanding his brand by fronting for the NRA would be to argue that Puff Daddy's arrest for weapons violations in 2001 was going to expand his brand because there are 2 million people in federal prisons who would now identify more directly with him. Brand identity is more important than expansion, and damaging the core brand in favor of the expansion runs the risk of destroying everything that has been accomplished up to the date of expansion. When I parted company with Charlton Heston, it was because I felt his brand identity was being compromised, and he would not heed my advice to repair it.

There are many more examples of Branding successes and failures throughout this book: Apple Computer's ability to make evangelists of its users; McDonald's stock market and market share decline, and the erosion of its brand integrity; the Walt Disney Company's almost obsessive attention to brand identity and detail. They are meant to illustrate Branding points, and to show the way for those who would care to follow in their footsteps or avoid the more dangerous paths.

Remember that the identity your brand develops is its own; no preconceived template can work for every possible brand. Use your judgment and your brand's identity, and remember: Those who do not learn from the past are condemned to repeat it.

Just the Best has to continue to maintain its identity as it grows as a brand. While expansion and extension might go on as a natural process, the core brand has to be constantly nurtured and reinforced. Sponsorship of family concerts on summer evenings, for example, might be a way to remind the public of the Just the Best brand, while constant quality checks are being made daily on manufacturing plants, customer service representatives, and delivery contractors.

The key is not to take anything for granted in Branding. As Just the Best becomes a familiar brand in consumers' lives, it has to remain what it has always been, while keeping open the chance that it might evolve and mature even as its consistency continues.

CHAPTER ELEVEN

DAMAGE CONTROL

"You can't control a divorce, for example; you can't control an ugly divorce. Look at Tom Cruise, Mr. All-America. You can't get any cleaner than that. It's continuing to hit the pages of the National Enquirer that he screwed Nicole Kidman over, you couldn't have gotten any cleaner than Tom Cruise. There are some things you can't control, and it's a risk you've got to take. You can reduce the risk considerably by being careful and being thoughtful about who you go with."

—NOREEN S. JENNEY, PRESIDENT OF THE CELEBRITY
ENDORSEMENT NETWORK

In 1993, it was reported on television and in newspapers that Michael Jackson, who was arguably the most popular entertainer in the world at that time, had been accused of (but not charged with) molesting a 13-year-old boy whom Jackson had befriended.

The world exploded.

While the allegations were never substantiated (the civil suit eventually was settled out of court, and criminal charges were never brought against anyone), in the court of public opinion this was the case of the decade. Brigades of reporters appeared near Jackson's home, and reams of unsubstantiated (and in almost every case, proven false) rumors were reported. The media feeding frenzy was beyond anything that had come before it, but would be eclipsed soon enough by the O. J. Simpson murder trial.

For people who weren't there, the Michael Jackson scandal is hard to describe. It was front-page news on virtually every newspaper; it was reported on television news with the weight of an international crisis. Reporters from countless countries were dispatched. Rumors that had no validity were never checked and printed as fact. The world's biggest enter-tainer was being held hostage in his own home, unable to do anything except watch the allegations against him grow. His reputation was being pummeled and his integrity questioned. And the Jackson camp was doing the worst thing they could possibly do under the circumstances: nothing.

When I was called to consult, the crisis had already reached its peak. But the people around Michael Jackson were not responding to the press. They were not getting their side of the story into the mix. And a rumor unanswered in 24 hours becomes truth. This had been going on for weeks.

No question, there was almost Chernobyl-like damage to the Michael Jackson brand. I came in about midway through the crisis. Jackson had been acting prior to my arrival as if he were a deer caught in the headlights, paralyzed and unable to respond. The first thing I did was try to create a feeling with the media, which were in a feeding frenzy, that we could at least communicate with each other. Previous to that, there had been no communication. Jackson's people were stonewalling, so the press was free to make up whatever they wanted.

The best defense is a good offense, and the best offense is relentless. I tried to take control of that situation, to the extent that any one person could, by creating open dialogue with the media. We were getting some-where around 150 to 200 calls from all over the world per day to my office, seven days a week. We were working feverishly to create dialogue with the media, which were acting in ways that I can only describe as utterly irresponsible.

Once we had opened up lines of communication with the media, it was easier to get Michael's story out. An article (with a cover photo) in GQ in 1994, entitled "Who Framed Michael?", put together all the evi-dence that had been built up against the people who were accusing Michael, and the fact that no evidence had been gathered that could impli-cate him in any wrongdoing was featured prominently throughout the long, well-researched article.

Clearly, in a situation like this, the public relations executive has to pay more attention to legal ramifications than Branding ramifications. But the damage done to the brand Michael Jackson was slightly lessened through our hardworking, constant efforts for the one-year period during which I represented Michael. My position coming into the situation was that I had to rock the boat, and the reason I thought it was okay to rock the boat was that so much damage had been done in the beginning. By the time we left, the boat had taken on some water, but the bailing had already begun and the leaks had mostly been repaired.

WHEN BRANDS STUMBLE

The fact is, nothing goes smoothly forever. All the enormous brands—Coca-Cola, Nike, Disney, Enron, Microsoft, Bill Clinton—have had times when things were going desperately wrong. The wolves were at the door, the vultures were circling, and the media was reporting on it all. In today's culture, it's difficult to maintain any kind of anonymity in business or personal matters. When you want to get press coverage to establish or reinforce your brand, it's very hard to convince the gatekeepers that what you're putting forth is news. When you have a situation you'd rather not have uncovered, the press is certain to find out, and will report upon it immediately, whether you present your side of the story or not. As Michael Jackson's case illustrates, it's best to present your side of the story.

Public relations is often the business of damage control. Publicists like myself are brought into situations like the Michael Jackson episode, where there has already been damage done to the brand that must now be minimized, or, if possible, reversed. The public's trust is essential to the Branding of any product, service, or personality, and when that trust is injured, it must be treated and cured as quickly as possible to ensure the brand's survival.

> More than any of the other disciplines, public relations deals with the perception of the general consumer. It is about how the public sees your brand and how the issues that face your brand are perceived by the people who keep the brand alive. And at the times when a threat appears, either internally or externally, the way the brand reacts—which will be seen through the prism of public relations—will determine its future. The public will accept or reject a brand based on one misstep or one redemptive move. It can be that simple and that imperative.

A BRANDED WORLD

In his book *Big Brands, Big Trouble,* Jack Trout, president of Trout & Partners, one of the most prestigious marketing firms in the country, writes, "Today there are so many competitors that they quickly take your business if you make a mistake. Your chances of getting it back are slim unless someone else in turn makes a mistake. Hoping for competitors to make mistakes is like running a race with the hope that the other racers will fall down. It isn't a very smart strategy."

Naturally, it is preferable to avoid mistakes rather than to have to compensate for them. But even public relations executives are human, and mistakes happen. How we react to our mistakes is the meat of the public relations business; in Branding, it can determine the direction, and in some cases the fate, of the brand.

Jack Trout lists any number of mistakes that extremely big brands (AT&T, General Motors, Pepsi) have made, and the ways they could have been avoided, usually by deciding not to take a specific action. For example, his absolute abhorrence of me-too products—such as Pepsi's response to Lemon Coke with lemon-flavored Pepsi—leaves only the solution that you shouldn't have done that in the first place.

Trout is a remarkable marketer; he knows his business better than almost anyone. Public relations, however, flexes a different set of muscles. It deals with perception and reality at the same time, and often is reactive rather than proactive. Jack Trout is right about everything he says. But in publicity, we have a whole separate set of problems.

For example, if a brand has been compromised by marketing a me-too product—for example, when McDonald's saw a trend in the fast food habits of the country and tried to inaugurate McPizza—there is little point in assigning blame and lamenting the decision to have made such a mistake, which seems so obvious in 20/20 hindsight. Instead, the brand must regain its footing through public relations techniques, by focusing attention on more positive aspects of the brand's activities and by letting the mistake die quietly, with little if any notice taken by the public and the media.

When McDonald's offered Chicken McNuggets for the first time, it was the same kind of gamble, but one that has paid off and extended the brand. There was no despair at the corporate headquarters about that decision, although the process was exactly the same as the one that produced a dismal failure. Market research and marketing technique can take you only so far, and then the public will either respond or not.

After all, there have been remarkably successful me-too products developed by large companies, too. Everyone in the electronics business agreed that Sony's Betamax was the first, and the superior, format for video recording in the seventies. VHS, developed by JVC and Panasonic, was a latecomer, a me-too product. Today, Betamax decks are located in museums, while VHS is in virtually every home in America.

Public relations certainly had some effect on the perception of the two video formats, but eventually, the practical aspects of the one product—VHS could record for longer, and store more programming on one tape—won out with consumers.

Damage control is best avoided, as Jack Trout clearly states. But when that isn't possible, *spin,* or public relations efforts, will be the best defense, which is based on the best most aggressive offense possible under the circumstances.

When Paul McCartney was arrested by Japanese police for marijuana possession in January of 1980, his brand was in peril. The family man, the "cute Beatle," the one whose music was most accessible and middle-of-the-road, was being detained (for 10 days, as it turned out) in a foreign country on drug charges. There was no point in lamenting the fact that the incident occurred, but the way the public was to perceive this arrest was going to be crucial to McCartney's image for the short term, if not for years to come.

Instead of denying the crime, McCartney's camp realized that the image of the former Beatle—who had already admitted, along with his bandmates, to using LSD in the sixties—was probably stronger than the charges against him. While it was illegal to bring marijuana into Japan, pot smoking was seen as a minor infraction in most countries, and the amount found in McCartney's possession probably would not have resulted in 10 days imprisonment in most other places.

Therefore, the McCartney camp decided to concentrate its news releases on the conditions the former Beatle was enduring, his state of mind, his separation from his wife and family. The fact that he had been denied access to his guitar to pass the time was made quite public. McCartney never tried to deny any knowledge of the drugs in his luggage and never attempted to suggest they didn't belong to him. Instead, the public was treated to an examination of Japanese prisons, discussions of overly harsh drug possession laws in that country, and a virtual hour-by-hour account of the amount of time it was taking to release the musician and send him on his way.

McCartney, released after 10 days, suffered no ill effects from the arrest in terms of his popularity or marketability. His brand remained untainted because the public relations efforts made on his behalf had managed to shift the focus from any wrongdoing (however minor) he might have done to the seemingly inhumane treatment by Japanese authorities. It was a publicity blitz that managed to change negative coverage of a brand into positive, sympathy-producing coverage that never tarnished the brand. More than 20 years later, the McCartney brand is still among the most popular in the world.

That kind of crisis control isn't always possible. McCartney carried with him a huge amount of goodwill from the public, built up over years. His brand was among the best-known in the world, and was regarded by a very large segment of the population as a friendly, accessible brand with pleasant memories attached to it. And he hadn't been accused of a violent crime that raised thoughts of a dark side to the brand that some hadn't considered before. Drug use, especially marijuana smoking, was not seen, in most countries, as a serious thing.

"When you have a person who's so closely linked to the brand, what happens to them certainly does affect the image of the product itself," says *Brandweek* editor Karen Benezra. "However, people are not necessarily looking to Martha Stewart and saying, 'Hey, she's being investigated by Wall Street; her sheets must not be fluffy any longer.' It probably sours you to seeing her flitting around a kitchen and chopping cabbage. Americans are very forgiving and even if she is convicted and all these other issues are worked through, there will still be a market for her stuff."

On the other hand, when O. J. Simpson was arrested in 1994 for two murders, and through the ordeal he underwent, his public relations never achieved the kind of brand acceptance that McCartney's did. Even after

Damage Control

Simpson was acquitted in a Los Angeles courtroom, public opinion polls indicated the general perception that (a) he was guilty; (b) he had been arrogant and unremorseful about the crimes; and (c) the system had failed. Simpson's acting career was essentially ended, his possessions were seized and auctioned off after a civil suit found against him, and his name was reduced to a punch line.

The circumstances were much different than in the McCartney case. For one thing, the crimes with which Simpson was charged were infinitely more serious, involving two deaths, and were reported on extensively before Simpson himself was even identified as a suspect, let alone arrested and charged. The public had no reason or encouragement from the media to see Simpson as a sympathetic figure. In fact, the first time he was spotted after being identified as a suspect, the former football player was in the infamous low-speed chase down California highways, holding a gun to his own head and threatening to kill himself.

On the other hand, the public was sympathetic toward the victims' families. Those who had lost their family members made statements to the press, made themselves available for interviews, and presented their side of the story, all of which was damaging to O. J. Simpson. While it might not have been an orchestrated public relations campaign, the handling of the media by the Brown and Goldman families certainly did have winning the hearts of the public as its goal, and it was far more effective than anything O. J. managed to do. After the verdict, when Simpson tried to tell "my own story" on a home video, he got a lot of publicity and sold few tapes. His brand had, in many eyes, gone from football hero and movie actor to murderer, no matter what the jury had declared.

In the corporate world, the very hint of scandal can be devastating to a brand. Procter & Gamble spent years and millions dispelling a rumor that its logo indicated the company was somehow affiliated with devil worship. While sales did not slip noticeably, the idea that America's soap company could have an unseen dark side was not acceptable to the brand, and public relations steps had to be taken.

By the same token, such companies as Enron (which handled its own disaster very poorly from a public relations standpoint) and Johnson & Johnson (which rebounded brilliantly from the tainted Tylenol scandal, as

I discuss below) have had to react to public exposure of very negative circumstances. Whether or not the revelations could have been avoided, or the situations themselves could have been prevented, is irrelevant. What is worth noting, from a Branding point of view, is the differences in the reactions companies have had to negative revelations and how their brands were affected by those reactions.

TYLENOL: HOW TO HANDLE A CRISIS

Johnson & Johnson was never considered responsible for the deaths of seven people in the Chicago area in 1982; an unknown person tainted Extra-Strength Tylenol capsules with cyanide and then set them in a number of area stores. But from the public's point of view, one of its most trusted pain remedies was now quite literally tainted; even advertising guru Jerry Della Femina doubted Johnson & Johnson's ability to recover. Della Femina was quoted in the *New York Times* as saying that Johnson & Johnson could never "sell another product under that name. There may be an advertising person who thinks he can solve this, and if they find him, I want to hire him, because then I want him to turn our water cooler into a wine cooler."

The drug company seemed to be in an inextricable situation. One of its core brands was under direct attack; Chicago police were roaming neighborhoods with bullhorns warning people not to use Tylenol. All major networks and news programs were advising viewers to avoid the pain reliever at all costs until the extent of the tampering could be determined. Tylenol jokes were starting to emerge. The brand was becoming a word that, in itself, was scary. Its doom seemed inevitable.

Instead, Johnson & Johnson responded with a stellar public relations campaign—one of the best imaginable. First, the company made sure consumers knew it was more concerned with their safety than with its own profits: It advised consumers not to take any kind of Tylenol product until the source of the tampering could be determined. It recalled about 31 million bottles of Tylenol—every single capsule in circulation, representing a retail value of more than $100 million—and stopped production and advertising of the brand entirely.

Not only was this the right thing to do from a moral standpoint, it began the rebuilding of trust for the Tylenol brand. Johnson & Johnson's message to consumers was: "We won't let you have Tylenol until we know it's safe." The company knew it would take a very large hit in profits, but it had long-term goals (not to mention safety issues) in mind, and it made sure the public knew where its priorities lay.

The media immediately announced the recall, but on-air and in-print analysts also praised the drug giant for doing the right thing. On October 11, 1982, the *Washington Post* reported that "Johnson & Johnson has effectively demonstrated how a major business ought to handle a disaster." The company also made a very public offer of $100,000 for information leading to the arrest of the killer (which has gone uncollected, since the killer has never been found).

Finally, since Tylenol capsules were the only ones found to be tampered with, the company offered to exchange any Tylenol capsules in consumers' homes for Tylenol tablets, which were considered safer.

While the company's integrity and moral fortitude were rebounding, there was still an enormous job ahead: reestablishing the Tylenol brand and resurrecting the trust the public had grown to have for the product. Before the tragic events in Illinois, Tylenol enjoyed a 37 percent market share among nonprescription painrelievers. With the recall and the hysteria surrounding the deaths from the Tylenol tampering, that was clearly going to change.

Before the Tylenol murders, over-the-counter medications had been packaged in bottles that could be opened by anyone at any time. Child-resistant caps were included on some, to prevent accidental overdoses, but it was usually possible to pick a bottle of pain medication off a shelf, twist it open, and then put it back. It had never occurred to anyone that someone might have the ability and the inclination to tamper with such products.

In response to the Tylenol incidents, Johnson & Johnson had to virtually invent the tamper-resistant packaging that is standard today. Less than four months after the murders, the company unveiled its new Tylenol packaging (which it also applied to its other over-the-counter medications;

competing brands followed suit), with careful instructions on the box never to take any of the pills in the package if the safety seals were broken.

Johnson & Johnson (through its McNeil Consumer Products subsidiary, the manufacturer of Tylenol) also offered $2.50 coupons toward any Tylenol product once the brand was back on the country's shelves. Consumers could find the coupons in local newspapers or call a toll-free number to have them mailed directly from Johnson & Johnson.

By December 24, 1982, a few months after the murders, the *New York Times* reported that Tylenol had achieved a 24 percent share of the pain reliever market, an astounding comeback considering the unspeakable events that had occurred so soon before.

ENRON: HOW NOT TO HANDLE A CRISIS

When it really started to go bad for Enron—when bankruptcy (the largest in history) was inevitable and allegations of financial wrongdoing throughout the corporation were about to become public—the reaction of the company was, from all points of view, wrong. From a public relations standpoint, responding to coming allegations by shredding documents and denying the truth is about the worst decision that can be made. But Enron executives, from the top down, have been accused of doing exactly that. While the actions of Enron's staff have not been completely substantiated, it is clear that the company did not do what a public relations executive would certainly recommend: tell the truth, try to create a positive image of the company by coming clean, and do what can be done for investors and consumers to lessen the blow. Johnson & Johnson lost millions recalling Tylenol, but the company did not have to go bankrupt and its executives were not brought up on charges afterward. In a remarkably short period of time, Tylenol was once again a trusted brand in America. Enron, by contrast, had its name taken off the baseball stadium in Houston where the Astros play.

One difference between the two situations, of course, is that the crisis for Johnson & Johnson came from outside the company, while the Enron situation was certainly an internal problem that grew beyond any reasonable expectations. That makes a large difference in the public's perception of the problem, since Johnson & Johnson could easily be characterized as the victim of a hideous crime, while Enron appeared to be more the perpetrators of more white-collar wrongdoing. It would have been harder to spin the Enron situation into something that would engender sympathy with the general public.

Still, steps could have been taken to maintain the Enron brand. With early public relations intervention, it would not have been out of the question to minimize the damage done to the public perception of the brand (although not the governmental controls or legal problems associated with the scandal).

First, it was absolutely essential to tell the truth early, and that was apparently never considered. Once mistakes are made within a company, it is not possible to make them disappear, but a public disclosure and a display of contrition go a long way with the public. After the New Coke debacle, consumers—who had been absolutely apoplectic over the move—quickly embraced Classic Coke and forgave the miscalculation the company had made, reestablishing Coca-Cola as one of the most dominant brands in the world.

In Enron's case, that would have been more difficult, but not impossible. Clearly, the political and financial ramifications of the Enron situation overreach the simple concerns of a product problem or a celebrity's peccadilloes. But a direct appeal to the public, explaining what had happened and how the company intended to reverse it, would have gone a long way toward repairing the brand.

Next, because the situation was an internal crisis, it would have been necessary to discipline—if not remove—the people involved. That may seem a naive solution in a situation like this, but we are examining the public relations opportunities and the impact on the company's brand. Identifying the responsible parties would make the scandal understandable, and making sure they were removed or disciplined would go part of the way toward a Johnson & Johnson-type solution in that it would give the public and the company's investors a clear indication that the problem was being dealt with internally.

Because Enron was not selling a typical consumer product, there was no way to compensate in the direct, easily understood way to which the Tylenol situation lent itself. But giving the impression of propriety (because, remember, public relations is about impressions and perceptions) would have gone a long way toward healing the brand, if not the company. By the time any steps were taken, the internal situation had gone much too far to save the brand that Enron had built. The rest of the story has not yet been written, but the Branding damage has already been done. It would be surprising if repairs could ever be made.

THE LAST WORD ON DAMAGE CONTROL

It is obvious that a strong brand is more likely to survive a crisis than a brand that is weak before hard times hit. But a situation like the one Tylenol faced could have destroyed the brand, if not the corporation that owned it, had the proper steps not been taken. The Enron situation was much more complicated, and might have been too deeply entwined throughout the corporation, for any public relations effort to improve the brand image. Still, the fact that Johnson & Johnson managed to make all the right decisions and did what needed to be done, no matter what the cost, in its crisis led to the positive outcome any brand would hope for when bad times crop up—as they inevitably will.

> The key to any difficult Branding situation is to keep the brand identity—the promise made to consumers—the brand integrity, and the unblinking dedication to keeping that promise, in mind when making all decisions regarding public statements on the situation. No brand has ever gone out of business by doing the right thing and telling the public about it, and no brand has ever overestimated customer satisfaction.

When Major League Baseball players went on strike in 1994 (a situation that could be blamed on the players, the team owners, or both) and canceled the World Series for the first time in 90 years, the baseball brand suffered untold damage. Even after the strike—a bitter, public one—was settled, fans were disgusted with what they saw as "millionaires fighting billionaires" at the expense of the national pastime.

Public relations could have done wonders for the situation, if either side had been willing to listen. Instead, attendance at baseball games dropped precipitously and remained anemic for years, until the 1998 season, dubbed baseball's best, found Mark McGwire and Sammy Sosa challenging the home run record and each other and creating a public relations bonanza that finally brought fans back to the ballparks.

The flip side of that coin was baseball's reaction to the 9/11 tragedy. Once the country could focus on things other than the attacks, baseball resumed its season and helped to provide much needed distraction—particularly in New York City, where the Yankees headed for their fourth World Series in a row (they lost to the Arizona Diamondbacks in a riveting series that was decided in its last inning).

Here, public relations efforts by the Major Leagues were going on for all the right reasons. Ballparks were instructed to play "God Bless America" and to have a special moment of remembrance during the seventh inning of every game. Players visited Ground Zero and victim aid centers and signed autographs at fire stations, and each team, as well as Major League Baseball itself, donated money to rescue efforts. All these facts were reported not by the baseball establishment but by the news media covering both the aftermath of the attacks and the sport. There was no attempt on the part of the Major Leagues to garner direct credit for any good works done in connection with the awful events.

That kind of campaign, not orchestrated by the desire to raise awareness of the brand or the brand's good deeds, has the residual effect of improving the brand's profile and its standing with the public. The brand benefits even as it does exactly what it should do under those circumstances. The crisis being controlled may not have been baseball's crisis, but it was a crisis for the country, and, as a representative of the nation, the sport did the right thing and was rewarded for it. Attendance at games—perhaps because fans needed a release from the tension of those days—increased to near record levels.

The ability to deal with something that could adversely affect the brand and turn it into something that actually enhances the brand integrity is exactly what public relations is meant to do.

PR isn't simply a publicity machine; it is a means of communication between a brand and the general public, or at least that segment of the public to which the brand appeals. When a crisis occurs, either from within or without, public relations executives should be in their element. The integrity of the brand is the paramount concern, and it must be maintained at all costs.

In Michael Jackson's case, the brand had to be reintroduced, since the allegations against it were eroding the initial brand promise. In Tylenol's case, the brand had to be reinforced and healed. For Enron, the damage to the brand was too deep, too wide, and too well developed for public relations to help. And for Major League Baseball, there were good and bad results. The key is to assess the situation as quickly as possible, and always to act in as honest and up-front a manner as you can. Branding demands consistency, and crises threaten consistency. Remind the public that you are consistent, that the crisis is either a fabrication from without or an aberration from within, and perhaps brand integrity can be salvaged.

CHAPTER TWELVE

SUCCESSFUL E-BRANDING

"The Internet is entirely a process, and one of the big problems is that people are so focused on the process that they pay very little attention to how they get there. They don't pay that much attention to the existence of a site as a company, where they might pay a good deal of attention to Michelin versus Firestone tires. Michelin might have a certain reputation and Firestone will have another reputation. In the Internet, it's much more a question of functionality than reputation. This Web site works really well, and this Web site gives me what I want really quickly. In the non-Internet culture, what you think of me is the most important thing. In the Internet culture, what you think of me is not as important as whether you enjoyed using me?"

—DICK MORRIS, POLITICAL CONSULTANT

On July 16, 1995, when Amazon.com first went live on the Internet, not many people had ever purchased anything online. Few would recognize the URL suffix .com, if they even knew what a URL was. They were aware the Amazon was a river, but nobody associated it with selling books.

Today, as Amazon.com is the most successful Internet start-up ever, its name and designation are considerably better known. And it could be argued quite easily that Amazon.com was the first, and to date the most successful, Internet brand.

Karen Benezra of *Brandweek* says, "A lot of people are still struggling to figure [Internet Branding] out. There are firms that have purported to get it; there are brands that have not used a lot of advertising dollars but have created a very good product and a strong presence and used PR to get their name out there. One example is Google, which seems to have come out of nowhere into very common usage. It's a reliable service that has somewhat of a personality behind it; for a Web brand, that's kind of intriguing. You have a very strong, devoted user base that relies on Google almost to the exclusion of a lot of other search engines."

E-Branding is not just the activity of creating a brand on the Internet. It's not just about making e-commerce sites famous and creating brands that end in .com. In spite of the dot-com debacle, the Internet remains a great place to publicize and sell. There are countless opportunities—most of them related to public relations—of which a brand can take advantage on the Web, and they can increase awareness, state the brand identity, and reinforce brand integrity as well as or better than most other forms of Branding communication.

Think of the Internet as a direct means of communication with the public. You can talk to the consumer you most want to reach—and who most wants to hear about your product or service—without any interference or editing from news media, reporters, editors, producers, or networks. You can reach millions of people for the price of one local newspaper ad, and you can do it in the time it takes for you to start to blink.

The Internet also has created a forum for directly interacting with consumers. As Elsie Maio, president of Maio & Co., says, "If you look at how we have run our companies historically, they've been command and control. They've been directed down from the top. That's been changing for years. The one piece that's been missing has been the voice of the consumer, the voice of the customer. The Internet has empowered that voice, and the company that is not receptive and responsive to that on an ongoing basis is going to be out of business, because its competitors will be those things."

A Web site for your brand would have been considered a luxury in 1995. Today, it is an absolute necessity. It is impossible to take seriously a brand that has no presence on the Web at all, but beyond that, it becomes almost inconceivable that any product or service without a Web presence could even become a brand in this day and age. Consumers have come to expect such things, and will look upon a company with no Web site as a minor leaguer, not to be taken seriously. Think of any brands you know, and search for them on the Internet. I'll be very surprised if you don't find all of them.

The Internet provides an unprecedented opportunity for Branding executives to carefully nurture and design a brand identity with every aspect from the color of the type to the wording of the message controlled entirely by those doing the branding.

The personality of the brand can never be as clearly and fully demonstrated as on the brand's Web site, since the brand identity, above all else, is the message being communicated there.

Prior to the Branding craze, businesses often maintained a utilitarian appearance, as though quickly furnished for a transient tenant. Today, style is a huge part of the message, and style simply oozes off a Web page, since everything has to be designed and planned from the ground up. Even newspaper ads don't offer as much freedom of expression; they can be published on a day when the news is especially upsetting and therefore taint the message, or the newspaper could be dropped in a puddle and be rendered unreadable that day while on its way to the consumer's doorstep. There is a lack of control in print and even broadcast advertising.

Not so on the Internet. When a consumer stumbles on your Web site, or seeks it out and finds it, he or she is going to see precisely what you intended to be seen. Your message is in every detail, every background, every carefully chosen color. The sounds the consumer hears will be the sounds you intended, and the images he or she sees will have been painstakingly constructed and placed in the area of the page that you have determined will create maximum impact.

That doesn't mean every Web site has to be the most elaborate and technologically impressive experience ever designed. Very simple sites can still provide the visitor with an interesting experience constructed with the brand's identity in mind. If it's not possible to actually experience the product or service through the Web, it *is* within the realm of possibility to have an experience in connection with that product or service that will evoke pleasant, perhaps exciting, memories and be mentally connected to that brand for the consumer.

A BRANDED WORLD

Consider the Web site for Mercedes-Benz (for Americans, www
.mbusa.com). The home page colors are elegant and cool: blue, silver,
gray, and white. The immediate feeling is one of tremendous luxury.
Every feature on the page is designed to move the visitor toward the purchase of a new Mercedes-Benz. There is no hard sell; it is assumed that if
you have chosen to seek out this site, you are the kind of person who
wants a Mercedes, so all that's necessary is to provide you with the information you need to make that purchase.

Linked pages are in the same vein: There are ways to select the best
Mercedes for you to drive, lists of manufacturer suggested retail prices,
comparisons of models, explanations of options, and a catalog of promotional merchandise. In the summer of 2002, there was also a link to a game
tied in with the Mercedes-Benz product placement in the film *Men in Black
II,* but that was clearly provided by the company that made the film, not
the car company itself, and no Mercedes appeared in the game. There was
no direct effort to publicize the game or gain public relations capital from
it; it was something that would hopefully boost the appeal of Mercedes-
Benz on its Web site and promote the connection to a popular movie at the
same time.

Everything on the site is cool, composed, and presented in an infor-
mational, logical manner. The site isn't about having fun; it's about the
feeling you get driving a prestigious automobile.

Contrast that experience with the feeling you glean from a visit to the
Web site for Saturn (www.saturn.com). Here, the home page's large picture of the product is displaced by an image that downplays the car but
offers a view of the company's successful "Maybe Too Honest" ad campaign, prompting the visitor to recall an amusing moment as well as reinforcing the company's current promotion.

Elsewhere, the links are focused more on Saturn's famous no-haggle
sales philosophy and on economy. Consumers are encouraged to calculate
monthly payments on a new Saturn equipped just the way they want.
They are treated to information on safety, one of the manufacturer's main
emphases. In a separate section there are some games to play.

The emphasis here, while still keeping the sale of vehicles in mind, is
on communicating the brand promise, since it might not be as well known

as that of Mercedes–Benz. The colors are warmer and more plentiful. Each screen comes with text explaining some point of Saturn's philosophy, whereas the Mercedes site offers facts on the performance and purchase options of the company's product. It is assumed that the Mercedes visitor wants a Mercedes, while the Saturn site's premise is that its visitor is shopping for a car, is seeing a number of different manufacturers, and is in need of an explanation as to the company's mission.

Saturn also emphasizes its community aspect, in that owners are often invited to the company's Tennessee headquarters for special events. The sales philosophy of a set price with no haggling is mentioned frequently. New and upcoming models are explained rather than announced. Saturn's commitment to environmental, social, and even labor issues is highlighted.

The two sites have the same goal: to help sell automobiles. But even when their approach appears to be similar, the tone taken is right for the brand in each case. That is essential to a Web site promoting a product or service, and it is the most important thing for any Web site that supports a brand.

THE BRAND SITE

The question, "Does my brand need a Web site?" is no longer valid; the answer is yes. You need a Web site in order to be a brand, let alone to enhance your brand. So a product or service without a Web site right now is like a politician without vocal cords: He or she might have great ideas, but who's going to know about them?

A proper brand Web site contains five essential elements:

1. Consumer information
2. Corporate information
3. Contact information
4. Product/service information
5. Brand information

There are several optional elements beyond these, but without those five content essentials, the site cannot be considered a true brand Web site.

Consumer information refers to the kind of content that consumers alone will seek out. It is not about product (as we will discuss), but is about brand promise and mission, purchasing options, finding a proper outlet to purchase the product or service, pricing (if appropriate), online commerce procedures (if selling the product on the Internet), and so on. It is consumer-based information about everything except the product or service being offered.

Corporate information is data about the company offering the product or service. It will appeal to investors, for the most part, and will contain such things (assuming the company is publicly traded) as the latest annual report, the current stock price updated as often as possible, news about the corporation's activities, press releases regarding the company, names and titles of key individuals in the company, subsidiary companies and their vital information, and other key pieces of data that the corporate investor will find helpful—particularly if that information makes the company look like an attractive investment.

Contact information refers to exactly what it implies: how to contact the company whose brand is being promoted on the Web site. This can be useful to consumers who might want more information about the product or need to speak to brand officials about a problem with the product or service. In the latter case, this information is central to the success of the brand. Every customer must be sent away happy, and if they don't know how to contact you to explain a problem, consumers are sure to be frustrated and will not consider their experience with your brand a positive one. Contact information is also useful to members of the press who might be visiting your Web site with a possible article or broadcast piece in mind. Make sure the name and contact information for the company spokesperson in each area is easy to find. Remember, public relations is all about media placements, and those can't happen unless reporters know how to contact the proper brand official.

Product/service information is what most people consider consumer information. It is, as expected, information about the product or service you're offering to the public—what it is, how it came about, what's new about it, if there are ancillary products, any coupons or special deals you wish to promote to online visitors, and, of course, how and where the consumer can find the product or service to purchase it.

Successful E-Branding

Brand information is not about the product or the company as a whole, but about the brand. It is a statement of the brand's promise to the consumer, a definition of the brand identity, an assurance of brand integrity, and, above all, a communication of the brand in its entirety, not product by product. Coca-Cola's Web site includes pages for Diet Coke, Vanilla Coke, and all the other products offered by the company, but every page and every aspect of the site itself is dedicated to the communication of the Coca-Cola brand as a whole. It is the personality, the identity of the brand that comes through more explicitly than any of the specific product information offered on any page. Coke's intention to be the drink you've always known it to be and always expect it to be is firmly imprinted on every decision made in building and maintaining that Web site. You couldn't possibly come away from a visit to www.coke.com and mistakenly think you had just seen a Web site dedicated to a stuffy financial institution.

In addition to these five essential data elements, some brands might find it helpful (depending on the identity being communicated) to add recreational aspects to the site, or links to sites that have agreed to ally themselves with the brand in question. Celebrity endorsements might be included on the site, with links to the celebrity's official page, for example.

Keep in mind that Saturn's Web site regularly offers games, while the Mercedes-Benz site's game was a cross-promotion with a movie and not a regular feature of the site. That is not a mistake on either company's part; it is a communication of the kind of brand being represented here. Mercedes does not wish to project a frivolous image, as it knows its consumers aren't buying the company's product because it's so much fun. Instead, the kind of quality, dedication to design and style, and the lifestyle being represented on the Mercedes site would cater more to a busy businessperson who probably doesn't have time to play Internet games, and would more likely have an upscale video game console at home to do so if that interest appeals.

Any Web site representing a brand has as its primary mission the communication of the brand identity. That is first and foremost in the mind of the Web site builder, since any information the visitor might obtain at the Web site will be infused with the brand identity in any case, and even a casual Web surfer should be able to recognize the personality of the brand and have a positive reaction to it based on a cursory look. It doesn't matter how strong your data might be, or how powerful your brand is, if the identity of the brand that you've constructed so painstakingly over time is not communicated when a consumer decides to investigate your Web site.

The Ben & Jerry's Web site (www.benjerry.com), for example, opens with an animated minibus decorated with hippie-style colors, while the visitor selects the country in which he or she is located. The Ben & Jerry's home page is equally lighthearted, with informal company history, a "flavor graveyard" where discontinued flavors are listed, and other information, all presented in the traditional Ben & Jerry's irreverent, easygoing manner. Lists of causes the company supports are also very easy to access, and the ice cream maker's commitment to social issues is explained clearly and informally.

What comes through immediately is the personality of the company. Pomposity would be ridiculed off this Web site; every element on display, all the way down to the job openings listed, is presented with humor and a sense of community. The bovine art decoration throughout is meant to reinforce this feeling.

All brand Web sites should have as clear a mission. While it is possible to conduct actual retail business on the Ben & Jerry's site, commerce is not the clearest memory the visitor will have after turning off his or her browser. Rather, the impression will be of color, social commitment, and above all lighthearted fun (what other ice cream company would sell you a "pint lock" to ensure others will keep their hands off your ice cream?) and an enjoyable experience.

JUSTTHEBEST.COM

Any potential Just the Best Web site would have to learn lessons from the competitors' existing sites. Ben & Jerry's site would be a model for fun and lighthearted information dispersal. But Just the Best would have to express its personality in a unique and unmistakable way.

Each product would have its own Web page, with tantalizing pictures of each flavor and close-ups of each novelty. But even as the images appeal to a visitor's taste buds, other aspects of the site—such as links to games and coupons for products create a sense of lighthearted fun.

The color scheme would be in line with the Just the Best logo and corporate colors; the logo with the hand offering a cone would be prominent. The accompanying sounds would start with songbirds and summer breezes and eventually end up with the sound of someone slurping the last ice cream from a cone. The one unmistakable feature would be the ability to find the Just the Best retailer nearest your home, with just a prompt to type in your zip code and one click of the mouse.

There can be no question that Just the Best needs its own Web site to communicate directly with the public and the press, for all the reasons detailed in the next chapter. The question is how best to illustrate and convey through the Web site the brand identity Just the Best has established, and what kind of information should be included and disseminated via the Internet.

Remember, the brand identity is one of lighthearted nostalgia and attention to quality and detail. Given that, the Just the Best Web site should include the brand promise, conveyed through descriptions of each of the products in the line. It should include access to video clips of the brand's (hopefully) popular humorous television ads. It should include downloadable coupons to stimulate new customers to sample the brand and to reinforce the brand loyalty of continuing customers. And it certainly should include the standards of most brand sites: contact information, customer service, press contacts, and links to related sites. Just the Best should also make sure its brand identity is underlined by including a games section for younger consumers and for those who want to take a quick, enjoyable break while surfing the Web.

Each of these sections serves a purpose. Naturally, product information is vital to any consumer Web site, so the original three flavors of Just the Best, available through quart containers in supermarkets, should be included in the information and described in sumptuous detail, encouraging consumers to rush to the freezer or the supermarket for a taste.

Access to the ad clips reminds consumers of the funny moment they enjoyed, and spreads the word on the product and the brand. If consumers weren't amused, they will not, in all likelihood, download the clips, so there is no danger of putting off potential customers. The coupons will serve the same purpose coupons have always served in retail transactions—to stimulate sales and encourage first tries. And the rest of the information, including the games installed on the site, will provide the basic data consumers need to find out more about the brand or solve a problem they are having with the brand. Even the games should relate to ice cream and brand identity—for example, trying to get a cartoon ice cream cone through a difficult intersection to a small child waiting on the other side of the street, or holding on to the ice cream on a cone during a wild hayride.

More than anything else, however, the site should serve public relations purposes. The customer service aspects of the site help by protecting and maintaining the brand promise. In times when the brand is under attack by competitors, or if a crisis has arisen internally, the Web site will be our first line of defense, where we can communicate information unedited and complete.

Colorful, vibrant, and above all fun, the Just the Best Web site should provide an enjoyable experience for consumers who seek it out or come across it while Web surfing. On the Web, the experience is everything, and while we can't convey the flavor of the ice cream across modem lines, we are able to communicate our brand identity. That should clearly be the goal here.

> On the Internet, the experience is everything. Creating a climate that speaks of your brand identity without having to state it directly will contribute mightily to the experience the visitor to your Web site will have. It is the goal to be achieved, at all costs, when designing a Web site for your brand.

BUILDING A BETTER BRAND SITE

Simply communicating identity, however, would be a gross waste of the vast potential an Internet site offers. Public relations can be done in tiny, subtle ways on the Web, starting with the domain name you choose for your site.

Making the Web address you choose fit your brand will direct interested consumers to your site much more quickly and efficiently than a URL that doesn't immediately leap to mind when considering your brand. If you type www.coke.com into your browser, you are whisked instantly to the brand site you want to find. If the Coca-Cola Company had decided instead to make its Web address www.refreshingcola.com, it would have made a crucial error.

Al and Laura Ries, in their book *The 11 Immutable Laws of Internet Branding,* write that in choosing a brand name for a Web site, "The first thing to ask yourself is, what's the generic name for the category? Then that's the one name you don't want to use for your site." For example, www.pets.com was a generic name that eventually failed, while www .amazon.com, which bears no direct link to the product the Web site initially sold (www.books.com was taken) was wildly successful.

Beyond the Web address, the tone of the home page must be reflective of the information you are dispensing and the personality you've chosen for the brand. Links to subsequent pages have to be easy to find and fast, as must the rest of the site. Press rooms and consumer contacts are recommended, since public relations is all about the communication between your brand and both the press and the consuming public.

Press releases you've issued should be available to both press and public. If your company is publicly traded, such information must be available to all investors and the public anyway. Such releases also give visitors to the site a clear image of the brand from the ground up, providing insight into decisions made and reactions to situations that arise from within and outside the company.

While the public might not find the information that you've just appointed a new vice president of investor relations fascinating, potential investors will find the press release of interest. And the fact that there are press and public contact people named in the release (with contact information where applicable) will only help.

Many Web sites include a link marked "contact us" that immediately activates the visitor's e-mail program and sends an e-mail to the brand contact listed. Making it easy for consumers to contact the company is never a bad idea; remember that there can be no such thing as a dissatisfied customer if you're building a brand.

The concept is one that may not register consciously with consumers, but will always create a favorable impression: If the brand is accessible—that is, if it is easy to communicate with the brand—the consumer will have a higher opinion of the brand generally, which is the ultimate goal of any brand Web site.

DAMAGE CONTROL

There are few if any tools as effective as the Internet when your brand is under attack from without. Because the message received from your Web site is unedited and unadulterated, it is the one place you have total control over the information the public receives. If rumors surrounding your brand are circulating (some of which could originate from the Internet), the quickest, most logical place for consumers to look for information is your brand Web site.

From a public relations point of view, it is always a colossal mistake to ignore negative rumors. As I noted with the Michael Jackson situation in the previous chapter, a rumor left unanswered for 24 hours becomes truth—or, at least, that is the way the public will perceive it, which is essentially the same thing. Even if the rumor is true, a swift, clear response (either explanation or apology and offer of retribution) is the strongest defense—a good offense.

Don't hide the message in some hard-to-access subsidiary page. Make sure that if a rumor is being circulated about your brand, you respond to it on your home page, even if the home page houses only a link to the response (particularly if the response is lengthy and will take up too much space on the home page).

For example, the Procter & Gamble site (www.pg.com) devotes an entire section to the unfounded rumors that the company's logo was somehow linked with Satanism. Testimonials from religious leaders and celebrities asking for an end to the rumors are featured, even though the response was made years ago. It is still very easy for any visitor to the Web site to find the company's response to the well-circulated rumor.

While there is little point in calling the public's attention to scandals or rumors that could deteriorate your brand's integrity, acting on such potential disasters on your Web site is absolutely essential. Ignoring a problem merely intensifies the danger; it doesn't make the negative information, right or wrong, go away.

The savvy public relations practitioner will deflect potentially damaging information with reasonable, sober, *true* information. The ludicrous idea that Procter & Gamble was linked with the Devil was an extreme example, but the company handled it well. It addressed the rumor directly, with no attempt to deny that such a rumor existed or to ignore it, hoping the company's refusal to dignify that suggestion with an answer would serve as a denial. If there's something to deny, it must be denied head-on, with substantiating information that proves the rumor or suggestion to be false and unfounded.

Today, the home page for Enron (www.enron.com) is devoted entirely to press release links that address the company's attempt to emerge from bankruptcy protection. While it does address the financial side of Enron's problems directly, for legal and public relations reasons the Web site does not discuss the wrongdoing behind those problems. Instead, a "frequently asked questions" link informs investors and other visitors that: "Despite our intensive efforts in recent weeks to stabilize our trading operations, reduce costs and maximize cash flow—while also pursuing the merger process with Dynegy—Enron's financial condition has deteriorated significantly. After Dynegy abandoned the merger agreement, we decided to file for Chapter 11 reorganization to enable us to preserve and enhance our liquidity, stabilize our operations, and restore relationships with our business partners."

Obviously, the Enron situation is a public relations nightmare, such as I faced with the Michael Jackson situation. But in that case we found that direct communication with the media helps to present the side of the situation that we wanted the public to hear, rather than hiding from the news people, which only makes the subject of the scandal seem more guilty than otherwise.

In Procter & Gamble's situation, the inclusion of testimonials from religious leaders like Jerry Falwell, Donald Wildmon, and the Billy Graham ministry, as well as from trusted celebrities like Sally Jessy Raphael, helped to target the very segment of the consuming public that might have been especially concerned with the subject of the rumors. Religious consumers would find a link to Satanism especially disturbing, so words directly from Christian leaders denouncing the rumors as false and urging their ministries in no uncertain terms to ignore the rumored links were extremely effective. Despite the fact that the rumors, which were potentially damaging to the Procter & Gamble family of brands, surfaced years ago and were given a good deal of media attention, the brands remain very strong, and no further public relations actions were necessary after the initial flurry.

As in the case of Procter & Gamble, continuing to post refutations of rumors on your Web site is a smart public relations move, designed to address those who might be hearing the worrisome information for the first time. It's also wise to keep the successful refutations available to anyone interested enough to seek them out.

BRAND MAINTENANCE

If a brand is strong and healthy and has established its identity firmly in the psyche of the consuming public, its Web site is a first-rate place to continue that process by reinforcing the brand identity and integrity via providing information and affirmation of the brand in the minds of the public. But once that Web site is set up and running, why is it necessary for a successful brand to update its site periodically?

On the Internet, change is constant. A consumer who visits your Web site today might very well come back for updates, for information on new products, or to search for sales or coupons. Today's consumer might be tomorrow's investor. But you have to give that consumer a reason to keep coming back to the Web site, or you'll lose his or her interest. And loss of interest on the Web is death; it is the end of the information flow, and at that point you might as well write that consumer off and try to find another one.

Does that mean the Web site has to have a new home page every week? Of course not. It's impractical to make that massive a change on a regular basis. But changes to the data pages linked to your home page can be made periodically, especially to add information about new products, press releases issued by the brand, new promotions, and the like. There should be something new on the Web site as a whole at least once a month, and large, top-to-bottom overhauls should be made at least once every 18 months.

It's also imperative to have an employee whose duties include reading and responding to every e-mail the site receives.

> Communication between the brand and the consumer is unquestionably important to the brand's success and survival; part of the brand identity must be to make a commitment to the consuming public, and part of that commitment must be to respond to inquiries from loyal consumers.

Expansion and extension are going to have a presence on the Net, too, although they will not be exclusive to Internet public relations. Publicity releases and events will be devised and scheduled for expansion and extension announcements, and the Web site will be the place for consumers to come for more information, special promotions, discounts, and games or contests tied to the brand expansion or extension.

Needless to say, any advertising, letterheads, or brand announcements made on paper must include the Web address for the brand. Any billboards that feature the brand name should include it as well. Radio ads should include the Web address as part of the copy. The Web address should be repeated as often as possible in communication with the public; it should become as much a part of the brand as the name of the product itself.

Online companies like Amazon.com already have their Web addresses in the brand name. Companies doing the bulk of their business on the Internet have a certain advantage in terms of their Web sites, but other products and services can use the Web to great effect. Retailers such as The Gap, Toys "R" Us, and 1-800-FLOWERS all have very strong Web presences that might eventually dwarf or displace their bricks-and-mortar stores.

Businesses that were originally telephone-based, such as Moviefone, 1-800-FLOWERS, and Federal Express, have all significantly increased their Web presence and shifted a good portion of their business to their e-commerce sites. Even the United States Postal Service now sells stamps on the Web. Barnes & Noble and Borders Books and Music have followed

A BRANDED WORLD

Amazon.com to the Net and have found success there while maintaining their presence in bricks–and–mortar stores. Catalog companies like L.L. Bean, Lands' End, and Harry and David have all made the Internet a significant segment of their retail business. All those businesses are seeing the percentage of their sales on the Net grow, even as smaller start-up dot-com businesses have failed over the past few years.

> The Internet and Branding will continue to impact each other significantly. The power of Branding on the Web is that it is worldwide and instantaneous. It expands any business to the entire planet and makes it possible to expand a business from the smallest possible beginnings to the largest of enterprises. Without Branding, however, the Internet is simply a commerce tool, and many dot-com businesses have already discovered that sites on the Web that have not been intelligently branded will fail.

E-Branding should be done with both disciplines—Branding and Internet design—in mind. All decisions made in designing the brand must have the Internet in mind, and every step of the Web site development must be made in line with the brand's identity and integrity as top priorities.

CHAPTER THIRTEEN

MAINTAINING THE WHOLE PACKAGE

"The graphic is important to the image of the company. Simplicity makes a good Branding graphic, and most of all conveying the message of the product. When I'm deciding a logo, I have to know from the company who they're gearing it for, which demographic."

—RUBY MAZUR, DESIGNER OF ROLLING STONES'
"LIPS AND TONGUE" LOGO

It has been said that the most recognizable sight on this planet is so ubiquitous that it transcends class, geography, and interest: People from every continent, virtually every country, and every walk of life from tribesman to President of the United States can identify it without hesitation. Children under the age of two know it, as do people over 100 years old. It requires no explanation, can be found almost anywhere, and is immediately associated with positive feelings, experiences, and possibilities by the vast majority of those who see it.

The most recognizable sight on this planet is a pair of Mickey Mouse ears.

A symbol of brand identity, the round black ears of an animated character engender more good feelings, more approval, and more giddy anticipation than the sight of a beloved world leader, a food that keeps us alive, or the most famous human entertainer on the planet. Tom Cruise may not be able to go outside without being recognized in Los Angeles, but the sight of his ears in Botswana would not be cause for celebration. George W. Bush has very high approval ratings among American voters, but his popularity is certainly not as strong in other areas of the world.

A BRANDED WORLD

Among corporate symbols, only the distinctive shape of the Coca-Cola bottle even approaches the Disney symbol in recognition potential. And the power of the Mickey ears is not measurable in conventional terms. It is a phenomenon that has had no rival.

Think about it: When you see those ears, you know exactly what they mean. No words are necessary; no message need be communicated. You can associate that symbol with experiences you have had before and anticipate experiences you are about to have. And while it is recognizable, familiar, and friendly, the Mickey symbol is not boring and predictable: It could mean an amazing thrill ride in a theme park, a new animated cartoon, a live-action film, a television special, or the purchase of a new piece of apparel. It promises quality, safety, and a family experience, and it almost never fails to deliver on all those counts. How many times were *Disney* or *Mickey Mouse* among the first words a child could recognize in print? How many babies pointed at a screen in delight and yelled "Mickey!" among their first words? Now, that's a packaging miracle.

It is a mistake to underestimate the importance of packaging for a brand. Consider that Ruby Mazur, who created the "lips and tongue" logo for the Rolling Stones, was paid $10,000 for his work. This was a good deal of money in 1971, but considering that the logo has made the Stones an estimated $200 million, it's the bargain of the century.

By *packaging,* we don't just mean the box, bag, or container in which a product is sold; a package is the presentation of the product or service that represents the brand. It includes the brand logo, the name of the brand, the type of lettering on the box, the material from which the package is made, and any visual image that represents the brand in the consumer's mind.

Packaging is the art of Branding in the most literal sense; it is the visual representation of the brand. As such, it must adhere to all the laws of Branding, like any other element of the process. Above all, the packaging must be consistent with the brand identity. The packaging also evolves over time as the brand is expanded or extended, as I discuss later in this chapter.

Public relations influences every aspect of Branding, including packaging. Public perception of the brand will certainly be affected by the visual image packaging offers, so the public relations professional working on the brand will have to determine whether the packaging communicates the brand identity so carefully developed. Some packaging and corporate images become so tightly associated with the brand that the public feels a sense of proprietorship over them, and when it's necessary to change these images, public relations gets involved in making the transition palatable and understandable for the public.

In 1975, NBC decided to retire its peacock logo, which had signaled the beginning of color broadcasts since 1957, and replace it with a more modern symbol. The broadcast giant spent well-publicized millions on its new emblem, a sleek, impersonal N in red and blue, and spent more well-publicized millions hiring Oscar-winning film composer John Williams (*Jaws, Raiders of the Lost Ark, Star Wars*) to write a five-second theme for *NBC Nightly News*.

What the company didn't anticipate was the loyalty the public felt for the peacock, and by 1979 the colorful bird was back, coupled with the company's name in a new logo designed by the New York-based firm Chermayeff & Geismar. The public had spoken, and it felt that the new, modern logo did not represent the corporate brand identity it wanted NBC to have. The more whimsical, colorful peacock was a fixture, and remains so (in clear form, in the lower right corner of the TV screen on every NBC program) to this day.

If a company like MTV, known for its lighthearted approach to business, had a logo that resembled that of Merrill Lynch, a company known for anything but a lighthearted approach to business, it would not resonate with the public MTV does its best to attract. The brand identity would be poorly represented, the public would be confused or repelled, and in all likelihood the brand would fail.

Consistency is the lifeblood of Branding; without it, a brand could hardly be considered a success. McDonald's reigned supreme among brands for so many years because the experience a consumer had at any of the 20,000 McDonald's outlets worldwide was consistent. When the public began to perceive that the consistency it was accustomed to was no longer a given, the brand began to lose its credibility with the public, and the stock price and earnings projections began to fall.

A logo must convey the brand's identity consistently and not try to redefine it. A logo is, after all, merely a symbol of the company and not the brand itself. Its job is to remind the consumer of the brand identity in a positive way.

In his book *Emotional Branding,* Marc Gobe, president, CEO, and creative director of d/g* Worldwide, one of the world's top 10 image creation firms, writes that "powerful logo identities . . . make advertising and public relations programs more effective by becoming a visual shorthand for the meanings attached to them and thereby influencing consumers to be receptive to a company's message." Consider that every computer hardware or software ad that mentions that its product includes or is compatible with an Intel Pentium processor must include the Pentium logo and signature four-note jingle, to remind consumers that something they have probably never seen or touched is doing a tremendous job for them every time they sit down at their PC. It is Tiffany wrapping at its best— the hardware or software brand being advertised benefits from the inclusion of Pentium's logo, and Pentium reinforces its name and function with the public without advertising itself.

PACKAGING JUST THE BEST

Just the Best's logo and packaging were in place at the brand's inception, and perhaps now is the best time to update them just a little. The public should not be allowed to consider these integral parts of the brand identity too familiar or tired before the brand has a chance to enmesh itself into the overall consumer consciousness.

On the other hand, change for the sake of change is not always a good idea. If the logo, for example (an adult hand giving an ice cream cone to a smaller, younger hand), has only been visible to the consumer for a few years, perhaps it's not yet time to worry about it becoming so familiar that it fades into the background and is no longer seen. The Coca-Cola logo has seen some renovations since its introduction, to be sure, but the original lettering in the red circle is still prominent and visible all over the world. No radical change has been necessary.

Just the Best's packaging, however, might be ripe for some upgrading. After all, the original quart containers were simple and understated, but did

Maintaining the Whole Package

not allow for the addition, later in the brand's life cycle, of novelty items that would be packaged in a box, not in round containers.

Just the Best's original quart packages prominently displayed the logo with a wood grain pattern around it, giving the impression of the sign hanging outside an old-fashioned ice cream parlor. The hands-and-cone logo was in color in the center of the wood grain sign and was large enough to be seen through a supermarket freezer door, even with some condensation on the outside. The top of the package held a smaller version of the same logo, with a cellophane window showing some of the product, and the flavor name (chocolate, vanilla, chocolate chip, or strawberry) printed underneath the cellophane, again easily visible. A band around the top of the container was also color-coded to convey the flavor contents: brown for chocolate, white for vanilla, white with brown spots for chocolate chip, and pink for strawberry.

With the introduction of the novelty bars, however, an overhaul of the packaging might be appropriate. For one thing, cellophane is a very difficult material to incorporate properly into packaging, especially of a liquid product. It tends to tear or wrinkle with shipping, and the product is not shown off to its best effect. Besides, quart containers in supermarket freezers are stacked one on top of another or placed on shelves between other brands, meaning that the purpose of the cellophane window—to show off the product—might not be achieved much of the time. In addition, cellophane will not work on a box, and the novelties will be shipped in cardboard box packaging.

So the cellophane should go. This frees up space on the top of the quart container and means the packaging can be consistent throughout the brand's product lines. The logo, however, will remain unchanged.

The new packaging will feature more color, with the entire quart containers designed in the color that emphasizes their flavors. The logo will be larger on the top, as will the type all around. The novelty boxes should feature the logo, with a design running across the top and bottom of each panel featuring a picture of an ice cream sandwich, pop, or cone, depending on the variety packaged inside. This redesign will maintain continuity with the old packaging while emphasizing the elements that communicate the brand identity and getting rid of distractions.

The public relations campaign for the new packaging should be aggressive. A news conference describing the changes will be held, and consumers should be treated to views of the new packages on television, in publications, and in advertising at the same time the new packaging hits supermarket shelves. The success of the company to date should be stressed in all releases, leading to a statement that the consumers' love affair with the brand prompted the changes in packages to make them more visible and easy to locate in supermarket freezers.

THE AMAZING CHANGING LOGO

One of the most distinctive logos to emerge during the 1980s was the logo of the company some think epitomized that decade: MTV. Distinctive and immediately recognizable, the symbol for Music Television was almost impossible to avoid during the eighties and nineties. It symbolized an attitude and a brand image that was absolutely unmistakable and immediately communicated. There could be no mistake about what the brand MTV stood for.

There's only one problem: There is no MTV logo. There never was. Or, to be more precise, there has never been one official design for an MTV emblem. The shape of the MTV logo (the huge outlined M with the small TV in the lower right corner) remains the same day to day, but its design, color, and even print font can change from moment to moment. In fact, the distinctive thing about the MTV logo is that it is always different. Particularly in its early years, the channel delighted in coming up with new versions of its logo, sometimes going so far as to show how a certain version had been constructed.

Doesn't that fly in the face of everything that Branding demands? Doesn't it completely dispense with consistency, making it difficult if not impossible to identify with the logo and therefore the brand? How could so revolutionary a concern as MTV establish its identity and build an audience with a logo that never stood still long enough to look the same?

It was exactly that inconsistency that defined MTV's brand identity in its early days. While the shape of the logo remained the same throughout, its look was never the same twice, and that communicated to the potential audience (teenagers and young adults) that there was one thing you could predict about MTV: It would never be predictable.

The other thing MTV's amazing changing logo did was define the attitude and the brand identity that MTV would offer its viewers. This was not your father's television network; it was something that would sneer at conventions and traditions. It would revel in the irreverence of its young viewership and satirize every aspect of network television, from the CBS eye logo to the newsbreaks between network shows. After establishing its logo, MTV even satirized itself, for example, in promotional spots that had laid-back TV painter Bob Ross painting an MTV logo on a canvas with "happy little trees."

In short, the MTV logo was perfectly consistent with the MTV brand identity because it wasn't ever the same thing twice. Made of clay, painted in patriotic stars and stripes, spray-painted on the side of a brick wall (and dripping), the logo was and is a clear, distinct statement of the brand identity. Like the MTV brand, it proves that it isn't necessary to follow the rules to succeed; it is only necessary to be true to your brand. And that has never been a problem for MTV.

LOGO AS BRAND STATEMENT: TARGET STORES

By making its logo a central part of its brand statement, Target Stores has managed to incorporate its symbol into its advertising, public relations, and marketing plans, and has given the circular red-and-white target symbol the same function as the Nike swoosh: It is a stand-in for the brand name in print.

This was accomplished chiefly in print and television advertising spots, where the Target symbol was used in models' clothing, set design, props, and straight graphics, constantly repeated until it was the symbol, rather than the word *Target* the consumer would remember from the ad. In some of the ads, the symbol was substituted entirely for the word, reinforcing in the consumer's mind the logo as a stand-in for the brand name.

The same thing has been done, over years, by Absolut vodka. By featuring its distinctive bottle in print ads (the only kind allowed for alcoholic beverages other than wine and beer), Absolut has made the product itself a substitute for its name. A consumer need not think of the name of the brand when shopping at the liquor store; the bottle itself, recognizable from the witty Absolut ads, will suffice.

Target's strategy is simpler: It doesn't require the mental step that Absolut's does. In that case, the consumer has to make the connection of bottle to logo to name brand. For Target, the connection is simpler: logo to name brand, period. From a public relations stance, it is important to establish the logo as an explanation and representation of the brand identity. Target's logo is colorful and distinctive, and while it doesn't convey the brand's promise the way the MTV logo does, Target's symbol will remind a consumer of the brand name and the fast-moving, upbeat advertising campaign that defines it.

The more a company's packaging—its visual imagery—is established in the consumer's mind, the easier it is to remind the consumer of the brand's personality. A strong, communicative logo eliminates obstacles in the consumer's mind and streamlines the process, simplifying the way a consumer thinks of the brand. A symbol like the Nike swoosh, which has no explicit meaning, can be an immediate reminder of both the brand name and the brand experience once it is established with advertising and public relations tools.

Nike's brilliant symbol, which surely caused some confusion when it was introduced, has become so well defined through advertising (since it is never directly explained by the company, but allowed to speak for itself) that every consumer believes he or she knows exactly what the symbol means: Just Do It. Just do what? Whatever it is you do in your Nikes: The publicity and advertising campaigns showcase individual sports, sometimes highlighting certain items in the Nike line and sometimes not. But the tag line remains, and with the slogan comes the swoosh. The two are so clearly linked in the imagery that there is no confusion: One means the other.

The Target logo isn't quite that well established, but it has been underlined with the advertising the brand produces, and it now symbolizes the speed and energy that Target emphasizes in its brand identity. It may not be the strongest tool in the Target arsenal, but it is certainly a very successful one. A logo won't bring people into the stores, but when it is joined in the consumer's mind with the positive attributes the stores emphasize, a logo can make a difference.

COLOR: BIG BLUE, BIG RAINBOW, AND THE WHITE ALBUM

There is no visual element of packaging more immediately striking—and therefore more important—than color. When advertising executives and others talk about something being "eye-catching," they are usually making reference to the color used in the packaging. Other visual elements contribute to the impact the packaging will have, but color is the first thing that registers in the consumer's mind, and first impressions are the most imperative ones in Branding.

Think about the IBM logo. That visual impact is so striking that the company it represents is often referred to as "Big Blue." The *big* part is a reference to IBM's enormous success in its marketplace, while *blue* refers strictly to design elements, chiefly the corporate logo.

Does that mean anyone could take the same shade of blue, use it in their company logo, and suddenly be a huge global conglomerate? Of course it doesn't. If the typeface, the design, and all the elements put together by IBM's art designers did not have the same type of striking quality, the color would make little difference. But because everything does work, the distinctive blue of the IBM logo gets its chance to stand out and symbolize the stable, dependable technology that is IBM.

The Apple Computer logo, on the other hand, is made up of horizontal stripes of rainbow colors. This example is just as striking as that of its competitor, but nobody refers to Apple as "Big Rainbow." The colors of Apple's logo, while they do attract the eye, are less important a design element than the color of IBM's emblem. In fact, Apple doesn't always use the rainbow colors, instead using the logo's immediately recognizable shape to symbolize the company in many print and television ads and on packaging.

Target Stores' use of red and white certainly helps distinguish its logo, and other corporate symbols, like Coca-Cola's red ball, *USA Today*'s blue box, and BMW's blue-and-white logo, all attract the eye and create a memorable visual impression. NBC's peacock logo is certainly another example of color combinations used to command attention and create a definable brand identity.

The Beatles, by contrast, decided in 1968 to package their latest and most ambitious recording in a package with absolutely no design elements at all, other than raised letters announcing the band's name. The two-album set, officially entitled *The Beatles,* was forever known as The White Album.

That packaging move, made by a brand that already had no peer in 1968, was an amazing example of the power of the unexpected. By draining the packaging of all color and making it the whitest white possible, Capitol Records and the Beatles managed to create something that would certainly stand out in a crowded record store (this was when records were 12-inch vinyl discs packaged in large, flat cardboard sleeves) and on store shelves. With the busy, colorful psychedelic packaging that was saturating the marketplace in the late sixties, the idea of a perfectly plain white cover was revolutionary and made exactly the impact its creators intended. The packaging, more than any of the music on the vinyl inside, is remembered to this day as a magnificent feat of Branding.

Color is a very important element of packaging as it relates to Branding. Besides drawing the eye to the product or the logo, color is another means of defining the brand identity. Would IBM convey the same message with a hot pink rendering of its name? Probably not. Would Apple Computer or Ben & Jerry's command the same kind of consumer loyalty with plain gray renderings of corporate logos? It seems unlikely.

Blue, gray, green, and brown are considered "cool" colors, akin to a silvery, metallic feel. They communicate confidence, competence, and stability. Red, yellow, orange, pink, and other "hot" colors are used in packaging to convey a feeling of unpredictability, strong emotion, friendliness, and warmth. Deciding on the proper color is a job for the design consultant and marketing executives. Public relations gets involved in introducing packaging elements or changing them, and at that point the logo or packaging should be well considered and aimed specifically at expressing the brand identity in no words or less.

Just the Best, for example, would use the wood tones of its sign with a blue sky, a yellow sun, and the richest chocolate brown for its ice cream.

The design would be palpable, almost three-dimensional, so that the consumer would feel the possibility of reaching out and touching the sign logo (made to look like an old-time ice cream parlor sign). The effect would be that of clear, bright days with rich ice cream as the treat at the end.

TYPEFACE: THE FONT, AND NOTHING BUT THE FONT

Typography—or the choice of the typeface used in print—is a science of repetition. If we had not seen numerous examples of a typeface like Edwardian Script ITC used for formal and elegant names, would we associate it with such feelings? Would Impact have the same, er, impact?

Conditioned responses are natural when we are given the same set of circumstances in repeated situations. When we see a typeface that has traditionally signaled a whimsical approach, we naturally expect that intention again. To use it in a staid, serious context would either be revolutionary and bold or simply unwise.

"The way letters conveying a message are designed is an important visual element of Branding that can utilize powerful emotional connotations," writes Marc Gobe in *Emotional Branding*. "It is a kind of science that can be used for a real strategic advantage, and it is unfortunate that it is not always given the attention it deserves."

The choice of a typeface to communicate to the public, then, is important. While it doesn't have the same immediate impact of a bold or unexpected use of color, typeface can just as effectively convey a brand identity to the consumer. Formality versus informality, stability versus unpredictability, warmth versus serious intentions—all these things can be expressed through the choice of a typeface.

Think of the logos you remember most vividly, the ones you have no trouble conjuring up in your mind's eye. What do you feel when you think of one of those images? What feelings do you get from it and why? Certainly the font used will make a difference in that message and the way you receive it.

All the examples used in this chapter—IBM, Apple, Target, and the rest—have distinctive typefaces they use to communicate a personality to the viewer. By the same token, the somewhat pompous, overly grand image of 20th Century Fox's logo, framed by klieg lights and a huge fanfare, would not be as effective with a whimsical typeface like Curlz or Hobo representing the company. Certainly, the message being sent would be different.

THE WHOLE PACKAGE

The material of packaging—the physical makeup of the package and promotional materials themselves—can also create a positive or negative impression. These, too, will be conditioned responses. Popcorn at the movie theatre can't come in a plastic bag; we won't tolerate it. The cellophane package we get at the supermarket can contain popcorn, but not at the movies.

At the same time, it is possible to combine elements that might seem contradictory and communicate two aspects of the brand identity at the same time. Bold colors with conservative typefaces, or a combination of typefaces, each conveying a part of the brand message, can be used. For example, Marc Gobe notes the use of several typefaces in Coca-Cola's sponsorship of the Olympics, with the traditional brand logo in its conservative script typeface coupled with more unusual, "outrageous" fonts that communicated the sense of urgency and excitement the company hoped the Olympics would bring to its brand.

It may sometimes seem odd when public relations professionals schedule and host news conferences to introduce a new logo or a change in an existing brand packaging component. For example, when FedEx decided to change its logo color for ground deliveries from the traditional blue and red to blue and green, press conferences were organized, the public was informed, and new trucks were painted with the altered logo.

This accomplished a number of benefits for the brand. First of all, it was covered in some news media, which meant that the name FedEx was mentioned on the evening news and in publications in a positive context. That is the basic element of publicity: coverage from third parties deemed credible.

Maintaining the Whole Package

Second, it informed the public that FedEx had a ground delivery service that rivaled that of the United States Postal Service. Many consumers were familiar with the overnight delivery FedEx so successfully offers, but weren't aware that a lower-cost, somewhat less immediate, option was available from the company. That piece of information alone, delivered to millions of consumers nationwide, would have meant the campaign had accomplished what it set out to do.

But the red-to-green announcement also had a simple nuts-and-bolts benefit to it, which was that consumers now knew what that green half of the FedEx logo on a truck meant. They had to be informed that the familiar, trusted company they'd been relying upon for overnight deliveries for many years wasn't changing—and if a consumer saw a truck with the green, rather than the red, logo, he or she might think something at FedEx had changed. The press coverage ahead of the move itself was insurance against such misconceptions, and reassurance for the consumer that everything at the most reliable delivery service was the same as it ever had been.

It is an easy mistake to assume that packaging is all about the surface: What goes outside the product itself, the nameplate a corporation shows the public, is an expression of image and flash, not identity. But the fact is that surface can express more inward motivations and qualities.

Think of the packaging as the face a brand shows to the public. In the course of your normal day, your face will convey much about your thinking, your feelings, and your character. They say the eyes are the windows of the soul, and in that way, a corporate logo or packaging elements can be the windows to the soul of the brand. As such, they must be consistent with the brand promise, message, and identity. Packaging materials, design elements (either designed in-house or by a contracted outside design firm), and all visual representations of the brand that the public gets to see must be conceived with the brand identity in mind, not twisted to conform to the brand identity. If the two are incompatible, the brand identity and its expression of brand integrity must remain intact and unquestioned. The visual element that doesn't conform must go.

CHAPTER FOURTEEN

BRAND LOYALTY AND CUSTOMER SATISFACTION

"A brand is not a tangible item; it's a space in an individual's mind. A brand does not mean the same thing to everybody. Different individuals are going to have different meanings for a brand. Some people can love BMW and others will hate it. Some think it's an unnecessary expense, and some people think it's a value added that's worth the money. A brand is space in someone's mind, and it means different things to different people."

—JOHN O'BRIEN, FORMER VICE PRESIDENT OF
MARKETING FOR SHERWIN-WILLIAMS

"A brand," says Sumner Redstone, chairman and CEO of Viacom, "is a special relationship that you develop with a particular audience, where they trust what you're doing, and you trust them."

A successful brand is not simply a product that has been launched to great press, strong sales, and customer satisfaction, although all those things are certainly desirable. Strong, enduring brands are built with the concept of brand loyalty in mind—the idea that consumers will develop a bond with the brand that will strengthen over time and will make changing to another brand feel like a betrayal of trust. If you know someone who will only drive a Honda, and no other car, you understand what brand loyalty is. If you never miss a particular television program—if you stay home on a Saturday night to see it or make sure your VCR is set well in advance when you will be out—then you know about brand loyalty.

BRAND LOYALTY

Brand loyalty is the look you get from a Coca-Cola drinker when you hand him or her a can of Pepsi. It is the snide remarks made in the press when Tom Cruise drops out of an upcoming film and is replaced with Steve Buscemi. Steve Buscemi is a fine actor, and Pepsi is a fine soft drink, but people who expect Tom Cruise or a Coke will certainly be confused by the substitution. Brand loyalty is a lifelong commitment to a political party or a sports franchise. It is a buying habit that wouldn't be broken even if the product in question was replaced by a new technology that was proven better by every scientist on the planet. It was the picket lines organized when New Coke replaced the original formula on supermarket shelves, despite studies showing that most people preferred the taste of the usurper.

In other words, brand loyalty is what every Branding executive in the world prays his or her brand will achieve. It is the Holy Grail of Branding, because with strong brand loyalty comes the one thing that is most elusive in today's business climate: stability. The greatest branders of our time have shown extraordinary sagacity in connecting with human nature.

While advertising has a hand in brand loyalty development, the two components that make the biggest impact in brand loyalty are product development and public relations. If the product or service doesn't measure up to the public's expectations, the best ads and publicity in the world won't create brand loyalty. But if the product being delivered is sound, advertising can only introduce it to the public. Public relations will build upon that introduction to create a solid brand that the consuming public will embrace.

Public relations is more responsible than any other element for the consumer's overall impression of a brand. It is the public relations campaign, viewed through the third-party news media, that adds credibility and weight to the brand's message, and it is through those avenues that the public deepens its knowledge of the brand identity. Think of advertising as setting up a blind date, while public relations is akin to forging a deep, lasting relationship.

195

A BRANDED WORLD

On December 31, 1993, Barbra Streisand ended a 26-year hiatus in her concert career with a widely publicized appearance (the first of two) at the MGM Grand Hotel in Las Vegas. I did some of the public relations work for that appearance, an event that was extraordinary for its anticipation as well as for the performance itself.

In this case, the Barbra Streisand brand was incredibly well established, and the loyalty to that brand was unprecedented. Streisand had, in a career that spanned 30 years, delivered for her fans so many times that there was no question of their loyalty to her brand. The fact that this would be her first full-blown concert appearance in so long brought people from around the world to the MGM Grand that night, strictly on the concept of brand loyalty. What was most amazing about the Branding, however, was the way Streisand's brand loyalty could be expanded and borrowed upon to create new brands in the course of one evening.

The locale of the concert had not been chosen randomly. MGM was anxious to put its new centerpiece hotel on the map, and coaxing the world's most famously elusive performer out of seclusion was conceived as a major coup to draw attention to the venue. If the MGM Grand had Streisand, it could be surmised, it must certainly be *the* place to see amazing entertainment in Las Vegas. So the corporation made a fantastically attractive offer to the artist, and the Streisand brand was lent to the MGM Grand for a night, helping to create a new brand for the hotel in the process.

Through the publicity process, however, we managed also to create a third separate brand that evening. "Barbara Streisand—The Concert" became an entity with a life of its own, and the merchandising of T-shirts, souvenir programs, silk jackets, souvenirs, and related merchandise brought in millions. It wasn't a brand that could develop strong loyalty, since it would last for only one night, but it was an ancillary brand that was extremely successful and that helped to promote and deepen the loyalty for the core brand—the performer herself.

All these things were possible because Barbra had carefully developed loyalty in her brand for decades. While she may have made some choices that didn't resonate at the box office, she has never betrayed the trust of the

196

consuming public (her fans) by delivering anything but her strongest effort and the best performance she could. She doesn't compromise, she doesn't relax, and she never, ever coasts. And the public knows that, so the brand development of Barbra Streisand started sound and remains so.

Public relations does the rest. We controlled the flow of information to the media very carefully for that concert. Only one 60-second clip could be filmed for news reports; there was no access to rehearsals or backstage passes for press. Many celebrities were invited (again, reinforcing the MGM Grand's own brand as well as Streisand's, and the brand we were creating for the event). I was never as popular in my life as when others perceived that I had access to Streisand tickets for the New Year's Eve concert.

The information that came out about the concert, then, was the information we released, and that made the event as special as it could possibly be. All three brands were enhanced, and the evening was a resounding success all around. Brand loyalty was maintained for the performer, established for the hotel, and exploited to the utmost degree for the event.

PR AND BRAND LOYALTY

There are plenty of brands that have been established with the public and then have failed to develop loyalty. Some were very successful in their initial incarnations—pets.com, for example, built itself into a name brand with its sock puppet advertisement campaign. But with maturity came no loyalty; consumers continued to buy pet supplies in stores like Petco and PetSmart or at local shops. The brand had failed to establish itself through public relations, and advertising (and, as it turned out, funding) wasn't enough. pets.com, despite its high profile, went out of business along with many other Internet concerns in the late 1990s.

In their book *Creating Brand Loyalty,* Richard D. Czerniawski and Michael W. Maloney write about the importance of a "brand character"— for our purposes, a brand identity. They cite Nike's advertising campaigns, but also the importance of public relations moves like alliances with star athletes.

"Perhaps one of the most successful trademarks to be built on brand character is Nike," they write. "Nike epitomizes the positive values of sports—marketing its products by lauding the exploits and personalities of alpha athletes such as . . . Michael Jordan. Who doesn't want to be like Mike? He's not just a winner but a hero. . . . The brand character is one with which every sports-minded individual would like to affiliate, regardless if you are a fan of the Seattle Supersonics or the Chicago Bulls, or a youth from America or Lebanon. Nike has successfully established an enduring brand character to differentiate its products from the competition."

Brand loyalty is built through a series of circumstances, such as the longevity and reliability of the product, but even more through the satisfactory execution of the consumer's experience. It is also developed through smart public relations strategies conceived and executed with the goal of brand loyalty never out of sight.

Creating a solid brand is your best opportunity to deny the fickle odds of the market, to make your enterprise more or less impervious to quarterly business cycles. Making sure your brand's winning personality is presented to the public is the key to brand loyalty once you have established that brand. And that is done through public relations.

Public relations is the art of drawing attention to the positive. A successful PR campaign should be expected to discover something positive about the brand, report on it to the media, and encourage the media to report the news it has received accurately. That seems simple enough, but the process is never that easy, and in fact is often fraught with difficult twists and turns and subject to disaster at various junctures.

With the Barbra Streisand concert, our strategy was to limit press access to the event but not to withhold information. We knew we were operating from a position of strength—the media already wanted to know about the event, and every detail could make news—so we used that to our advantage and doled out pieces of information at regular intervals to keep the event in the news. On a certain day, we would disclose the length of the concert; the next, we'd divulge some of the guest list, as celebrities responded to invitations. There would always be a nugget of news for the press to report every day. We didn't choose to announce ourselves that way, however. Choice of words is a very important factor in brand identity, and hence brand loyalty.

Brand Loyalty and Customer Satisfaction

Obviously, the choice of words in any message to the public—especially one that can reflect upon the brand—is critical. We did not issue a press release from the Barbra Streisand camp saying, "Press access will be severely limited." Instead, we emphasized the information that *was* being released.

Positive words will yield a positive message. We avoided words like *familiar* or *comeback* in our Streisand releases, instead concentrating on *excitement, once-in-a-lifetime, event,* and *long-anticipated.* There wasn't much of a negative story to tell in that case, but we still did our best to accentuate the positive.

The message itself, however, is positive whenever there is no crisis to overcome. The news releases public relations will send to media outlets highlight a positive, newsworthy aspect of the brand—perhaps an event being planned or a charitable contribution made by the brand—and report it accurately. Naturally, the language will all be upbeat, but the item itself must be true and worth the reporter's time, or it will not be reported and the effort will be wasted.

Finding such an item shouldn't be difficult, assuming the product or service that is the core brand is sound. After seven decades, Disney still manages to find something new to talk about in the press regularly. In fact, the 100th anniversary of Walt Disney's birth became a yearlong celebration (and a yearlong source of feature items) for the company's theme parks.

Use the facts about the brand to generate publicity. Explain brand extensions and expansions. Introduce changes to your Web site. Let the press have access to market research that shows your brand gaining market share or becoming the most requested product in your category. Mention an affiliation with a celebrity spokesperson or a charitable organization. If your business does good works, let them be known. You're not only bolstering awareness of your brand; you're also heightening publicity for the charitable organization, the cause you support.

When Mercedes-Benz affiliated itself with the movie *Men In Black II,* the company did more than supply a black car to the filmmakers, and the www.mbusa.com Web site was not the only place Mercedes mentioned its alliance. Press releases were sent to the media and clips of the movie were supplied to television programs, and a glimpse of the Mercedes in the film was sure to be included. Both brands benefited from the publicity generated from either company's public relations corps. That means each brand benefited from the brand loyalty already established by its temporary partner.

By the same token, contests, events, and promotions generated by brands like AT&T, the Gap, Coca-Cola, and Nike can all be tied to other brands, and the brand loyalty already enjoyed by the partner brands will rub off on the brand now allying itself. The Tiffany Theory weighs in here, as the affiliation with another successful brand can transfer some of that brand's loyalty to another company. And when the publicity is generated through a third-party media outlet, the brand loyalty commanded by *Good Morning, America* or the *Wall Street Journal* can be associated with the brand being reported on.

When a brand is extended through merger or acquisition, the brand loyalty—good or bad—enjoyed by both the parent company and the new brand being absorbed will affect the other. When Disney bought ABC, it not only acquired one of the largest broadcasting networks in the world, it also bought the brand loyalty of programs like *NYPD Blue* and *The Drew Carey Show*. There were millions of people devoted to those programs who now were—whether they realized it or not—devoted to products of the Walt Disney Company, which now owned ABC.

Public relations devotes itself to building brand loyalty in any endeavor, since the dissemination of positive information will always have some effect on the consumer loyalty to a brand. When more difficult information surfaces, public relations strives to minimize the damage done to brand loyalty. Classic Coke managed to repay consumers for their loyalty to the brand. The O. J. Simpson brand did not do as well.

As I've noted in previous chapters, the difference between public relations, which serves as the conduit of information between the brand and the public, and publicity, which exists only to promote the name and identity of the brand with the public, is not always easy to see. But in cases of brand loyalty, the difference is simple: Publicity will not engender brand loyalty, and public relations can.

Brand Loyalty and Customer Satisfaction

The public might sample something because it has heard the name, but the overall impression of that brand, and the chance that it will become something to which the consumer can remain loyal, is very much a function of public relations.

Keeping consumers engaged in the brand is paramount to continued success. For Just the Best, brand loyalty over the coming years will be more important than the addition of new consumers, because ice cream is the kind of product that can become a family tradition. Once our brand is established in a child's mind, that child can grow and continue the tradition as he or she starts a family.

Naturally, the quality of the product is going to be central to the establishment and maintenance of brand loyalty. But public relations will also play a large part. The message that the brand is continuing to deliver on its promise, and is in fact expanding that promise, is crucial to brand loyalty. But it must not be communicated as directly as that; a press release reading that "Just the Best is continuing to deliver on its brand promise" would not only sound silly, it would be a serious embarrassment for the brand rather than an asset to marketing.

Instead, publicity about the expansion of the brand and its packaging are a start. But stories from within the company about employees doing charity work or the company donating ice cream to an area whose children have been badly hit by a natural disaster (also mentioning a donation of money the company is making) should continue to deliver the message that Just the Best is a brand that connects to its consumers in an emotional, real way. Once a year, on the anniversary of the Election Day promotion that launched the brand, Just the Best can hold a National Ice Cream Social, in which tables are set up in various supermarkets that carry the product and company employees in vintage ice cream fountain uniforms offer samples to customers who wish to sit down and relax for a moment during a shopping trip.

Loyalty is also garnered through the word of mouth generated by employees of the brand. Treating employees like individuals (as companies like Ben & Jerry's have done) is an excellent way to get the word out about the practices of the brand, and bolsters the message of the brand promise. Many companies have employee programs that encourage participation in stock ownership, making each ᴄmployee a part-owner of the company; Just the Best should explore the financial implications of such a move. Employees who discuss their employer in a positive light have an effect on the general public by extension. They should never be underestimated.

> Brands expecting loyalty from the consumer should not change too radically or too often, however. Further changes, such as overhauling the ad campaign or adding more flavors to the mix, should be postponed until a time when no changes have been made in the recent past. After all, consumers can't be expected to remain loyal to a brand that doesn't respect that loyalty enough to maintain the basic promises it made when it was being introduced. Major overhauls are for brands that are experiencing declines.

CUSTOMER SATISFACTION

Some Brands mistakenly present themselves as Xanadu. But there is a correlation in the human between expectations and happiness.

If I tell you that I'm going to accomplish for you tasks A, B, C, D, and E, and I accomplish only A, B and C, you will be disappointed, and my brand identity will suffer in your eyes. In all likelihood, you will not develop brand loyalty for me, and you will search for someone else who can perform all five tasks.

If, however, I promise to do tasks A and B, and I perform A, B and C, you will be thrilled with me, and my brand identity will become that of an overachiever in your eyes. My chances to establish brand loyalty will increase dramatically, and you will probably ask me to perform those tasks for you, or similar ones, the next time a need arises.

Customer satisfaction is absolutely central to the idea of brand loyalty. Common sense dictates that a consumer whose hopes are dashed by a brand time and again will seek out another brand to replace it, while the same consumer, when his or her hopes are exceeded by a brand, will feel more loyal to that brand and will be much less likely to abandon it just because a newer, sexier, or trendier brand is developed.

Brand Loyalty and Customer Satisfaction

It should be obvious that too many businesses aren't paying enough attention to customer satisfaction. And it doesn't matter how large a brand you own, if the consumer's experience with your product or service is an unsatisfying one, you are asking for trouble.

L.L. Bean does not allow there to be such a thing as an unsatisfied customer. Ever. If there is a problem with a product the company sells or the sales experience the consumer has had, online or in a bricks-and-mortar store, the customer service department is absolutely devoted to pleasing that consumer before the contact between brand and consumer ends. If that means replacing a product, giving a refund, or simply providing an explanation, it will be done before that customer leaves the store or hangs up the phone. No exceptions, no excuses.

Oddly, however, not many brands are performing with the same kind of zeal or with the same commitment to the multitudes who pay the bills. Too many brands consider themselves clearinghouses, selling product and then forgetting about the client entirely but expecting him or her to return the next time a need for that product arises.

The computer industry is among the worst at this. The public's opinion of Microsoft is not always a positive one, given antitrust proceedings and the fact that any question about a software program downloaded free from the company's Web site will cost the consumer $35 when he or she calls for technical support. Making consumers pay for customer support (which is not by any means exclusive to Microsoft) is an astounding show of arrogance by a consumer company, and while the consumers pay the fee, the move does not by any means help engender brand loyalty. On those occasions when consumers have been given a choice of suppliers for programs that do the same thing as Microsoft's they have often opted for one of the company's competitors, depending on price and circumstances. Yes, consumers have to pay for tech support at the second company as well, but if there were brand loyalty to Microsoft, they wouldn't weigh price and circumstance, but would buy from the company that had established itself as an ally in the consumer's mind.

The paradox of extraordinary Branding is that it should be strong but not crude, soft but not weak, bold but not bullish, humble but not timid, and proud but not arrogant, and should include humor without folly. But there is one constant: Without customer satisfaction, there will be no brand loyalty.

Most consumer brands have a problem: Either they have lost sight of the initial promise they made to consumers or they have lost focus. Those that have lost their promise are in danger of betraying everything they have worked for because they are arrogant and detached. Those that lose focus do care about customer satisfaction, but don't stress it enough to make it a clear priority all of the time. They are simply lazy.

> Any product or service that relies on the public for its income must be considered a consumer experience. It is the experience a brand promises, and delivers, that will determine its measure for any consumer, and eventually for Wall Street and potential investors. Carvel doesn't sell ice cream cones; it sells the experience of eating an ice cream cone. If the Carvel experience is more pleasing to the customer than the Baskin-Robbins experience, the consumer will become a "Carvel person." A consumer who finds the experience of driving a Buick more satisfying than the experience of driving a Pontiac might very well become a Buick driver for life.

"Howard Schultz (chairman and CEO of Starbucks) did an amazing brand campaign," says Grace Ascolese of Ascolese Associates, the market research firm. "He was able to craft together a set of values that speaks to where we are and where we want to be, even though it has nothing to do with coffee. He tapped into this well of unmet needs that consumers have. Can you sell people things that they don't want if it's a brand? I think paying $4 for a 20-ounce coffee is getting them to pay for something they want because you're telling them they want it. You've created a need for them where they didn't see a need, and the need is an emotional need. It's not massive quantities of coffee that they need. I think that's the goal, and then there's brand loyalty, where people will go to Starbucks."

Companies like Starbucks and BMW provide more than coffee and cars; in fact, Starbucks is designed around providing the consumer with a place to sit and drink the coffee as much as around the coffee itself. BMW provides an experience from its showrooms to its carefully cared for "previously owned" vehicles: There is snob appeal, certainly, but it is well deserved, based on the kind of one-on-one care and attention to detail the car manufacturer offers.

At Starbucks, the environment is every bit as important as the product being sold. Before that chain erupted out of the Seattle area, coffee was something people bought at the local mini-mart or Dunkin' Donuts, then took to work in the morning. To sit and drink coffee, which was usually priced at under $1.50, a consumer would go to a diner or restaurant and generally would have something to eat at the same time.

Starbucks changed that. With its comfortable furniture and welcoming, relaxing environment, the chain actually invited consumers to come in and spend time, in contrast to the rushed, urgent atmosphere in most places where coffee was sold. Customers came to Starbucks to talk, read the newspaper, relax, and enjoy the many different varieties of coffee the chain offered. The average time of a consumer's visit to Starbucks was considerably longer than at Dunkin' Donuts.

The chain made up for that lag in traffic flow by the experience it offered, and consumers did not balk at the increase in the cost. It was the perception of a fine product and especially the easy, welcoming environment that created brand loyalty for Starbucks and helped the chain become a huge business, with retail outlets on thousands of corners, coffee products sold in supermarkets, and a following that can only be described as devoted.

BMW approaches its business differently, emphasizing the product's high quality and reputation rather than the environment in which it is sold. Yes, BMW dealerships are very well appointed and the sales staffs are extremely well versed in the product and accommodating to the consumer, but the experience of buying a BMW is not the selling point. The experience of driving a BMW—and, more to the point, owning a BMW—is.

Upscale car buyers who are deciding among luxury models are already convinced, at least to some extent, before they enter the BMW showroom. They undoubtedly have Internet access, and have done research on all their possible choices before deciding on a test drive. In fact, if they have been to www.bmwusa.com, they may have taken a virtual test drive in a BMW model and compared its features with any of a number of competing cars. So the visit to the showroom is not what the consumer is looking forward to here. The customer's goal is in the BMW slogan: The Ultimate Driving Experience.

The brand loyalty enjoyed by BMW is more product-based, but is still tied to the experience the consumer expects and receives. Once behind the wheel for a test drive, the consumer is given the type of driving experience he or she expects from a luxury car, and the perceived experience of the prestige and status of driving a BMW is reinforced. Both the physical and emotional experiences of the test drive have been accomplished. In most cases, the vehicle will be purchased and brand loyalty—because BMW is extremely attentive to its customer satisfaction ratings—can be established.

ENSURING GREAT CUSTOMER SERVICE

Customer satisfaction is essential to brand loyalty, and smart companies make sure it is maintained with the use of *mystery shoppers*. This process, which sends people employed by an independent firm into the company's outlets to evaluate the average shopper's experience, has gained popularity in recent years and is an excellent way to gauge the effectiveness and stability of the brand's promise. A mystery shopper coming into the McDonald's restaurant I sometimes patronize could open a good number of eyes in the company's Illinois headquarters.

According to Jim Robinson, chairman of Partners in Charge, a consulting firm, "[Mystery shoppers] is one element of a management system. It's very important in every industry where there's customer contact. There's also a system that tracks how long customers are on hold, how many customers are hanging up, and how many customer opportunities are they losing."

Tara Griggs is a researcher who has done some mystery shopping for a number of companies, and she says that the process is essential for both small and large businesses that deal with the public. "There are a lot of policies in place for each company, and 99 percent of them are not being followed," Griggs says. "Management has to have the biggest responsibility. Small businesses need it more."

Brand Loyalty and Customer Satisfaction

The problem, once again, is that management personnel in some large companies (and some small ones as well) pay lip service to the idea of customer satisfaction, but don't follow through. Brand promises are made and not kept. Arrogance in larger companies leads to laziness and indifference due to a belief that the public will remain loyal to the brand out of habit.

Of course, even mystery shopping has pitfalls. Duane Knapp, president of Brand Strategy, Inc., says the forms given to mystery shoppers can answer the questions without addressing the problems. "Mystery shoppers can be helpful, but that is a misused term and a misused science, because what they're doing is examining the technical aspects of the process of the brand," he says. "For instance, a mystery shopper goes in and says, 'Was I greeted within the first five minutes of entering a retail store?' So they check that off. Then it says, 'Did the person say thank you?' and they said thank you, so they check that off. It could be that the customer service level in that store is declining in the customer's mind, while you could have positive mystery shopper scores. There's no comparison to the competitors. The technical aspects are interesting, but the real key is to be talking to your customers every day."

That's why the concept of *wandering around,* which means high-placed executives in companies actually walking the floor at stores and getting into the trenches with the employees (and sometimes, the customers) is so important to Branding. Wandering around is an excellent tool for learning about Branding, and the giants of the Branding kingdom often have the souls of nomads.

As Duane Knapp points out, "The presidents of the companies of great brands, like Lexus, are out there on the floor talking to the customers. Lexus is getting 10,000 comments a day from customers." Only in that way, with direct consumer contact, can the company determine if the initial brand promise is being kept. If it is not, changes must be made quickly and definitively, because brand loyalty is already suffering, and erosion in loyalty can be deadly to a brand.

It is possible to restore some lost loyalty among consumers, but it is not easy, and it takes time. The Tylenol example is an anomaly; brand loyalty stayed high because the public understood that the tampering was not the fault of the manufacturer, and Johnson & Johnson took immediate, dramatic steps to alleviate the problem. So Tylenol's rebound was truly remarkable.

In most cases, as with McDonald's, brand loyalty has eroded over time and must be restored over time—assuming the company has the time and money to spend reviving its brand promise. From a public relations standpoint, the effort to repair the brand promise must be made in full view of the consumer, admission that the promise has slipped must be acknowledged, and the solutions must be clear and to the point. That doesn't mean a public apology is necessary, but a public declaration must be made.

Consider the brand image of Oldsmobile, which by the 1980s had become a tired, old me-too car company with no appeal to younger car buyers. The company acknowledged that image and tried to update it with an ad campaign whose slogan was, "This Is Not Your Father's Oldsmobile," and sales increased for a time. The problem was, it really *was* your father's Oldsmobile. The product hadn't changed substantially, and now the brand is reportedly being phased out by General Motors.

The company tried to repair what it saw as a flaw in its brand promise by acknowledging that flaw. But it didn't go the extra mile and actually change the product being delivered, so the updated image did not stand.

On the other hand, there is the image of Hugh Grant. Grant, who became one of the most sought-after leading men in Hollywood after the success of the romantic comedy *Four Weddings and a Funeral,* saw his popularity soar as his public persona—that of the slightly embarrassed, humble Englishman—became a brand.

Then Grant was publicly humiliated when he was arrested for soliciting a prostitute in Hollywood, and a huge scandal erupted. For a while, it seemed that the public would not retain its brand loyalty for Hugh Grant.

But the actor made a self-deprecating appearance on *The Tonight Show,* that was well orchestrated by his public relations staff. He spoke about the situation directly, although not in a graphic way that would offend viewers, and didn't offer flimsy excuses. Grant admitted his transgression and performed as a slightly embarrassed, humble Englishman, and his career has certainly not suffered. Brand loyalty remains strong.

In that case, public relations did exactly what it should do for a brand under fire. Grant admitted that he had not maintained his public brand promise, and while he didn't apologize directly to the public, he did present the face of someone who was sorry and wouldn't do such a thing again. The consuming public forgave the transgression and moved on. What could have been a career-ending episode became an embarrassing footnote.

That is public relations and brand management at work beautifully. It shows that brand loyalty can be repaired when necessary, but that honesty and public relations techniques—particularly those that relate to customer satisfaction—can make all the difference.

CUSTOMER SATISFACTION AND JUST THE BEST

Our fictitious ice cream brand, Just the Best, has come a long way since its imagined inception. What started out as a concept for a broadly distributed, high-quality ice cream that would concentrate on the three most popular flavors and sell through supermarkets and not storefronts has evolved into a brand with a strong, personable identity that has successfully expanded into a limited line of novelty items, with a name that we hope can rival such industry heavyweights as Breyer's, Edy's, and Häagen-Dazs.

Still, as the Branding process continues, Just the Best will still have considerable hurdles to jump. It will have to deal with the inception of a Web site, upgrades of its packaging, establishment and maintenance of brand loyalty, continued efforts to increase customer satisfaction, questions about sponsorship, attacks from its competition, and the natural process of evolution as the brand continues to mature and remain vital and important in the minds of the consuming public. And it will have to do all this simultaneously, since life does not proceed in a linear fashion. The greatest brands on earth handle these situations with grace and acuity, while those that have no strategic planning become reactive and defensive and end up among such names as Studebaker, Fresca and pets.com.

The role of public relations in each situation is central. In all of these cases, the perception of the general public will color the brand, and in some cases will determine the brand's future, if not its very survival. Just the Best, as a relatively new brand, still has something to prove. But its

greatest challenges will no doubt lie less in being what it is than in growing into what it will eventually become. As we have seen, that process
continues into perpetuity.

Because the ice cream market was not dominated by one huge brand
before we began our Branding journey, the original goal of Just the Best
was to become that dominant brand, to be the giant in the ice cream market where none had existed before. At this point in its evolution, we cannot assume Just the Best has accomplished that goal, so that will remain the
ultimate aim of the brand. With that in mind, how will our brand handle
the hard ground balls hit to its right and its left?

The key to Branding success and brand loyalty is customer satisfaction,
and in this area, Just the Best must shine brighter than its competition.
While the quality of the product will comprise a good portion of the customer satisfaction the brand will enjoy, it will be the job of the customer
service staff and the public relations professionals involved to make sure
the brand, rather than the product, is appreciated for all it can be.

Constancy is the key to customer satisfaction. If an e-mail from a disgruntled Just the Best customer is received, it must be answered that day,
and the answer must contain the solution to the customer's problem. If the
packaging leaked or the product was for some reason unacceptable when
the customer brought it home, the customer must be provided with a
coupon for a free exact replacement. If a local store has stopped carrying a
certain product, the consumer must be provided with a nearby alternate
supplier. No problem must ever be shrugged off, and no consumer must
ever go away unhappy. The last thing public relations people need to deal
with is bad word of mouth, and if it is in any way avoidable, it should be
avoided.

Surveys showing high levels of customer satisfaction (which would be
compiled by market research professionals) should be released to the press
and posted on the Web site. Customer testimonials should be solicited on
the Web site and posted with the permission of the consumer involved.
In short, customer satisfaction must be guaranteed and then delivered
unquestionably and publicized unreservedly.

Advertising can become involved, guaranteeing to the public that they
will never be disappointed by Just the Best and making sure consumers

Brand Loyalty and Customer Satisfaction

know how to get in touch with the company via an 800 number or e-mail to gain that satisfaction. Phone personnel must be trained to be unfailingly polite no matter how rude the consumer might act; e-mails must be answered promptly. Another news conference mentioning the high level of consumer satisfaction and explaining the system by which Just the Best ensures such exemplary ratings can be scheduled.

While the nature of the product makes selling Just the Best directly through the Web site impractical, it is possible to sell gift certificates and ancillary merchandise for consumers who might want to express their brand loyalty. Customer satisfaction breeds loyalty, and letting consumers act as walking advertisements for the brand can never hurt.

At the same time, the highest quality standards for the production and distribution of the product must be maintained at all times, and mystery shopper must be employed.

The concept of a mystery shopper applies to Just the Best peripherally, since the brand is being distributed through supermarkets, so a mystery shopper is not able to go into a company-owned retail outlet and report on the service he or she receives.

Still, customer satisfaction can be experienced, and it can be measured, and that is what a mystery shopper does, in the most realistic circumstances possible. A consumer who would be interested in Just the Best would approach it in one of two ways: at the supermarket or on the Web site.

A mystery shopper hired by an outside firm would then do the same: Go to a number of local supermarkets to determine how well the retailers are handling distribution, then to evaluate the product itself. At some time, the mystery shopper would investigate the Just the Best Internet site to determine how well the information and entertainment there serve the average consumer and how well the site staff responds to concerns from consumers.

Evaluation forms would be filled out, measuring the retailer's place-ment of the product, how well the product presented itself in supermarket freezers, and how well the retailer managed to stock each item in the prod-uct line. The number of shelves available for the product in the freezer, as compared to other brands, would also be counted and evaluated. The mystery shopper would also determine how hard the frozen ice cream is by the time it arrives in a consumer's home. This will help retailers decide at what temperature their freezers should be set.

Once in his or her home, the mystery shopper would evaluate the product itself for consistency, flavor, and texture, as well as the container for its stability and attractiveness. The mystery shopper would also examine the Just the Best Web site for quality and quantity of information and the overall experience of visiting the site, as well as how well it conveys the brand identity developed by the company. The mystery shopper would call the customer service phone number and contact the customer service link on the brand Web site to determine how well customer service responds to a problem with the product. The customer service representative would be rated for promptness, politeness, and ability to solve the problem satisfactorily.

The information gathered by the mystery shopper would be extremely valuable to public relations representatives for Just the Best. Knowing where weaknesses exist before they can be exploited by competition is the best way to avoid a possible attack from without, while seeing the strengths of the system expressed in clinical terms and statistics can help identify possible news stories that can be publicized in future campaigns.

In working with Hollywood celebrities, I don't often use mystery shoppers, but I have represented such corporate concerns as Pizza Hut and other retail chains that do. The information they gather, because it is dispassionately reported and observed, can be invaluable to the task of customer satisfaction, which is the heart and soul of any Branding objective.

CHAPTER FIFTEEN

BRANDING THROUGH SPONSORSHIP AND ENDORSEMENT

"We have to define Branding as systemized reputation. Everyone you know has a brand: This friend is funny; this friend is compassionate. This guy is a son of a bitch; this person is a warm, kind, sweet, decent human being. These things are all brands. It's important that we see Branding as part of that progression. It really relates to the level of privacy that you shed. People have behaviors which nobody knows about. If they're willing to share that behavior with a small group of people, it becomes a characteristic. If they're willing to share that with a wider group of people, many of whom they've never met, it becomes a reputation. If they're going to sell it and gain benefit from it, it becomes a brand."

—DICK MORRIS, FOUNDER OF VOTE.COM

The Tiffany Theory allows for the benefit of association. That is, if a brand becomes associated with another brand, the identity of the associate brand can rub off onto the original one, and at least some of that personality will become part of the original brand identity. The Tiffany paper wrapping is the associate brand, and the package inside is the original brand.

In other words, if Jason Alexander (George Costanza of TV's *Seinfeld*) appears in a series of television ads for Kentucky Fried Chicken—which he has—the brand Jason Alexander becomes associated with KFC. People seeing the ad might think that the character they saw on television is now endorsing a product, and if they identify strongly enough with the actor or the character, they might sample that product.

213

This association immediately becomes complicated. If viewers find Jason Alexander or his famous *Seinfeld* character unattractive or annoying, the KFC brand may suffer. By the same token, vegetarians or people opposed to fast food restaurants might lower their estimation of Jason Alexander because of his association with the Colonel's chain of restaurants. To take the example to its extreme, other *Seinfeld* cast members could find themselves unconsciously associated with the chicken stores in the public's mind. Jason Alexander could find that when he plays a role in a new film or television project, he is too closely associated with Kentucky Fried Chicken for the audience to forget that attachment. Clearly, the business of celebrity endorsement is complex.

ENDORSEMENT

Branding is the business of creating and communicating a personality. When a brand—either new or established—associates itself with an already established personality, it can enhance its own brand identity or be swallowed up by the larger identity it has annexed. Identifying the proper celebrity to endorse your brand can be difficult, and, once that is done, convincing the celebrity can be more difficult. In my capacity as a Hollywood publicist, I've seen more than my share of bad behavior by celebrities, and when that behavior becomes public, a brand endorsed by that celebrity can be tarred with the same brush in the court of public opinion.

Sometimes, as in the case of Nike's endorsements by Michael Jordan, the marriage of celebrity and brand works remarkably well. Jordan did a wonderful job for Nike, but when he endorsed Hanes underwear, neither brand (Jordan or Hanes) experienced much benefit. The lesson here is that celebrity endorsements are the equivalent of swimming in a murky lake: The water could be still and calm, or there could be piranha just below your kicking feet. Before you dive in, there's no way to tell.

When determining if a celebrity endorser is right for your brand, it's necessary to determine if there is a need for a celebrity endorsement. After all, many brands get by quite nicely without them. Coca-Cola does not rely much on star power, emphasizing its brand (although it did create some waves a number of years back with Diet Coke ads that starred Elton John and a number of deceased celebrities like Humphrey Bogart). Pepsi has featured advertising with Michael J. Fox, Cindy Crawford, and Britney Spears, among others, in the past few years. United Airlines doesn't feature any celebrities on camera, but has Gene Hackman do its advertising voice-overs. Jamie Lee Curtis appeared on camera for VoiceStream Wireless, while Barry Bonds has joined Jason Alexander in the KFC ads. George Hamilton, among others, has appeared in ads for Old Navy.

Noreen S. Jenney is president of Celebrity Endorsement Network, an extremely successful agency that matches advertisers with celebrities. She says there are certainly times when there should not be a celebrity endorsement for a brand. "If you don't match celebrity properly to appeal to the market that is buying that product, then you're just wasting your money," Jenney says. "It's got to be a good match. You can't just pull a celebrity out of the air. The most important thing is matching the celebrity's image and the way the public relates to them. You have to tap into that to be effective."

A brand might think a celebrity endorsement is a good fit if it is trying to establish or reestablish (or in some cases deepen) its brand identity and there is a celebrity who epitomizes the identity that brand is trying to communicate. For example, if your brand identity is brash, irreverent, and not terribly serious, Chris Tucker might be the perfect fit for a spokesperson. If the target demographic is a little older, and the image is friendly, warm, family-oriented, and familiar, Bill Cosby might be your man.

As Noreen Jenney says: "The most effective way to use a celebrity is that you want people to relate to the product through that celebrity. So if you have a beauty product and you have Cindy Crawford doing an endorsement for Revlon, women around the world are going to look at that and say, 'Look at her! If I use this, I'm going to look like that,' and that's going to help you. They're going to relate to that product, because they believe that celebrity uses it and that's part of the reason that celebrity is as beautiful as she is. If you have a bank and you have a very reputable kind of celebrity who has credibility to make people believe that this person invests in this brokerage firm or deposits their money in that bank, then that's going to be an effective endorsement."

But there is evidence that celebrity endorsements, particularly in advertising, don't necessarily translate into increased sales or even better awareness of the ads in question. An article in the April 22, 2002 issue of *USA Today* stated that the national newspaper's weekly ad poll, Ad Track, was not endorsing the idea of endorsement. "Results for some recent star-capped campaigns in Ad Track . . . suggest star power may not be as bright as advertisers think," the article read. "Just seven percent of those polled liked ads for TD Waterhouse featuring actor Steven Hill, the former district attorney on *Law & Order,* 'a lot.' Only nine percent really liked Pier 1 ads featuring *Cheers* star Kirstie Alley. Ad Track's average is 22 percent."

Indeed, the article went on to say that the Britney Spears Pepsi ads "chalked up Pepsi's worst showing in years in *USA Today*'s annual Super Bowl Ad Meter. Viewers ranked the $5.8 million ad as the third-lowest spot among the 52 rated by Ad Meter." Noreen Jenney adds: "I'm still questioning the Britney Spears for Pepsi; I'm not sure that works for them. I think there are better things they could have done with her and better things Pepsi could have done. I think Michael J. Fox for Pepsi was great; that was a great campaign." So even a teen pop idol can't guarantee high consumer ratings for ads, and consumers are the ones an advertisement wants to reach, aren't they? And after spending almost $6 million on an ad, shouldn't the impressions among the audience be higher?

Celebrities commanding six-figure fees for an endorsement should at least represent the brand identity being promoted. So before signing up a celebrity just because he or she is a celebrity, a careful brander must make the proper match between the product's brand identity and that of the celebrity being contacted.

Through my years working with the biggest stars in entertainment, I can also tell you there are some celebrities who won't endorse any product, no matter how hefty the fee. Barbra Streisand was very good about promoting her own concert event with merchandise, but will not appear in advertising or promotion for another brand. Likewise for Tom Cruise, Julia Roberts, and most of the A-plus list celebrities in film. Sports figures are more likely to endorse sports-related brands, while television actors, musicians, and some film actors will be available for endorsements (many have contracted with agencies that seek out endorsements) as long as the product is consistent with the celebrity's persona or brand identity. News personalities almost never agree to do endorsements, nor do politicians (until they are out of office, like Bob Dole in the Britney Spears Pepsi ad), for fear of compromising their credibility or creating a conflict of interest.

Endorsements also run the risk of overshadowing the brand being promoted. Audiences may remember seeing Mr. T in a commercial, but will they remember it was an ad for 1-800-COLLECT? When they see Mike Piazza and ALF discussing something with Fran Tarkenton, will they know it's the same service? And when they see Carrot Top in hockey paraphernalia endorsing AT&T's collect call service—well, who knows what the audience will think?

In advertising, the impression must be made quickly and dramatically or the consumer will not recall the important information: the brand name and identity. Sometimes the presence of a recognizable face from another context can hurt more than it helps. If the viewer is so busy nudging his wife and saying, "Look, it's that guy from *NYPD Blue,*" that he misses the information about the product, the brand is no longer the star of the commercial, and the point has been missed.

Keep the "got milk?" ads in mind. While the print ads especially get their point across, and catch the eye with celebrity glitz, milk sales have not increased significantly since the extremely popular campaign began. It is possible to interpret the figures to argue that the campaign has been a success, but it does not immediately prove the idea of celebrity endorsements as surefire Branding tools.

"They only paid $25,000 per celebrity for the 'got milk?' ads," says Noreen Jenney of Celebrity Endorsement Network. "But Annie Leibovitz was shooting it, and everybody wanted to be a part of the campaign. That was more identity than it was anything else. It was to get attention. It was not a brand of milk; it was just Milk. So I don't know whether you can even figure out if milk sales went up. That was more an identity issue. It started and it went on a roll, and it just kept on going and going. Celebrities wanted to do it."

On the other hand, Nike's initial brand identity was practically invented with the idea of athletes like Michael Jordan, Derek Jeter, and Tiger Woods doing nothing more than publicly wearing shoes and clothing with the swoosh on them. (It should be noted, by the way, that the designer of the swoosh was originally paid $35 for her efforts, but was later given healthy stock compensation after the logo had helped earn the company billions.) The athletes wore the items in advertising spots and personal appearances—in some cases while they participated in the sports that made them famous—and made both advertising and public relations points by acting as human billboards for Nike. The effect certainly can't be denied; Nike became one of the most recognizable and successful brands on earth, and practically invented the product category of athletic apparel out of virtually nothing.

The power of celebrity can't be overestimated; when Clark Gable took off his shirt in *It Happened One Night* in 1934, and the public saw that he wasn't wearing an undershirt, sales of men's undershirts dropped like a stone. When Sarah Jessica Parker appears on *Sex and the City* drinking a cosmopolitan, the cocktail immediately soars to untold heights in the country's lounges. When she wears a gold nameplate necklace, sales of such jewelry increase to unprecedented numbers. The designer for the HBO series was quoted in *TV Guide* saying the show doesn't "sit there consciously trying to create trends," but the effect is unmistakable.

In the mid-1960s, martinis that were shaken, not stirred, were all the rage because of James Bond films. In the seventies, John Travolta led a disco invasion in *Saturday Night Fever*. Each decade has its cultural touchstone, and sometimes it is difficult to tell if the trend was started by popular entertainment or if Hollywood noticed a blip on the radar and fanned the flames.

It is difficult, therefore, to determine if an endorsement from a major celebrity helps a brand. When a brand is new and trying to establish and define itself with the public, a star can be either a boost in brand identity or a distraction from the brand message. From the public relations stance, the execution of the endorsement is key.

"A lot of times the reason people use celebrities is to get attention," says Noreen Jenney. "If you have 14 brands of toilet tissue and you need to break out of the pack, a celebrity is a way to do that. It's a way to sort of get through the clutter of TV commercials. The perfect example is infomercials. They use celebrities as channel stoppers because as people are flipping through the channels, they see the celebrity, and they stop. I think it's the same for a commercial. You see a celebrity doing it; it gets attention, and people tend to remember what that celebrity was talking about—if the creative is well done. If the creative is not, people tend to remember that a celebrity was doing a soft drink, what the heck soft drink was it? If the creative is done well, you tend to remember the celebrity and the soft drink, and you begin to brand them together."

The emphasis must always be on the brand, not the celebrity. Entertainment figures are employed to enhance the brand, not to become the brand. When Robert Young endorsed a brand of decaffeinated coffee in the seventies, to capitalize on the medical image he enjoyed as the star of the top-rated *Marcus Welby, M.D.,* he became the focus of the attention and the brand was lost in the shuffle. But when Bill Cosby performed in a series of Jell-O Pudding ads in the 1980s, he made sure the product was the thrust of the campaign, and both are remembered well.

Sometimes, a celebrity who is well recognized but has not branded himself might be a better fit for an endorsement. Edward Herrmann is a well-respected character actor, but is not a brand in the way that Tom Hanks or even Sylvester Stallone would be; he doesn't always play the same type of role, and isn't seen as having one particular character trait that would define him. When he began doing ads for Dodge in the 1990s, he added weight to the brand without overwhelming it, and gave the message being delivered extra credibility.

Some successful brands create their own spokespeople and don't have to pay a celebrity top dollar to define the brand identity. Ronald McDonald speaks to children in a way that Britney Spears couldn't possibly do; Geoffrey the Giraffe is a recognizable and characteristic symbol of Toys "R" Us. Folgers Coffee used the fictional "Mrs. Olsen" for years in its ads, and later created a mini-soap opera between two anonymous neighbors who seemed to be heading closer toward a romance with each successive advertisement. Expensive celebrities weren't necessary, and the product remained the focus of the advertising and public relations message.

Keep in mind, too, that the most successful spokesman in the history of Branding is an animated rodent named Mickey, who can be identified by virtually every child on the face of the planet. It's amazing how little Mickey costs, considering his remarkable fame.

When I first met Vanna White, she was a down-to-earth, lovely young woman who had not yet surfaced on a game show that somehow captured the country's imagination like nothing else. White, who understood her own appeal, became a huge celebrity in 1982 by turning large letters around on *Wheel of Fortune* and saying very, very little.

She could endorse beauty products, based on her wonderful looks. She was considered friendly and approachable, and could certainly endorse products the average American woman might use. Men found her sexy in a nonthreatening way, and so she could be seen endorsing virtually any family-oriented product and be counted on to get the attention of the man of the house.

Because Vanna, at the height of her celebrity, was still something of a mystery to the public, she didn't bring the baggage of a particular character trait with her to a brand. She was the perfect spokeswoman for products like Sealy mattresses: instantly recognizable, extremely credible, and not so distracting that she overwhelmed the product.

Ed McMahon, who spent decades on the couch next to Johnny Carson on *The Tonight Show* and hosting *Star Search,* was also a fine celebrity spokesman. He was very famous, considered a friend by the consumer, and was not tied to one characteristic. To this day, he is just as well known for some of his endorsements—such as magazine subscription company sweepstakes—as for his years on late-night television.

When an actor becomes a spokesman based on a role he has played, rather than on his own personality (like Jason Alexander playing a variation on George Costanza for KFC), the brand risks having the role overwhelm the commercial and push the product out of sight. Sometimes, the off-screen behavior of the celebrity is also a factor. Stars who get themselves into trouble are one problem for a brand; another is the star who skyrockets to fame in a particular role or because of a particular event. The sports hero who wins a national championship on prime time television might decide not to honor the conditions of a spokesperson contract now that his asking price has gone through the roof.

"O. J. had a contract with Hertz," Noreen Jenney says. "Those contracts have morality clauses in them. And they're very clear about saying, 'If you do this, this is over.' They get invoked if something happens. It's damage control at that point. It's a chance you take. We try and use diligence if we put a celebrity into something and we try to warn the client if they're going to go with a celebrity who is a potential risk factor in that area. There are some celebrities you don't worry about. You don't worry about Dick Clark; you don't worry about Patricia Heaton—she's married with four kids. There are some advertisers that are willing to go out on a limb and use a celebrity even though you know three weeks later they're going to be on the cover of the *National Enquirer*. You've got to be really careful about that, and you can't always control it; that's the function and a risk of using a celebrity."

Brand executives who decide to employ celebrities can't let the reputation of the star go unheeded; if someone is known within the industry to be difficult and unreliable, then no matter how well known a celebrity, that star is going to be a problem for the brand. Wrapping your brand in that kind of Tiffany paper might end up being the wrong move.

A celebrity endorsement can cut both ways: It can be the best possible situation for an undefined or newly defined brand, or it can be an unfortunate distraction for a brand trying to communicate a message and being shouted down by star power. When it works, it is an undisputed boon; when it doesn't, it can be an unmitigated disaster.

SPONSORSHIP

Sponsorship is more than simply buying airtime on a particular television program every week. It is the business of allying your brand with a particular athlete, entertainment project, or event by lending the brand's name and image—and, usually, a good deal of money. It is, in fact, the flip side of a celebrity endorsement—the brand name is the star chosen to speak for the sponsored event or individual.

When Budweiser creates a television commercial and buys time during a New York Yankees telecast to show that commercial, it is sponsorship. So is the billboard in right center field at Yankee Stadium that reads *Budweiser*. So is Budweiser Cap Day during the Yankees season. Print ads in the Yankees program, sold during the game, are sponsorship. Calling yourself "the official beer of the New York Yankees" would be sponsorship as well. Making sure that the television broadcasters highlight the "Budweiser Play of the Game" or "Budweiser Starting Lineups" is sponsorship. That sign behind home plate that seems to change every half-inning, right in front of the guy in the rainbow wig with the placard that reads *John 3:16?* When that sign bears the legend *Budweiser,* that is sponsorship.

Seven examples of sponsorship in the course of one baseball game, and we're just getting started. Sponsorship can take on many different forms. The difference between sponsorship and endorsement is that the brand seeking an endorsement is hoping to trade on the cachet of the endorser, while the brand sponsoring an event or personality is lending its name to another brand in the hope of reiterating its place in society. One is establishing a brand identity, while the other reminds the consumer of the brand identity.

The *New York Post* reported in June 2002 that 15 major brands, including The Gap, Guiness, Lexus, Nokia, and Ben & Jerry's, were all featured prominently in the Steven Spielberg–Tom Cruise collaboration *Minority Report.* In such cases, the small thread of sponsorship becomes a huge web of benefits and potential risks. The Tiffany Theory is being used in several different directions at once to grab some star power and apply it to various brands.

When a company like The Gap, whose sales have been slightly off in the past few quarters, involves itself with *product placement*—the process by which brand names are included in films and television programs for a fee paid by the brand—it is attempting to accomplish a number of Branding goals at once. The Gap, for instance, is reminding the public of its brand name and brand identity as well as aligning itself with the high-profile talents Steven Spielberg and Tom Cruise in a very highly anticipated film. In other words, the Spielberg and Cruise brands are being manipulated to include association with the brand The Gap. But the process of product placement goes deeper than that.

It's one thing, after all, to place a brand in a Steven Spielberg film that caters to the audience's expectations and presents a fun, exciting view of the world: Think of the colossal boost the product placement of Reese's Pieces in *E.T.—The Extraterrestrial* had in the 1980s (after M&M's had turned Spielberg down). It's quite another thing to offer your brand identity to a dark, challenging story like Spielberg's *A.I.—Artificial Intelligence,* which did not strike a responsive chord with audiences in 2001. With *Minority Report,* a film based on the darker vision of the future from author Philip K. Dick (of *Blade Runner* fame), it could have been possible to associate a brand with a film audiences would not find appealing. Even with Tom Cruise and Steven Spielberg, it is possible to do damage to a brand identity with product placement.

Minority Report opened in first place at the box office with over $35 million its first three days, so brands that placed products in the film were probably quite pleased with the decision to spend that money. But product placement is always a gamble; Tom Hanks has made *Big* and *Forrest Gump,* but he also made *Joe vs. the Volcano.* There are no guarantees.

What can be controlled is the use of the brand in the film. Companies offering to pay for product placement often contract the way their brands will be portrayed; while not reigning in the filmmakers' artistic vision, brand identity must be protected with specific provisions before the placement is finalized. Scripts are often shown to the Branding company before the deal is completed to ensure that the brand will not be ridiculed or seen as a negative in the finished film.

In the film *Cast Away,* Tom Hanks played a supervisor for Federal Express who survives a plane crash in the ocean and is marooned on a desert island alone for four years. He survives partially by opening a number of the FedEx packages that were part of the plane's cargo and using the contents for purposes for which they weren't initially intended. VHS video tape is used for rope; ice skates are used to perform necessary dental surgery. At the end of the film, after being rescued and brought back to society, Hanks' character delivers one remaining FedEx package he had kept unopened for four years on the island.

"If you've seen *Cast Away,* you know it's a FedEx movie," says Duane Knapp. "They were very careful to deliver on their promise, that at the end of the movie, he had to go and deliver that package to that lady in Texas. That movie couldn't end until he delivered that package to that person in Texas."

Such treatment does not happen by accident. Federal Express surely stipulated as part of its cooperation with the film that Hanks deliver his package in the movie, and that FedEx is always seen as competent,

223

dependable, and efficient—the key elements of the brand's identity. Using that same logic, a film with a product placement for McDonald's would never show the restaurant in question as dirty, the employees as ineffectual or indifferent, or the food as anything other than wholesome and tasty. Otherwise, the company would not agree to the product placement, and the filmmakers would not benefit from the brand's product placement fee.

From the filmmakers' point of view, product placement is done to shave money off the shooting budget. If a company pays, say, $100,000 to place its brand name in a movie, that $100,000 is added to the shooting budget of the film, so the same movie can be made for $100,000 less. Add enough product placements, and a decent percentage of the product budget can be offset. The *New York Post* cited an article in *Variety* estimating that "the use of brand names in *Minority Report* could have contributed up to $25 million to the film's $102 million budget."

Branders, however, have another agenda: Their goal in product placement is to raise the brand profile and recommunicate the brand identity and brand message to consumers who might not have expected such information in their movie entertainment.

Product placement does not always imply a direct fee paid, however. Jay May, president of the Los Angeles–based product placement brokerage company Feature This, created a deal for Samick guitars in the film *Josie and the Pussycats,* having the fictional band use Samick's guitars without the instrument manufacturer paying a fee—but making sure that Samick promoted the film in its 40,000 retail outlets with posters and other promotional items.

Of course, product placement has now become somewhat routine in films, and audiences do tend to notice such deals with a slightly more cynical eye. When James Bond decided to forgo his traditional Aston Martin in *The Man with the Golden Gun* and drive an AMC Gremlin instead, audiences were not amused. These days, after a brief fling with a BMW, Agent 007 is back in his British Aston Martin V12 Vanquish again.

Sponsorship, of course, is not limited to product placement in movies. One look at the average NASCAR driver's uniform will acquaint the viewer with any number of brand names, many of which have nothing whatsoever to do with driving a racing car. Yes, Pennzoil and STP are still prominently displayed, but so are Budweiser, Skoal, Wendy's, and Winston. Anyone who expects the drivers of NASCAR to succeed while drinking beer, chewing tobacco, eating hamburgers, and smoking cigarettes is probably not paying much attention to the race.

What those brands are trying to accomplish is the repetition of their brand name in association with personalities with whom their target audiences identify. Maybe Dale Earnhardt, Jr. isn't drinking a Budweiser while he's competing, but his fans, sitting in the bleachers, certainly can, and seeing the name emblazoned on his car and his uniform reminds the audience that Budweiser made it possible for Earnhardt to participate in the race today by supplying him with some of the operating capital he needs.

As with celebrity endorsements, however, sponsorship can be a dangerous proposition if the personality, event, or programming the brand sponsors becomes associated with unattractive incidents, attitudes, or trends. When Bill Maher of *Politically Incorrect* made comments about the 9/11 bombers being braver than the American troops lobbing shells into Afghanistan, advertisers who sponsored the program felt the heat from their Wall Street backers and consumers. Many pulled their sponsorship of the program, and eventually ABC canceled the show.

Such incidents can have ramifications that go beyond the initial brand into a larger core brand. When Disney bought ABC in the 1990s, it also inherited programming including *NYPD Blue,* which at the time was a controversial program including profanity and partial nudity that had not been featured in broadcast network shows up to that point. Some conservative groups protested to Disney executives and tried to organize a boycott of Disney theme parks, and the core brand could have been threatened.

Disney's public relations stance was to answer the protests with statements reiterating the producers' right to present the program, noting that *NYPD Blue* offered parental warnings before it began and not at all tinkering with the content of the show, which drew high ratings and high advertising fees. To have ignored the protests would have been a mistake; they would only have escalated. But caving in to the protestors would have been worse; then a profitable show would have been extinguished, and special interest groups would have felt they could dictate the artistic point of view presented on television and in film through pressure on the producers. The

Disney boycotts never really materialized, and eventually the protests ended without any further incident. *NYPD Blue* remains on ABC, and is making the network a tidy profit in advertising and syndication fees.

Lending the name of a brand to an event or a venue has become very big business, and also assumes certain risks. When the Houston Astros decided to abandon their historic Astrodome (the first domed stadium) for a more modern arena, the team and the city managed to defray some of the costs of the construction by selling the right to the name of the new stadium. After only two seasons, however, the name Enron Field was no longer an asset but a liability. The team ended its 30-year deal with the energy company in February 2002 and had the name taken off the stadium (the company could no longer afford the licensing fee to maintain it), and now the Houston Astros play at Minute Maid Park after a $100 million over 28 years deal between the team and the juice company, which is owned by Coca-Cola.

Sponsoring an event usually requires more than paying a fee; public relations personnel from the brand also help organize the event itself, and must protect the brand identity from association with elements that won't be consistent with the identity being conveyed. For example, if a brand sponsors a concert tour by a well-known singer, and that performer includes a song that might be contrary to the values being espoused by the brand identity, the event itself could be a public relations nightmare for the brand. Discussing content is important, but censorship is not good business. Decide before signing the contract if there is a potential problem and then determine whether the difficulties with a particular lyric or content element will be enough of a deterrent to avoid sponsoring the event.

The key in that situation is to make the determination before the agreement is signed and the event is well into its planning stages. Brand executives have to have such a strong view of their brand identity that any potential conflicts with artistic content will leap out at the observer like a cheetah on Ritalin. Not paying attention to details—even small, hard-to-see details—is anathema to the great brander.

Not every sponsorship opportunity is appropriate for every brand. Again, brand identity, coupled with a deep, thorough knowledge of the target audience, is essential. Winston Cup Racing is appropriate for a cigarette company because (a) it does not cater specifically to children; (b) its target audience is more likely to include smokers than that for, say, a PETA event; (c) sponsorship promotes the sport and the sponsor at the same time; and (d) it is unlikely that the topic of smoking or the type of illnesses it causes will be brought up during a car race.

If, on the other hand, an appearance by the Teletubbies was sponsored by Winston or Smirnoff, the public relations damage done to both the sponsoring brand and the credibility of the children's program would probably be irreparable.

Sometimes, sponsorship means just that: to become a sponsor, a mentor, or a patron of an artist, company, or charitable cause. When MTV very publicly promotes a voting registration campaign every election year, that is sponsorship. When a struggling band's instruments onstage are provided by Yamaha, that is sponsorship. When Johnson & Johnson underwrites a program on PBS that deals with a health issue, that is sponsorship.

But when Yamaha provides the piano for a Billy Joel concert, that is also sponsorship, and it associates the instrument manufacturer with a famous virtuoso on the instrument. If Manhattan's Fourth of July fireworks are sponsored by Macy's, the department store chain reaffirms its roots in the New York community and buys itself some goodwill with the public in its hometown.

> Sponsorship is a Branding tool that must be used carefully, but can be extremely effective when done well. It employs the best elements of the Tiffany Theory while also reaffirming the brand identity that has been so carefully constructed. The pitfalls are significant and plentiful, and must be considered before any action is taken, but sponsorship is certainly an option for the savvy brander with a public relations sense.

JUST THE BEST ENDORSEMENTS?

Earlier, we determined that a celebrity endorsement for Just the Best was most likely a mistake. That still holds true, even after the brand has gone some way toward establishing itself in the consumer's mind. There isn't one particular celebrity who is especially associated with ice cream, and even if there were, having him or her endorse the product in advertising and public relations campaigns would not necessarily drive sales higher or help the brand identity come through more clearly. A friendly, nostalgic, playful celebrity who embodies high quality and ideals? Garrison Keillor comes to mind, but his following might not turn Just the Best into the most dominant ice cream brand in America.

Still, with a celebrity endorsement dismissed, the idea of sponsorship and product placement for Just the Best is not out of the question. Having Robert Redford and Debra Winger eat Häagen-Dazs onscreen in *Legal Eagles* helped establish the brand as an upscale indulgence, even though the movie wasn't a wild box office success. When *E.T.—The Extraterrestrial* was lured out of hiding by Reese's Pieces, it put the candy on the consumer map for the first time.

It's impossible to speculate about future entertainment projects, but let's assume that there is an upcoming film from a major studio that will feature an ice cream parlor, perhaps set in the 1950s or 1960s. Placing a Just the Best sign in the window wouldn't hurt the film (even though the product didn't exist at the time), and as long as the script treated the product fairly (for example, there would be no comments about what awful ice cream is being sold), the placement could prove a public relations coup for the brand. Besides Just the Best's publicity machine mentioning the placement, the filmmakers' public relations staff would be making mention of the product, and perhaps press junkets could feature Just the Best as well. It's a small outlay of funds for that much exposure.

At the same time, sponsorship has the advantage of not having to wait for exactly the right project to come along. Sponsoring a television program that reflects the brand identity—something on the order of *The Wonder Years* or *Everybody Loves Raymond*—can raise the profile of the brand and align it with a successful, enjoyable experience the viewer already likes.

It might also be a good idea to sponsor a pop singer's summer tour so that Just the Best can introduce small cups of ice cream to its product line and have them available exclusively at tour venues. This would test market a possible future product for the brand while generating public relations material through the sponsorship and the special product available

228

only in conjunction with the tour. In keeping with the brand's nostalgic, family-friendly image, the singer would need to be carefully selected.

Sponsorship and product placement are complicated, difficult deals to complete. The brand's presentation in entertainment events or venues is delicate and important; there must be approval of the way the product is referred to in scripts and where signage would appear when outdoor presentations are involved. But with the right planning and foresight, Just the Best or any brand could definitely benefit from the right kind of sponsorship or placement scenarios.

CHAPTER SIXTEEN

DEALING WITH COPYCAT BRANDS

A brander's greatest dream is to create a brand that so resonates with the consuming public that it becomes a trusted household name—something that is sought out and welcomed into millions of homes based on its carefully constructed identity. The same brander's worst nightmare is that his or her tactics would be used to take that same brand and make it seem passé or irrelevant, and to have it replaced in millions of homes by a pretender.

They say imitation is the sincerest form of flattery. That is little comfort when a successful Branding formula, painstakingly developed over time, is copied by the competition.

In any business, there is always going to be competition. All the great brands have competition: The New York Yankees are always fending off the Boston Red Sox; Coca-Cola is constantly at war with Pepsi; Susan Sarandon and Meryl Streep are often up for the same role. Direct competition can, in fact, keep a brand healthy and active—it can enliven the thinking behind the brand, and therefore make the brand more vital than it might have been otherwise.

It can be infuriating, however, when a competitive brand notices the delicately crafted Branding plan you have devised for your own, sees the positive results, and copies what you've been doing, making it seem like it was all the other brand's idea to begin with. This is not petty and childish; it is cutthroat business tactics, and can mean a very serious threat to a well-established brand.

In Hollywood, new actors are constantly being touted as "the new

Tom Cruise" or "like Helen Hunt, but younger." These performers don't necessarily steal the brand identities of those who have come before them, but they clearly exude, at least physically, some of the same qualities, and can therefore be branded in the same way.

The same is true in virtually any other business. McDonald's was followed into the market by Burger King, Wendy's, Roy Rogers, Kentucky Fried Chicken, Arby's, and a host of others, some of which survived while others have disappeared. The marketing plan and brand plan were not vastly different than the McDonald's mold, although some did vary in terms of product (Kentucky Fried Chicken, for example, has never sold hamburgers). The brand identity for each was a variation on the McDonald's promise—wholesome food, clean restaurant, quick service.

Copycat brands, or any brand that follows yours into the marketplace, will always exist. There is no point in trying to fight their existence, crying foul and expecting them to fold up their tents and go home; they are a fact of business life. It is irritating to have pretenders claim to be first to the market when you have been there already, and it can be infuriating to see your brand strategy imitated with slight changes to create a new, competing brand identity. The smart brander just sucks it up and moves on, not bothering to acknowledge the new presence on the scene. Getting into a war of words with a new brand cheapens your identity and can only elevate the newcomer by association.

On the other hand, public relations has always allowed for competition; in fact, a savvy public relations practitioner knows how to use competition to inflate the value of the brand and substantially bolster the brand identity, based on the reinforcement of the brand promise. Not only is competition healthy; it can be a benefit to the strong, smart brand.

One tactic for dealing with competitors is to make your brand ubiquitous. For example, IBM promoted its brand and its type of computers by allowing other manufacturers to clone the hardware itself, while IBM retained control of certain crucial parts of the computers. Because of that, and because Microsoft designed its Windows operating system to operate on the IBM-style computer and all its clones, that system has managed to retain better than 90 percent of the overall personal computer market.

Apple Computer, on the other hand, for a very long time did not allow any cloning of its computers or operating system, and then only did so for a limited period of time and to a limited degree. Despite having a system than many, if not most, in the computer world believe is more efficient, easier to use, and, in a word, better, Apple still commands only 3 to 4 percent of the overall personal computer market. Its customers are devoted to the point of obsession, but there are still far fewer of them than there are for IBM-type PCs.

In other words, IBM strengthened its brand by allowing competition, while by forbidding competition and obsessively protecting its proprietary information, Apple limited its brand to a small fraction of the available market. It was a very intelligent move on the part of IBM, and perhaps a shortsighted one by Apple.

The question becomes one of control. By trying to hold onto an unrealistic degree of market control, Apple Computer does damage to its brand in the marketplace. But IBM, while it strengthened its brand identity, did lose a good amount of the direct PC market by allowing its technology to be used by other manufacturers, and now is not one of the top consumer brands in that market. IBM does manufacture a good number of parts necessary for computer design and production, however, and retains its brand identity as well as market share in that area.

IBM did not see that one of its suppliers, Microsoft, was usurping the hardware manufacturer's place by creating a powerful operating system that would revolutionize the operation of IBM-style computers. Once clone companies like Dell, Gateway, and Compaq were using the Microsoft Windows system, the operating system developed by IBM was no longer relevant. IBM is now a manufacturer of hardware for computers, and has a very considerable percentage of that market. But it did not retain the huge market share it had before cloning began.

Apple retains control of its operating system and manufactures all its hardware, but that doesn't mean the company has expanded its market. In fact, only a few years ago, Apple had to recruit its cofounder Steve Jobs to come and resurrect the brand's identity with the iMac computer and the various models that have come since. These models succeeded in reinstating the innovative and informal brand Apple had always cultivated, but they only managed to retain the brand's market share, not to substantially expand it.

Control, then, is a double-edged sword. Too little of it will result in the market overtaking an existing, even powerful, brand, while too much can guarantee that the brand will not be able to increase its awareness and familiarity in the public eye. Striking a balance, then, is certainly essential.

Of course, in most cases, you'll have very little control over your competition. They will be devising strategies and brand identities behind your back at all times, and will not warn you in advance of the coming campaign. Most of the control you'll have will be reactive. Your brand identity might come under attack, and your best strategy is to be ready at all times, and never, ever to acknowledge the attack under any circumstances.

Attack ads in particular are seen by the public as intrusive, desperate attempts to undermine the credibility of a more powerful brand. The only time to attack another brand is when you are trying to conceal something you'd rather not have revealed, and the public is often aware of that motivation even if they don't know exactly what you're trying to hide.

The key to stopping a business decline today may rest with the person in charge, who has to make a central choice: Do I want to conduct an autopsy or a resurrection? Given that choice, some managers make the desperate decision to attack the competition rather than focus on their own internal problems and strengthen their brand's identity. I confess that watching businesses blow opportunities to deliver on their primary brand promise gives me an eerie sense of watching self-destruction in slow motion. The promise is everything to the consumer; fail to deliver on that promise, and it simply doesn't matter how badly the competition is doing. What the consumer will remember is that you didn't do what you said you would do.

Of course, this doesn't mean you can ignore your competitors entirely. Obviously, it is very important to keep track of the competition's moves and plans in order to stay one step ahead. But it is far more vital to stay obsessed with your brand's performance for the consumer, which will be the key to the brand's performance in the marketplace. There is no way to overstate the central place of the brand promise to Branding overall; it is all Ten Commandments rolled into one. Fail to give the consumer what you promise, and you will not be a true brand for very long, if ever.

Keep this in mind: A brand with no competition should be wary of that fact. If no one else wants to be in your business, perhaps there's no business there to be in.

For a new brand, the competition is more than likely already well established and entrenched. The idea, then, is to develop a brand promise and a brand identity that are different than those of the existing brands. This doesn't mean that a cellular phone supplier entering the market has to sell popcorn to be different. It means the brand promise should be more specific: "We're going to be the lowest-price cellular phone supplier" or "We will provide the highest-quality, most technologically advanced phones on the market." It also means the brand identity has to differ from the established brands to be noticed. If the bigger brands in the market are appealing to corporate clients and upscale businesspeople, perhaps the identity to explore is that of the offbeat, friendly, youth-oriented cellular phone company whose phones come in flashy colors and whose features are geared toward teens and young adults.

Established brands whose competition is either long standing or new upstart companies have more complex, although equally difficult, tasks in keeping ahead of the competition. Their goal must be the same: to stay true to the brand identity, keep delivering on the brand promise, and remain noticeable, identifiable, and well considered in the marketplace. The consumer is the final arbiter.

The first and best defense against any challenger, of course, is a strong offense: Be the best at what you do. That doesn't mean every company has to be Mercedes-Benz and make the most upscale, cutting-edge product possible. Some companies' missions are to be Honda or Toyota or Saturn, and make extremely dependable products in mid-price ranges that those who don't make millions every year can afford. But it is necessary to be the best at that: If you're going to make soft chocolate chip cookies, make the best ones for your market, whatever that is. Know your brand identity based on the market to which you are hoping to appeal.

It's also important, as has been chronicled, to let the public know you are the best in your market. Benjamin Franklin noted: "Hide not your talents; for use were they made. What's a sundial in the shade?"

That, of course, is the job of public relations and advertising. Branding does not end when the brand is established; it continues to remind the public of the brand's identity and accomplishments as the brand progresses. Disney did not stop sending out press releases when it became a multi-billion-dollar corporation, because the company knows it has competition and does not wish to become second best at what it does.

People believe that obsession is a negative thing. On the contrary, those who are obsessed with what they do, and obsessed with doing it the right way all the time, are the ones who succeed the most in business and in Branding.

The Branding process is best done in anything but a limp fashion. To work, it must be strong and ubiquitous. Vigor and dedication are necessary in every employee, not just the marketing executives, not just the CEO, and not just those who are directly involved in Branding. Obsession isn't present in every individual, but it can be taught.

Coming into a relatively crowded market with no dominant single brand, Just the Best knew it would be dealing with competition. That was the philosophy behind the brand identity: fitting into a broad-based hole in the market where none of the other brands had yet managed to eliminate all competition.

Now, however, the brand has established itself as an ice cream that is readily available in convenient venues and is both affordable and high in quality. It has the two-pronged task of having to fend off competitors while trying to expand its reach and become king of the hill.

It's always necessary to stay ahead of the competition. That means keeping very close watch on the brands with which Just the Best is most likely to rub elbows: Breyer's, Edy's, Ben & Jerry's, and Häagen-Dazs. I'm not suggesting that corporate spying is the way to go, but it is imperative to watch the activities of suppliers, distributors, and other ancillary businesses that service the competition to see if new products, new marketing tactics, and new attacks on Just the Best might be on the way from the loyal opposition.

A BRANDED WORLD

After a few months of testing in the sponsorship program, the Just the Best ice cream cups might be ready for supermarket distribution, as brand expansion is always a way to keep the brand current and stay ahead of the pack. But a brand can't always have a new product ready for introduction. Current stories from within the company, promotions being devised, or changes to the Web site can be publicized to make sure the brand name is not disappearing from the public's consciousness.

But let's assume that suddenly a new brand appears on the market that seems to have studied our own success quite closely. It isn't projecting a nostalgic image, but one that is up-to-the-minute. Its commercials feature a hip-hop beat, but its ice cream flavors are chocolate, vanilla, and strawberry—nothing else. It will be sold through supermarkets but also through cone shops, aligning itself with a chain of fast food restaurants for space. The name of the new brand is Outrageous!

The appearance of a direct competitor is something every brand has to face, assuming there is no such thing when the brand itself is conceived. But in some cases, a brand must compete with something new that has learned from the lessons the original brand taught the market and is therefore getting a faster start. In this case, public relations assumes that Just the Best must go into attack mode.

Noting the overwhelming typhoon of messages that attacks us virtually every minute of every day, the power of Branding is hardly stochastic. It is actually a very logical, sane market response to the times in which we live. What Branding does is to elevate one product or service above its competition, which is the ultimate goal in business. Through Branding, the product or service takes on a personality of its own that is definable and identifiable on an emotional level. The consumer knows the brand in a way he or she does not know a product or service that has not been properly branded; those are strangers, and the carefully branded product is a friend.

Attacking the smaller competitors would be like a trusted family pet German shepherd snarling at a smaller, weaker beagle. The family member walking the dog would be shocked, and the battle would be pointless; everyone would know the bigger dog would win.

Dealing with Copycat Brands

Even if the beagle growled first, the Shepherd would be seen as the aggressor, a mean old dog whose manner can't be trusted.

It's better to be seen as the calm, trustworthy friend, the accepting type who exudes confidence without having to preen or show off for the crowd. New York Yankees manager Joe Torre once described his superstar shortstop Derek Jeter as having "that look in his eye: 'I know I'm good, I don't have to tell you I'm good.' " Leaders inspire with cool, deliberate actions that prove their talents, not with shortsighted, adrenaline-driven outbursts that tend to mark one as a bully or an insecure king uncertain of his ability to hold the throne against the onslaught of upstarts brandishing torches at his castle gate.

Still, the upstarts can't be defeated without action. A good king has already made the decisions and initiated the policies that will endear him to his subjects, and an insurrection would therefore be less likely and less apt to succeed should one be mounted. But there are always pretenders to the throne, and the wise monarch must be ready to defeat them no matter how popular he may be.

The smart king always keeps his profile high with the public he commands and makes sure his name is mentioned whenever his government enacts an especially popular law or stops to help a citizen who has fallen on hard times. In this way, the leader can be seen as compassionate and fair, vigorous and progressive, as he goes about his daily business.

A brand can be seen in the same way. In the year 2000, McDonald's and Disney, two of the largest corporate entities on earth and two of the most high-profile brands in existence, teamed to honor 2,000 young people (under the age of 18) who had performed a good deed or overcome great odds. The Millennium Dreamers program, heavily promoted on both Disney and McDonald's Web sites and elsewhere, encouraged entries from around the world on behalf of young people whose dedication to a larger community made them worthy of a reward. Applicants had to be nominated by an adult, had to write a description of their accomplishments, and were judged not only for their deeds but for the way they carried themselves and considered others ahead of themselves.

The reward, once the 2000 were chosen, was substantial: The Millennium Dreamers and one of their parents were treated to an all-expenses-paid four-day stay at Walt Disney World in Florida. Flights and hotel reservations were handled by the Disney staff; food was provided by McDonald's and by Disney at its theme park restaurants, sections of the park were closed to anyone but Millennium Dreamer participants, and a celebration was held in Epcot park with a keynote address from Christopher Reeve.

While it is certain that the two conglomerates rewarded these 2000 youths because of their dedication to the world community and in appreciation of the young people's accomplishments, Disney and McDonald's did not hide their light under a bushel: There were reporters and television news crews from large cities, states, and countries around the world. Coverage was immense, and the two sponsors made sure each element of the event, down to the interviews with Millennium Dreamers themselves, was handled with tact, but also with maximum visibility.

Is it crass to exploit the altruistic deeds of 2000 young people to reinforce your brand identity? If that were the whole reason these two companies had sponsored the event, it would have been true. But it would have been just as easy to select 2000 young people at random, from a drawing held in every McDonald's restaurant, and given them the trip. Instead, the two companies planned an event that would attract attention to the charitable and in some cases courageous work of 2000 youngsters, and only peripherally managed to make their own brand identities more friendly and positive at the same time.

This kind of aggressive planning, coupled with a genuine desire to do good, is the ultimate Branding experience. It draws attention to the company in a positive way, is always good copy for a newspaper or an excellent story for television or radio news, and manages in the context of Branding to elevate the profile of the brand and perform a public service at the same time.

HANDLING ATTACK CAMPAIGNS

It happens in politics all the time: One brand, usually the more successful of two, finds itself suddenly under attack, often by a newer, or less established, brand that believes it can exploit a weakness in the stronger entity. Out of the blue, the established brand finds itself acting on the defensive, fending off charges that have been exaggerated (or in some cases fabricated entirely) and acting very much like a guilty party trying to control damage to its reputation.

Attack campaigns, which are mostly conducted in advertising, are a fact of life in the business environment. They can be very damaging: Barry Goldwater never recovered from one of the first TV attack ads, which Lyndon Johnson's campaign devised to paint the Republican as likely to start a nuclear conflict.

Vince Lombardi said, "The best defense is a good offense," and even if he was talking about football, he was correct about Branding as well. Making the attacker look petty and uninformed—without doing the same kind of attacking and leaving your brand open to criticism for using the same tactic—is the clearest, most effective way to fend off an unwarranted and potentially damaging attack from a competitor.

Notice that the attack has to be unwarranted. When a competitor uncovers a real flaw in your brand, or a true scandal that has emerged from your company, attacking back is not only a bad idea; it's Branding suicide. In that case, public relations practice is (as with any other negative news) to admit to the problem, apologize for it, and rectify it as quickly and clearly as possible.

However, when the attack comes without significant truth attached, firing back with facts is a very effective weapon, and still an opportunity to take the high road. Consider the Cola Wars of the 1970s and 1980s, when the "Pepsi Challenge" was being held in shopping malls (and on television sets) around the country, giving consumers the chance to drink samples of Coca-Cola and Pepsi without knowing the brand of either sample. Pepsi's data indicated that a very large percentage of the public preferred its taste, and the company was not timid about announcing that fact often and loudly in television commercials.

Coke eventually responded with the Branding error of the century, New Coke. If, instead, it had relied on its consumer base, flaunted its brand loyalty, and not panicked, the brand could have avoided the embarrassment that came with its about-face after the fanfare of New Coke, the reintroduction of Classic Coke, and the millions of dollars spent in the process. But it also would have avoided the mountain of press coverage and publicity that surrounded the New Coke debacle. Oscar Wilde once said, "the only thing worse than being talked about is not being talked about." In the 1980s, Coca-Cola was certainly being talked about, and it remains one of the five most successful and recognizable brands on earth to this day.

Nothing has happened internally that could possibly damage the reputation of Just the Best. But a threat from outside—the introduction of a new brand that emulates many of our brand identity tenets—requires quick and intelligent action.

Of course, the best way to act quickly is to start planning for such an emergency long in advance. Strategic planning allows for preparation for any scenario. A new competitor borrowing some of our tactics isn't so far-fetched a situation that it wouldn't have been anticipated months—sometimes years—ahead of time. It is simply the circumstances surrounding the new competitor, and not the concept of a copycat competitor itself, that couldn't have been foreseen, so they must be dealt with reactively.

Given that Outrageous! is aiming at a slightly younger market than Just the Best (although we concede no ice cream eater), one reaction could be to try and shore up our consumer base on the younger end of our demographic. We could begin using hipper advertising jargon and change our graphics to be more appealing to teens and young adults.

However, that would probably be a mistake.

Fighting a newcomer on its own turf weakens the established brand and makes it look frightened and shaky. It is better to deal with the upstart in the way any strong, confident champion should: by emphasizing our strengths and ignoring the competitor entirely. This means increasing some advertising buys, but also creating a public relations campaign that will overwhelm the new brand and steal its thunder.

Sponsorship of a highly visible event, like the Major League Baseball All-Star Game (since it is one game, it will be less expensive than a playoff series of the World Series) during our core summer months might make a big splash. Of course, publicity surrounding such an event would be extremely lavish, and would provide opportunities for press coverage.

Beyond that, holding a publicity event designed to capture the consumer's attention is the key to a large scale campaign. A contest offering $1 million (paid over 25 years) to the person who best describes the joy of Just the Best in five words or less could be organized, with entry forms in supermarkets placed adjacent to the freezers containing the product. The best slogans could be broadcast in commercial spots leading up to the crowning of the champion, best accomplished during a Just the Best-sponsored event such as the All-Star Game.

While such a campaign would cost a good deal of money, it would also provide public relations opportunities for months, with press coverage of the many entries arriving at company headquarters, profiles of the finalists, and coverage of the naming of the winner. With reality programming dominating much of television these days, the real-life drama of a consumer being awarded such a large sum can only make the brand look benevolent and vital. No mention ever need be made of any competitor, especially not Outrageous!

EVOLUTION

Without question, the best and most effective way to react to strong competition (and while weak competition must always be monitored, it doesn't usually merit reaction) is to keep your brand strong, vital, and progressive. That often means the brand must continually evolve.

Certainly, New Coke was an attempt at evolution; it was the wrong attempt and the wrong way for the brand to evolve. The product itself need not change for the brand to evolve. The brand identity, while not changing on a daily basis, needs to stay current, or Coca-Cola would have stayed a remedy for an upset stomach and never have become the universally beloved soft drink we know today. Honda would still be known as a company that makes motorcycles and cute, inexpensive little cars. Ronald Reagan would have been a respected but unremarkable B-movie actor, interviewed whenever a documentary about the Golden Age of Hollywood was being produced.

A BRANDED WORLD

Brand identity is determined at the inception stage of the Branding process, and it must not be abandoned at any time in a brand's evolution, but it can be altered, updated, and tweaked as the brand matures and time passes. For example, Kellogg's Tony the Tiger for its Frosted Flakes brand was once a somewhat elegant, authoritative figure who would growl, "They're grrrrrrrrreat!" about the product. Now, Tony still intones his famous slogan, but he appears on skateboards, playing soccer, and participating in the active lifestyle Kellogg's wants its young consuming audience to identify with.

When a person or a business begins a serious Branding journey, a metamorphosis is often soon to follow. The brand has to be free to morph into the best version of itself for the current time. For example, Frosted Flakes were known as "Sugar Frosted Flakes" in the 1960s, just as Golden Pops were "Sugar Pops" and other cereals used *sugar* in their names before dietary concerns changed. Likewise, if Aunt Jemima and Uncle Ben's were still trading on the racial images of their inceptions, or if Hoover vacuums were still advising housewives on the best way to clean the rug before Hubby gets home and expects a hot dinner, these brands would be considered archaic and probably would not have survived into the twenty-first century.

Instead, Aunt Jemima concentrated on the brand loyalty it had built, and stressed the quality of its products and the familiarity consumers had with the brand. Uncle Ben's extended its brand into frozen foods and other related products. Both brands deemphasized the stereotypical figures in their logos, making the images smaller and smaller but not eliminating them completely. Hoover now stresses the speed and efficiency of its vacuums to accommodate the two-income lifestyle of many of its customers. There is no mention of pleasing one's husband, although he is sometimes seen behind the vacuum, chipping in on the household chores and splitting the responsibility. By making these changes, these brands managed to preserve what was positive about their brand identities—familiarity, trust, quality—and still evolved into products to which present-day consumers can relate.

As years and decades pass, brands we consider to be cutting-edge today—Microsoft, Cingular Wireless, BMW—will have to evolve in order to stay relevant. Otherwise, they could meet the same fate as the cutting-edge brands of yesteryear—Ipana, Burma-Shave, Metracal—that didn't see the changes in lifestyle as threatening to their extant brand identities and therefore failed to evolve. Simple belief in the brand identity, and unwillingness to tamper with it as if it were set in stone, can signal deeper problems in the Branding process, since inability to bend will always snap even the strongest brand in half. Things can't stay the same just because that's the way they always have been. The world around every brand is evolving, and if the brand isn't evolving, as well, it will suffer the fate of the unfittest, Darwin's less hearty group.

Some brands, of course, are meant to hearken back to a different time. When Chrysler introduced the PT Cruiser in 2000, it was meant to look like a car from another era; that was the intended appeal, and the gambit worked. PT Cruiser sales were very strong, but Chrysler recognized a novelty when it saw one, and to date has not tried to expand that brand beyond one model. Just the Best, as well, was designed to capitalize on nostalgia and evoke warm feelings for fresh, pure ice cream.

By the same token, brands like Pepperidge Farm make use of their nostalgic personas to suggest a higher-quality, less gimmicky brand identity, and that works well for them. It would be difficult to translate that success to a product with a higher-tech purpose. Nostalgic computer chips or cellular phones would be a very hard thing to sell convincingly.

That doesn't mean Pepperidge Farm hasn't evolved; its brand identity has been able to survive the decades while the brand itself (with a slogan that once reminded us "Pepperidge Farm Remembers") still takes in such items as frozen cakes and desserts, toaster pastries, and microwave-ready snacks. Pepperidge Farm may remember, but it doesn't miss much in the present day, either.

Evolution is not revolution; things don't have to change completely and immediately. Tony the Tiger didn't put down his fountain pen and pick up a Walkman all in one day. Betty Crocker's image on a box of cake mix didn't go from timid hausfrau to power-suited executive in the blink of an eye.

Change is gradual, and done by degrees. Public relations opportunities can be made when a well-established brand changes its familiar mascot or tweaks the look of its logo to keep up with the times. But it is not necessary to call a press conference every time you change the typeface on your packaging copy; nor is it a publicity opportunity when it is decided behind a boardroom door to make a 1 percent change in the brand identity to accommodate current lifestyles. It's one thing to toot your own horn, and another to go out in the meadow and cry wolf every time you haven't been in the business pages for a couple of weeks.

The purpose of evolving is to survive and thrive; changing for the sake of change is pointless. So, in making adjustments to your brand identity, take great care not to destroy what has come before, but to enhance it; make sure the changes are consistent and not a radical, jarring change of direction for the consumer. That would signal desperation and invalidate all that has come before. Make evolution natural and logical for the consumer, and brand loyalty will not just hold firm, but also actually increase.

THE EVOLUTION OF JUST THE BEST

Over time, Just the Best has managed an evolution of sorts, from fledgling brand in an already competitive market to established household name that can be trusted and relied upon to deliver what it promises. But, before it becomes tired and predictable, the brand must decide on the course of its next evolutionary stage.

This will not be an abrupt process. Evolution of the human species took millions, if not billions, of years, and Just the Best, while a nicely familiar brand now in consumers' homes, is still relatively young as a brand, and should not expect its transformation to take place overnight. The question is: How should the brand change? The next questions are: Where should the brand expect to end up after the change, and How should it go about getting there?

Of course, the stated goal of the brand from the beginning has been to become the dominant brand in the ice cream market. To achieve that, Just the Best must appeal to the widest possible demographic and make its brand identity practically universal, without trying so hard to be all things to all people that the brand ends up with no real identity at all.

Right now, the brand's identity is one of a friendly, self-effacing product that harkens back to a simpler age when ice cream was a pure and uncomplicated treat. That's a fine image, but it will tend to skew more toward those 35 and older, and eventually the brand could be perceived as out of touch and aimed at older people alone. That might not be a problem now, but it certainly could evolve into one over years or decades if left unchecked.

The tweaking of the brand's identity must be extremely gradual, but purposeful. It will take years to shed the nostalgic image we have been endeavoring to create, but in the long term that will be the appropriate choice. And the process can begin almost immediately, but with subtle enough strokes to avoid seeming a reaction to a younger-skewing competitor.

First, the changes made to the packaging should extend to the logo. The wooden "frame" around the Just the Best trademark hands-and-cone logo will be made a solid color to look less like the sign over an old-time ice cream parlor and more like something you might see over a store today. Once the logo is adjusted, advertising spots can be made more contemporary, with the ice cream parlor spots giving way to people shopping in a supermarket. Perhaps the 1950s soda jerk character established in the original advertising will continue to appear, but as a figure out of his own time, conveying information about the product to modern-day consumers who look at him with a certain wonder.

These changes will not be accompanied with public relations campaigns, although the changes will be noted in press releases. There is no reason to explain that the brand is trying to adjust its identity, since that would require an admission that the current identity needs adjustment. This could point out the problem to competitors and consumers and alienate consumers who are loyal to the brand. Instead, the changes will be seen as a natural evolution of the brand, an effort not to repeat itself endlessly.

Over years, new products will join the brand line, and the advertising and public relations efforts will be coordinated to update the brand image, but not so much that it appeals only to younger people. The idea is to have the most universal appeal such a product can achieve, and that means expecting everyone to be a Just the Best customer.

Evolution is not something to be ashamed of; when a brand evolves, PR should trumpet the coming "next phase" proudly. But as with all other elements of Branding, the evolution of a brand will have positive and negative connotations. PR is the process of accentuating the positive.

CONCLUSION

"If your business doesn't stand out in today's world, you will be shut out, and indeed you may be shut down. Nine out of 10 businesses fail the first year. Having a brand allows you to promote your business with a bang instead of a whimper. First of all, if you have a brand, your business must offer your customers an advantage."

—ADAM CHRISTING, FOUNDER OF CLEAN COMEDIANS

I wrote earlier about the McDonald's restaurant in Los Angeles where I had difficulty getting ice in my drink because the counter help didn't speak English. The overall rating I'd give that fast food outlet was clearly an F, only because the grading system we know doesn't have anything lower than that.

Masochist that I am, I continue to stop in at that restaurant from time to time, perhaps proving the power of Branding after all: I go to McDonald's expecting the McDonald's that the company promises. I am happy to report that a new manager has been assigned to my local franchise, and she has made a significant difference.

I don't frequent the place; I'm there once a month, perhaps. But sometimes, that's the best way to notice a change. The counter help has become not only more fluent in my mother tongue; they are more helpful and more efficient. The cleanliness level has increased noticeably, if not dramatically. The food is, if not gourmet fare, at least consistent. It is what you expect from a McDonald's, which is to say about average.

Today, I'd give that restaurant a C. That's quite an improvement, and a testament to the power of one person to change the perception of a brand in the consumer's mind.

When I met Demi Moore, she was an actress on the soap opera *General Hospital* who was married to a convenience store clerk and had made a few films, none of which was terribly memorable. But she was ragingly ambitious, quite beautiful, and had a memorable, husky voice. I represented her for a number of years, during which she first came to great fame as a member of the Brat Pack, a group of young actors who starred in movies like *St. Elmo's Fire*. Rob Lowe, Emilio Estevez, Judd Nelson, and Andrew McCarthy joined Demi in this group, which became a brand in itself.

Through the next few years, Demi became arguably the biggest star to emerge from the Brat Pack, and her career took off wildly when she starred in *Ghost* with Patrick Swayze and Whoopi Goldberg, and when she began a romance (and later a stormy marriage) with Bruce Willis. While Demi was very ambitious, her marriage to Willis, and their children, which brought her *National Enquirer* fame, was not part of her career plan, and eventually she left the Hollywood merry-go-round to raise her children in a quieter environment. She had had enough of being a brand.

Consider the number of brands Jane Fonda has been in her lifetime. Starting her career known as Henry's daughter, Jane later had a reputation as something of a sex symbol, thanks largely to her first husband, Roger Vadim, and his vision of her in movies like *Barbarella*.

Then came the political period, during which Jane married liberal politician Tom Hayden and traveled to North Vietnam in protest of the American involvement in the Vietnam War. Earning the unwanted nickname "Hanoi Jane," she became a figure of great controversy, vilified for what some saw as giving aid and comfort to the enemy.

For a number of years thereafter, Jane became a respected actress, earning Oscar nominations and two Academy Awards and also producing some films in which she appeared. In the 1980s, she became a fitness guru, making a fortune on exercise videotapes in which she appeared and which she helped to create.

In 1991, Jane married media mogul Ted Turner, immediately quit acting and the fitness video business, and took to supporting her husband, showing up at Atlanta Braves games and staying out of the public life for the most part. Her brand now was Mrs. Ted Turner.

Since that marriage ended, Jane has become somewhat more active, but has not yet rebranded herself for the seventh go-round. But it will certainly be only a matter of time before she reemerges with another

Conclusion

enthusiasm, and it will certainly become another brand with the name Jane Fonda.

These stories illustrate the wide scope and endless depth of Branding. The McDonald's manager is the best example I know of a single employee—not an executive—of a huge corporation doing good work to improve the image of the overall brand by doing her job well. Demi Moore's story is about the Tiffany Theory, using associations with others, both intentionally and unintentionally, to elevate and create a separate brand that is the self. And Jane Fonda illustrates the endless flexibility of a brand, particularly a successful one, that can redefine itself at will and maintain contact with and loyalty from the public.

The subject of Branding is a large, vast canvas. It's hard to think of a better example of an idea whose time has come. The true nature of Branding is that it presents itself to each person with a unique face; what is Branding to you may not be Branding to me. The key is that if it works, it's Branding.

In the business world, Branding is the same as anything else: a sales tool. One of the key things a brand is supposed to do is create an inducement to do business. In the entertainment business, Branding is a way to achieve a new level of acceptance, a very high tier of celebrity. Madonna is a brand, and maybe Britney Spears is a brand (we'll see in 10 years), but Jeff Bridges, fine actor that he is, is not a brand.

As former *Brandweek* West Coast bureau chief T. C. Stanley says, "We at *Brandweek* felt it was so misused in our opinion that we wrote a big missive on: These Things Are Not a Brand. People would call us and try to tell us that Adam Sandler was a brand. No, he's not. Madonna stands the test of time, and that's a key element. Some don't. I reject the J. Lo thing and lean more toward Madonna as a brand because we're looking at 20 years now, and when you say Madonna, it doesn't just mean one thing now. It means a lot of things. People know exactly what you mean when you say that, and that's the test of a brand. Mary-Kate and Ashley are not a brand; they're a franchise, as many celebrities are. Michael Jordan is more than just a basketball player; he stands for so much more than what he does."

In politics, it is essential to be a brand—or you can go unnoticed, which is death to an office seeker. A nonbranded product or service (or politician) that finds itself in competition with a well-branded one may truly understand what it must feel like to be a eunuch.

Virtually all of us are associated with Branding in some way, even if it's simply fitting into a certain crowd, and not another one, in our high school cafeteria. Branding has encompassed our lives and changed the way we think about almost everything, even—perhaps especially—when we don't notice it.

Branding existed as a concept before there was advertising or public relations. It was evident at the time that Julius Caesar, and not Brutus, was emperor of Rome. It was present when Michelangelo, and not some other painter, was commissioned to decorate the ceiling of the Sistine Chapel. The first time all the cave women lined up behind the biggest, strongest man when there was danger, Branding was born.

Public relations has existed longer than it is given credit for, too. These days, with degrees in PR offered at major universities and publicity being studied like a physical science, it's hard to remember the time 20 years ago when I first came to Hollywood and had to explain to people what I thought public relations was all about. These days, it is a given.

Branding and public relations are bound together inextricably. Without one, the other would collapse. And while the techniques I've described in this book tell the story of PR in Branding, they do not encompass all that can be, because each practitioner will approach the subject with his or her own perspective.

Public relations has long been the forgotten stepchild of the Branding process, an important component that is overlooked or taken for granted. This book is meant to reintroduce PR to those who have underestimated its importance in Branding, and, hopefully, to make the case that PR isn't just a useful tool, but perhaps the linchpin of Branding, the sine qua non that makes the process work.

To dismiss public relations from the Branding process is to say that Paris would be the same without bistros, or that the computer is a useful tool but not integral to modern life. Public relations makes Branding work because it establishes credibility and brand integrity. As I have illustrated here, it is

Conclusion

without question the most natural and effective way to communicate and maintain brand identity, which is the absolute center of Branding.

This is not to say that advertising and marketing aren't important parts of the Branding phenomenon; they are. But without well-executed public relations efforts, the impact on a market would not be nearly as great.

The brand you are contemplating, developing, or maintaining must be nurtured and cared about. It must be cultivated, nourished, and defended. It will face challenges from outside, the natural predators of the marketplace, and threats from areas you haven't begun to consider. It's a scary, dangerous, brutal place out there.

Do you really want to brave such an environment without the public on your side?

NOTES

All of the direct quotes in this book are the result of personal interviews with the subjects, conducted between December 2001 and July 2002, with the following exceptions:

- Sumner Redstone is quoted from an interview with Sky Radio.
- Joe Torre is quoted from various interviews following the 2000 World Series.
- Yogi Berra is quoted from *The Yogi Book*.
- Benjamin Franklin is quoted from *Poor Richard's Almanack*.

Other quotes from various publications and Web sites are cited in the text. The author wants to sincerely and warmly thank everyone who agreed to submit to an interview. Without them, this book would not have been possible.

—MICHAEL LEVINE
Los Angeles

FURTHER READING

Berra, Yogi. *The Yogi Book*. New York: Workman Publishing, 1998.

Czerniawski, Richard D., and Michael W. Maloney. *Creating Brand Loyalty: The Management of Power Positioning and Really Great Advertising.* New York: AMACOM Books, 1999.

Davis, Scott. *Brand Asset Management*. San Francisco: John Wiley & Sons, 2000.

Evans, Robert. *The Kid Stays in the Picture*. Beverly Hills, CA: New Millennium Press, 2002.

Franklin, Benjamin, *Poor Richard's Almanack*. New York: Random House, 1988.

Gobe, Marc, and Sergio Zyman. *Emotional Branding: The New Paradigm for Connecting Brands to People*. New York: Allworth Press, 2001.

Knapp, Duane E. *The Brand Mindset: Five Essential Strategies for Building Brand Advantage throughout Your Company*. New York: McGraw-Hill, 1999.

Levine, Michael. *Guerrilla P.R.: How You Can Wage an Effective Publicity Campaign without Going Broke*. New York: HarperCollins, 1993.

McNally, David, and Karl D. Speake. *Be Your Own Brand: A Breakthrough Formula for Standing Out From the Crowd*. San Francisco: Berrett-Koehler, 2002.

Nelson, Bob. *1001 Ways to Reward Employees*. New York: Workman Publishing Co., 1994.

Ries, Al, and Laura Ries. *The Fall of Advertising and the Rise of P.R.* New York: Harper Business, 2002.

Ries, Al, and Laura Ries. *The 11 Immutable Laws of Internet Branding*. New York: Harper Business, 2000.

Ries, Al, and Laura Ries. *The 22 Immutable Laws of Branding*. New York: HarperCollins, 2002.

Trout, Jack. *Big Brands, Big Trouble*. New York: John Wiley & Sons, 2001.

Michael Levine is a frequent speaker at corporations and schools throughout North America. To contact him:

Michael Levine
Levine Communications Office
1033 Ashton Avenue
Los Angeles, California 90024
Tel (301) 248–6222 ext 10
E-mail levinepr@earthlink.net
www.levinepr.com

INDEX

255

Index

Index

Index

Index

Index